# GOSPEL PERSPECTIVES

*Studies of History and Tradition in the Four Gospels*

---
Volume I
---

*Edited by*
*R. T. France*
*and David Wenham*

JSOT Press

First published by JSOT Press 1980
Reprint edition by JSOT Press 1983

Copyright© 1980, 1983
JSOT Press

ISBN O 905774 21 3

Published by
JSOT Press
Department of Biblical Studies
The University of Sheffield
Sheffield S1O 2TN
England

Printed and bound in Great Britain by
Redwood Burn Ltd.
Trowbridge, Wiltshire
1983

# Contents

# Preface

Few questions have received more attention from Christian scholars and theologians during the past two hundred years than the question of history and tradition in the four gospels. But despite the amount of study that has been done and despite the real advances in understanding that have been made, there is still quite fundamental disagreement among scholars on how far we can regard the gospels as historically reliable, and indeed on what the notion of 'historicity' involves in this context, or whether it really matters. To thinking Christians this scholarly disagreement is a source of perplexity. It may be true that the theology of the New Testament is a more important object for study than its historical details; it is certainly the case that much of the past search for the historical Jesus has led into dead ends. But, despite the attempts of some to suggest otherwise, the conviction remains that the Christian faith is closely and essentially tied up with the history of its founder figure, so that the question of the historical value of the gospels cannot be dismissed and should not be left unanswered.

The Gospels Research Project of Tyndale House, Cambridge, of which *Gospel Perspectives* is the first fruit, was set up to look further into this question. It involves some thirty New Testament scholars who share the conviction that the question is important for Christian faith. Papers have been circulated, discussed, and revised, and this first volume contains some of those considered at a meeting of participants in Cambridge in July 1979. They range from discussions of method and of the nature of the gospel tradition to studies of particular parts of the gospels; one paper is an examination of an alleged contradiction between Paul's view of Jesus' resurrection and the account in the gospels.

This selection makes no pretence to a complete coverage of the area. Further papers on a wide variety of topics are being prepared for the Project; but to have waited for all to be ready in the interests of an ideal table of contents would have meant a long delay in publication. So we have thought it better to publish papers as they have become available. A second volume is already well-advanced and should be ready for publication in a year from now. We hope that the total results of our Research Project will add up to a fairly comprehensive study of our chosen area; but meanwhile we believe that each paper in this volume will contribute in its own way to a responsible discussion of the subject.

Within such a group there will inevitably be differences of opinion and of approach, and no attempt has been made to iron out such differences. But the contributors share a common respect for the historical value of the gospels, and a desire to provide answers to the questions of historicity which will stand up to serious academic scrutiny and will provide some help for those who are perplexed by scholarly disagreement.

We are grateful to the Council of Tyndale House through whose encouragement and support this Project has been launched and is continuing.

R. T. FRANCE

DAVID WENHAM

Tyndale House, Cambridge.

# The Trial of Jesus in the Fourth Gospel

F. F. Bruce,
2 Temple Road,
Buxton, Derbyshire.

## Preamble

John the Evangelist's narrative of the trial of Jesus
provides an excellent instance of what C. H. Dodd calls
'historical tradition in the Fourth Gospel'. Certainly this
narrative, like all other narratives in the Fourth Gospel,
serves as a basis for the Evangelist's theological reflection
and exposition, as he brings out the permanent and universal
relevance of the events he records. A notable instance of such
Johannine redaction is the falling back of the soldiers and
police who come to arrest Jesus when they hear his word of
power 'I am he' (18:5-8) - evidently with the same force as it
has in John 8:24, 28 (the force, probably, of the OT *ᵓanî hûᵓ*).
Readers are thus reminded of Jesus' true identity and realize
that his captors could do nothing against him except by his own
consent. At the same time the narrative preserves features
which, sometimes more tellingly than the parallels in the other
Gospels, belong to the course of events 'wie es eigentlich
gewesen' /1/.

## Preparation

The initiative in putting Jesus on trial, according to
John, was taken by the high priest Caiaphas in consultation with
'the chief priests and the Pharisees' (i.e. the Sanhedrin) after
the raising of Lazarus from the dead and the consequent public
excitement. This excitement, they feared, might well precipitate
riots which would invite repressive action from the Romans. In
such an event, there was a risk that the Romans would 'destroy
both our holy place and our nation' (John 11:48). Caiaphas cut
into their agitation by reminding them that it was better that
one man should die for the people than that the whole nation
should perish for one man: it was resolved therefore to seize
Jesus and put him out of harm's way. Any one who knew where
Jesus was must inform the Sanhedrin, so that he could be
arrested.

Surrounded by crowds of eager listeners, Jesus was
adequately protected while he taught in the temple precincts
during the few days before the last Passover. Any attempt to
arrest him in such an environment would stir up the very kind
of riot that the authorities feared. Their fears, indeed, grew
from day to day, especially as they noted the enthusiasm of the
crowd which greeted and escorted Jesus on his entry into
Jerusalem. Whether or not the palm-branches carried by the
crowd indicated their hope of imminent national liberation /2/,
their words of acclamation were eloquent enough, 'You can't do
anything', said the religious leaders one to another; 'see, the
whole world has gone off after him!' (John 12:19).

The authorities must have hailed it as a windfall when
Judas undertook to show them how and where to arrest Jesus
after nightfall, in circumstances when no inconvenient crowds
would be around. John gives no hint of Judas's conscious
reason for doing this: he puts it down to the devil's entering
into him.

It was Judas, then, who guided the men who were sent to
arrest Jesus in the garden east of the Kidron ravine, to which
Jesus and his disciples went after their meal and conversation
in the upper room.

### The Arrest

John's account of the arrest of Jesus contains a feature
not paralleled in the Synoptic Gospels. A posse of temple
police is mentioned, but before he mentions them John speaks of
a detachment of Roman troops: 'Judas, taking the cohort (*speira*),
and officers from the chief priests and Pharisees, comes there
with lights and torches and weapons' (John 18:3). /3/ Judas is
subject of the sentence, but his role was that of a guide: it
is absurd to suggest that John meant his readers to suppose
that Judas was commander of the Roman troops, or even of the
Jewish police. /4/ The commander of the Roman troops is
expressly mentioned in verse 12: 'the cohort and their
military tribune (*chiliarchos*), and the officers of the Jews,
seized Jesus, bound him, and led him away.' (By 'the Jews', as
regularly in this part of his Gospel, John means the chief-
priestly establishment.) The 'cohort' was based in the
Antonia fortress (cf. Mark 15:16). If the whole cohort (an
auxiliary infantry unit of a paper strength of 1,000 men) was
present, a full-scale band of insurgents must have been

expected; but this is an unnecessary inference from John's language.  His language would probably be satisfied if a detachment from the cohort was present - but it was a detachment large enough to call for the presence of the commanding officer (a predecessor of Claudius Lysias). /5/

What are we to make of this?  Mommsen says that the inclusion of the military tribune and the cohort in the arrest narrative is 'certainly wrong': it was the responsibility of the Jewish authorities to make the arrest. /6/  But what if the Jewish authorities, taking note of the strength of Jesus' following on his entry into Jerusalem, were afraid that their own officers might find themselves faced with opposition too great for them to cope with?  Might they not have arranged for a Roman military presence just in case?

As against Mommsen, it has been argued that the involvement of Romans in Jesus' arrest runs so counter to John's supposed tendency to emphasize Jewish responsibility for his death and to exonerate the Romans as far as possible, that the Roman presence at this stage in the narrative must be based on historical fact. Maurice Goguel went so far as to think that *only* the Roman soldiers were involved; /7/ Paul Winter, on the other hand, thought it more likely that Jewish police were also present. Winter distinguished two traditions in John's narrative of the arrest: (i) the distinctively 'Johannine tradition according to which Jesus was arrested by Roman troops, under their own commander, and assisted by a posse of the Temple Police', and (ii) the basically Markan tradition in which Jesus is arrested by a crowd (*ochlos*) led by Judas.  It was, in his view, only the former of these two traditions that had any historical foundation. /8/

One does not lightly disagree with Mommsen on a point of Roman judicial procedure, but it does seem more probable that the presence of at least some members of the cohort and their commanding officer belongs to the historical tradition on which John draws.  Indeed, John implies that the Roman troops did more than stand by in case of need; he ascribes to them an active part in the physical arrest of Jesus (John 18:12). /9/

If, then, their presence at, and indeed participation in, the arrest belong to the historical tradition, this points to an antecedent approach by the chief priests to the Roman authorities.  Such an approach is further presupposed in the

chief priests' dismay when Pilate, instead of ratifying their
judgment on Jesus out of hand, shows signs of opening the whole
case *ab initio* (John 18:29 f.).

Another incidental token of the historical tradition is
the remark that the high priest's servant whose ear was sliced
by Peter's sword was named Malchus (John 18:10). Malchus is a
common enough name in the Graeco-Roman Near East, and there is
no probability in the view that it is here a lectionary-
inspired inference from *malkô* ('his king') in Zech. 11:6. /10/

## In the house of Annas

John is the only Evangelist to record that Jesus, after
his arrest, was taken to Annas first. True, Mark and Luke do
not name the high priest who presided over the Jewish court
which examined Jesus, but the very fact that he presided over it
indicates that he was the reigning high priest (i.e. Caiaphas,
as is said explicitly in Matt. 26:3, 57). John knows that
Caiaphas was the reigning high priest - 'high priest that year',
as he puts it (John 18:13; cf. 11:49). /11/ Although John does
not describe a trial over which Caiaphas presided, he agrees
with the Synoptists in stating that it was from the house of the
reigning high priest (i.e. Caiaphas, not Annas) that Jesus was
taken to Pilate (18:28).

If, then, John calls Annas 'the high priest'
(*archiereus*), he knows and means that Annas was high priest
emeritus (owing his influence, no doubt, to his status as
senior ex-high priest).

The inquiry conducted by Annas, as recorded by John, has
nothing in common with the examination before the supreme court,
as recorded by the Synoptists. Annas questioned Jesus about his
disciples and his teaching; the issue before the supreme court
was his alleged threat to the temple and the nature of his
messianic claim. The Geneva and Authorized Versions follow the
'Received Text' in omitting the particle *oun* from John 18:24; by
rendering 'Now Annas had sent him bound unto Caiaphas the high
priest' they imply that the inquiry of verses 19-23 was conducted
by Caiaphas. Codex 225 and the Sinaitic Syriac, by bringing
verse 24 forward to an earlier point in the narrative, similarly
identify 'the high priest' of verses 19-23 with Caiaphas. The
Greek text is perfectly plain. There is no need by textual
corruption or rearrangement to harmonize the Johannine and
Synoptic accounts. John says nothing of what happened between

Jesus' being sent to Caiaphas and his being taken to Pilate, but that something decisive did happen is implied by his record, which leaves room for the Synoptic narrative of the examination before the supreme court.

The harmonizing effort was perhaps encouraged by the fact that John places Peter's denial (or at least the first phase of it) in the courtyard of Annas's palace, whereas the Markan record seems to place it in the palace of the reigning high priest, during the hearing before the Sanhedrin. But one point that Mark and John have in common here is the fire in the courtyard (Mark 14:54; John 18:18). The fire is an incidental feature which confirms the holding of a night session. Such an exceptional session was necessary because the time was short. The festival was drawing near, and if Pilate was to be approached before the festival, he would have to be approached next morning. Roman officials liked to complete the transacting of daily business between 6 and 10 a.m. So what A. N. Sherwin-White calls 'the quite unessential detail of the fire' confirms the account of both Mark and John, both of whom add that it was 'early morning' (*prōi*) when Jesus was brought before Pilate (Mark 15:1; John 18:28). 'Why light a fire - an act of some extravagance - if everyone was sleeping through the night?' /12/

Annas, then, having conducted a preliminary inquiry which does not seem to have been very productive, sent Jesus to Caiaphas. John, as has been said, is silent on the proceedings before Caiaphas, but the sequel indicates that at these proceedings one thing at least was determined - the wording of the charge against Jesus to be laid before Pilate.

## The question of capital jurisdiction

Why go to Pilate? According to John, the Sanhedrin lacked the authority to carry out the death-sentence. Jesus, they affirmed, had been convicted of a capital offence under Jewish law, but the provincial prefect's authorization was required for the execution of the sentence. The situation is made quite explicit in the Jewish leaders' words to Pilate in John 18:31b: 'we are not permitted to put any one to death'.

This account of the matter has been vigorously contested by J. Juster and a number of other writers, /13/ but their arguments are insufficient. For one thing, the account is *a*

*priori* probable, being in keeping with all that we know of
Roman practice in the provinces. 'The capital power', says
Sherwin-White, 'was the most jealously guarded of all the
attributes of government, not even entrusted to the principal
assistants of the governors.' /14/

There was indeed one area in which the Jewish authorities
were allowed to retain capital jurisdiction - that of offences
against the sanctity of the temple. There is a well-known
passage in Josephus where Titus reminds the Jews that Rome
was so mindful of their religious susceptibilities that it
allowed them to execute a Gentile who trespassed in the inner
courts of the temple even if he was a Roman citizen. /15/ This
agrees with Luke's account of the arrest of Paul when he was
suspected of aiding and abetting precisely this offence: 'he
tried to profane the temple', said Tertullus to Felix, 'but we
seized him and intended to judge him *according to our law*' (Acts
24:6, Western text). If offences against the sanctity of the
temple included offences in speech as well as in action, this
could cover the trial and execution of Stephen (Acts 6:12-8:1a);
it would also throw light on the attempt, in the Markan narrative
of Jesus' trial before the Sanhedrin, to convict him of a verbal
threat to the temple (Mark 14:57-59). Had this attempt succeeded, it might not have been necessary to secure Pilate's
confirmation of the death-sentence. But this question requires
further investigation.

The Sanhedrin's loss of capital jurisdiction is attested
by a *baraitha* in the Palestinian Talmud: 'Forty years before
the destruction of the temple the right to inflict the death
penalty was taken away from Israel.' /16/ The exceptions
alleged as arguments against the Sanhedrin's loss of this right
are all exceptions that prove the rule. The execution of James
the Just was acknowledged to be *ultra vires*. /17/ The execution
of a priest's daughter for adultery, witnessed in his childhood
by Eliezer ben Zadok (who was lifted on to his father's shoulder
to see it), /18/ probably took place during the reign of Herod
Agrippa I. Other arguments against the position stated in John
18:31b are weaker than these.

### Appearance before Pilate

To Pilate, then, Jesus was brought from the headquarters
of Caiaphas. Into the location of Pilate's praetorium we cannot
enter here, /19/ nor yet into John's passion chronology, which

is bound up with his statement that Jesus' accusers would not
enter the praetorium lest the defilement so incurred should
incapacitate them from eating the Passover (John 18:28b) - a
nice example of Johannine irony.  Pilate heard them in the
paved courtyard of the praetorium, having his tribunal set up
there for the purpose (19:14).

The right and execution of *coercitio* by Roman provincial
governors may be found conveniently set out in Mommsen's trea-
tise on Roman penal law.  This work, published at the end of
the nineteenth century, remains the standard treatment of the
subject, requiring amendment only in a few particulars. /20/

The provincial governor's *imperium* was confined within
the frontiers of his province and limited further to his
physical presence there and to the duration of his appointment,
but within these limits it was subject only to the supreme
authority of the emperor.  In Judaea indeed the prefect's
authority was subject in measure to that of the imperial legate
of Syria-Cilicia, but more in military than in judicial
matters.  Roman citizens in the province, while they were
subject to the governor's *imperium*, had certain rights and
privileges safeguarded to them by Roman law; but ordinary provincials had no special protection.  They did have some general
protection in the fundamental principles of Roman judicial
practice, as expressed, for instance, in the words of Festus:
'it is not the custom of the Romans to hand any one over
before the accused meet the accusers face to face and have
opportunity to make his defence concerning the charge laid
against him' (Acts 25:16).  This principle operated in Jesus'
trial before Pilate - certainly in the Johannine account.

The trial took the form of a *cognitio* or inquiry
designed to elicit the facts of the case: the governor might
enlist the aid of well-informed parties as his *consilium*, but
the decision was his own responsibility.  Unlike the judge in
Rome, he did not have to instruct a jury.

There were native courts which took care of ordinary
cases arising among provincials, but the governor was responsible
for cases affecting the welfare and security of the empire, and
also for ratifying the death penalty, which native courts were
not normally authorized to execute.

From John 18:29 onwards, according to Paul Winter, 'the
Fourth Gospel contains nothing of any value for the assessment
of historical facts'. /21/ This is not so. From the standpoint
of Roman procedure, says A. N. Sherwin-White, 'there is no
historical improbability' in John's technical variations from
the Synoptic accounts. John's 'framework of the trial is not
notably inferior to that of Luke. It begins with a formal
delation - "What accusation bring ye against this man?" - and
ends with a formal condemnation *pro tribunali*.' /22/

John's framework for the Roman trial is judicially
accurate, though he fills it in with theological as well as
historical content (the theological interpreting the
historical).

Jesus' accusers seem to have been taken by surprise when
Pilate's formal question indicated that, instead of rubber-
stamping their judgment, he proposed to open the trial *de novo*.
Hence their protest: 'If he were not a criminal, we would not
have handed him over to you' (John 18:30). To Pilate's
rejoinder, 'If you have reached the appropriate verdict, then
inflict the appropriate penalty', they replied that the penalty
for Jesus' offence was death, which they were debarred by Roman
law from inflicting by their own authority.

But Pilate did receive an answer to his question: 'What
is the accusation that you bring against this man?' The
accusation, he was told, was that Jesus claimed to be king of
the Jews. For when, according to John, he summoned Jesus into
the praetorium to interrogate him, the first question he put to
him was, 'Are you the king of the Jews?' (John 18:33). Jesus'
reply is transposed by John into his own idiom in such a way as
to bring out for his readers the true nature of Jesus'
kingship -- which is not to say with Paul Winter, that Jesus
'treats Pilate to a course in Johannine theology'. /23/

Jesus, in fact, is represented by John as doing before
Pilate something of the same kind as Mark says he did before
the Sanhedrin. When the high priest asked him if he was the
Messiah, he replied in effect: 'If "Messiah" is the word which
you insist on using, my answer can only be "Yes"; but if I were
to choose my own words, this is what I should say' - and then
follows his declaration about the Son of Man (Mark 14: 62).
So, when Pilate asks him if he is a king, he says, '"King" is
your word; if I were to choose my own words, this is what I

should say' - and then follows his declaration about truth
(John 18:34-37). /24/

At this point John introduces the Barabbas episode
(18:38b-40). Whereas in the Markan record it is the crowd
(*ochlos*) that reminds Pilate of his custom to release a
prisoner annually at Passovertide (Mark 15:8), John makes
Pilate take the initiative in bringing up the subject. Pilate
tells the accusers that his interrogation of Jesus has satisfied
him that his claim does not amount to sedition, and asks if he
may release this 'king of the Jews' in accordance with the
paschal custom. In our ignorance of the background to this
custom, we can but note that its independent attestation in the
Johannine alongside the Markan tradition strengthens the case
for its historicity. /25/ John's statement that Barabbas was a
*lēstēs* - Josephus's common designation for Jewish guerrilla
fighters - chimes in well enough with Mark's association of him
with violent insurgents (*stasiastai*).

When Pilate's offer to release Jesus is met with the
demand, 'Not him; we want Barabbas!' (18:40), he proceeds to do
what in Luke's narrative he proposes to do. In Luke 23:22
Pilate says that, since Jesus has committed no capital offence,
he 'will therefore chastise him and release him'. In John 19:1
he has Jesus 'scourged'. This scourging (*mastigōsis*) is not
the *phragellōsis* of Mark 15:15, which was a preliminary stage
in the process of crucifixion, but a less severe beating, a
punishment in itself, intended to teach the accused to be more
prudent in future. /26/

For the actual *cognitio* the soldiers' horse-play (19:2 f.)
is irrelevant; in their dressing up Jesus as a carnival king
and paying him mock homage John sees a deeper significance.
(The narrative at this point bears a superficial resemblance to
that of the Alexandrians' treatment of the idiot Carabas by way
of insulting Herod Agrippa. /27/) But Pilate's presentation of
Jesus - bruised, battered and dressed up in ridicule - to the
chief priests as a fitting king for them was partly an act of
mockery of them and partly an attempt to make them drop the
charge: this sorry figure, he implied, could be a threat to no
one.

The chief priests and their attendants, however, refused
to withdraw the charge. Instead, they changed its wording.

Jesus, we may be sure, had not claimed expressly to be
king of the Jews.  This was the construction put on his claim
by his accusers, in order to give it a form of which Pilate was
bound to take cognizance.  If Jesus had accepted the designation
Messiah in any sense (as Mark says he did), this could well have
been represented to Pilate as a claim to be king of the Jews.

The claim to be Messiah, however, is bound up in the
Markan record with a claim to be Son of God.  Jesus is said to
have replied 'I am' to the high priest's question: 'Are you the
Messiah, the son of the Blessed One?' (Mark 14:61 f.).  In the
Johannine record Jesus, on an earlier visit to Jerusalem, had
used language which not only constituted a claim to be Son of
God but was taken to imply equality with God (John 5:18; cf. 10:
33).  A claim to be king of the Jews, in the absence of a
reigning and recognized Jewish king, was not presumably a
serious offence in Jewish law, but anything which amounted to a
claim to equality with God was held to be blasphemy, a capital
offence.  We need not bring forward into the period of the
second temple the restrictive Mishnaic definition which
recognized blasphemy only when the ineffable name was
pronounced. /28/

Now the chief priests press the plea that, since Jesus
has been found guilty of a capital offence in Jewish law
(blasphemy), Pilate should confirm the death-sentence for this
offence.  After a further brief interrogation of Jesus, Pilate
shows himself unwilling to grant their plea.

But this time the chief priests play their last card, and
it proves effective.  'Never mind about the charge of
blasphemy, then', they say in effect; 'come back to the charge
of sedition.  Any one who claims to be a king infringes
Caesar's authority, and if you release him you are no friend of
Caesar's' (19:12).  According to Sherwin-White, 'the telling
phrase - "If you let this man go, you are not Caesar's friend"
- recalls the frequent manipulation of the treason law for
political ends in Roman public life, and uses a notable
political term - *Caesaris amicus* - to enforce its point'. /29/

'Caesar's friend' is not an official title here, nor is
it used to denote personal friendship, as when Philo speaks of
Herod Agrippa as 'Caesar's friend'. /30/  It has reference to
Pilate as Caesar's legal representative.  For the prefect to
be 'no friend of Caesar's' implies his disloyalty to the
emperor.  To Pilate the message was plain: the chief priests

had independent channels of communication with the imperial
court.  Bowing to their scarcely veiled threat, he sustained
the charge of sedition and sentenced Jesus to be crucified,
taking his seat formally on his tribunal to do so.  That it was
on the charge of sedition that sentence was passed is confirmed
by the wording on the placard fixed to the cross: 'Jesus of
Nazareth, the King of the Jews' (19:19).

John sees a wealth of theological significance in the act
of passing sentence: he draws attention to the place (The
Pavement) and the time: towards noon on the Friday of Passover
Week (the trial lasted longer than had been expected).  He
dramatizes the scene: Pilate presents the chief priests with
their king rather in the manner of the 'recognition' ceremony
at the beginning of the British coronation service.  But the
historical and judicial data are accurately reproduced.

It must be accounted a curiosity of translation and
exegesis that a number of versions (e.g. those by Moffatt,
Goodspeed and C. B. Williams) say in verse 13 that Pilate made
*Jesus* sit on the tribunal.  It is true that the first aorist
*ekathisen* may be transitive as well as intransitive (although
it is regularly intransitive in NT).  But the determinant point
is simply this: there are many things which a Roman judge might
do in the exercise of his wide discretion, but there are some
things which he would not do, and to make the accused sit in
the judge's seat is one of the latter, whether the accused
himself or his accusers were the target of such mockery.  Some
of the translators in question would agree that Pilate did no
such thing, but would maintain that John represented him as
doing so, for purposes of symbolism (as though to suggest that
from a higher point of view it was Pilate who was being judged
and Jesus who was the real judge).  But John's purpose is to
record events that really happened; if he sees (as he does) a
deeper significance in the events, they are none the less
historical events.  Some second-century writers, like Justin
Martyr /31/ and the author of the docetic 'Gospel of Peter',
/32/ might represent Jesus as being placed in mockery on the
judge's seat, but they were influenced by a misinterpretation
of Isa. 58:2.

When John says that Pilate handed Jesus over 'to them'
(*autois*) to be crucified (19:16), he does not mean, as Paul
Winter thought, /33/ that 'Jesus was physically handed over to
the Jews for crucifixion'.  As Winter himself points out, John

makes it plain that the crucifixion was carried out by Roman
soldiers, acting of course under Pilate's command.  When John
says that Pilate 'handed him over to them', he probably means
the same as Luke means when he says that he 'delivered Jesus
up to their will' (Luke 23: 25).  The sense of John 19:16 is
conveyed admirably in NEB: 'Then at last, to satisfy them, he
handed Jesus over to be crucified.'

## Concluding comments

The use of nails on this occasion to fasten the crucified
man to the wood, explicitly attested by John (20:25), is
illustrated by the discovery in an ossuary in 1968 of the bones
of a young man who had been nailed to his cross through each
wrist separately and through both heels together.  He had also
been subjected to the *crurifragium*, like the two criminals
crucified along with Jesus (John 19:31 f.). /34/

It has been emphasized already that the presentation of
data in a theological manner does not diminish their historical
validity.  This is illustrated afresh by the incident of the
dividing of Jesus' clothes.  John quotes the words of Ps. 22:18
as being fulfilled in the action of the soldiers at the foot of
the cross (19:24).  (The other Evangelists have the OT text in
their minds, although they do not introduce it as a formal
quotation.)  It would be easy to regard the incident as an
invention in the primitive church, fulfilling a detail in what
was in any case recognized as a passion psalm - were it not that,
'as has been familiar since Mommsen, legal texts confirm that it
was the accepted right of the executioner's squad to share out
the minor possessions of their victim'. /35/

John presents the trial and execution of Jesus, as he
presents everything else in his record, in such a way as to
enforce his theological *Leitmotiv*: Jesus is the incarnate Word,
in whom the glory of God is revealed.  But the events which he
presents in this way, and pre-eminently the events of the passion,
are real, historical events.  It could not be otherwise, for the
Word became flesh - the revelation became history.

## NOTES

/1/ L. von Ranke, preface to *Geschichten der romanischen und germanischen Völker, 1494-1535* (Berlin, 1824).

/2/ Cf. W. R. Farmer, 'The Palm Branches in John xii.13', *JTS* n.s. 3 (1952), pp. 62 ff.

/3/ RSV is quite misleading in representing Judas as 'procuring a band of soldiers and some officers from the chief priests and the Pharisees'; the reader could not guess that the 'band' consisted of Roman soldiers. NEB and NIV make the distinction clearer.

/4/ In John 18:3, according to P. Winter, Judas is 'said to have been in charge of the cohort'; Winter sees that this is inconsistent with verse 12, but mistakenly ascribes the inconsistency to John (*On the Trial of Jesus* [Berlin, 1961], p. 44).

/5/ Cf. Acts 21:31 ('the tribune of the cohort'); 23:26.

/6/ T. Mommsen, *Römisches Strafrecht* (Leipzig, 1899), p. 240, n. 2.

/7/ M. Goguel, *The Life of Jesus*, E.T. (London, 1933), pp. 468 f.

/8/ P. Winter, *On the Trial of Jesus*, pp. 45 f.

/9/ The *koustōdia* of Matt. 27:65 ff. is not a parallel case; it consisted of temple police, not Roman soldiers, as appears from the fact that they reported to the chief priests, not to the commanding officer.

/10/ Cf. A. Guilding, *The Fourth Gospel and Jewish Worship* (Oxford, 1960), pp. 165 f. The idea that explicitness in the ascription of proper names is a mark of lateness (cf. R. Bultmann, *The History of the Synoptic Tradition*, E. T. [Oxford, 1963], p. 40 *et passim*) is rightly criticized by E. P. Sanders, *The Tendencies of the Synoptic Tradition* [Cambridge, 1969], pp. 10, 24 f., *et passim*): as a criterion it is inconclusive, being both a feature of eyewitness narration and elsewhere a mark of lateness.

/11/ Meaning perhaps 'in that momentous year', 'in that year of all years' (Caiaphas was high priest from A.D. 18 to 36).

/12/ A. N. Sherwin-White, *Roman Society and Roman Law in the New Testament* (Oxford, 1963), p. 45.

/13/ J. Juster, *Les Juifs dans l'Empire romain* (Paris, 1914), ii, pp. 128 ff.; cf. P. Winter, *On the Trial of Jesus*, pp. 75 ff.

/14/ A. N. Sherwin-White, *Roman Society and Roman Law in the NT*, p. 36.

/15/ Josephus, *BJ* vi.124 ff.

/16/ TJ *Sanhedrin* 1.1; 7.2.

/17/ Cf. Josephus, *Ant.* xx.200.

/18/ M. *Sanhedrin* 7.2; Tos. *Sanhedrin* 9.11a.

/19/ Cf. P. Benoit, 'L'Antonia d'Hérode le Grand et le Forum Oriental d'Aelia Capitolina', *HTR* 64 (1971), pp. 135-167.

/20/ *Römisches Strafrecht*, especially pp. 229-250.

/21/ *On the Trial of Jesus*, p. 89.

/22/ A. N. Sherwin-White, *Roman Society and Roman Law in the NT*, p. 47.

/23/ *On the Trial of Jesus*, p. 89.

/24/ Cf. C. H. Dodd, *About the Gospels* (Cambridge, 1950), pp. 37 f.; *Interp. of the Fourth Gospel* (Cambridge, 1953), pp. 88 f. L. Janssen, '"Superstitio" and Persecution', *Vig. Chr.* 33 (1979), p. 155, takes the passage as a factual report and considers that Pilate understood what was being said to him better than is commonly supposed.

/25/ The provision for slaughtering the paschal lamb 'for one whose release from prison has been promised' (M. *Pesaḥim* 8.6) is adduced as throwing light on the Barabbas problem by C. B. Chavel, 'The Releasing of a Prisoner on the Eve of Passover in Ancient Jerusalem', *JBL* 60 (1940), pp. 273-278; J. Blinzler, *The Trial of Jesus*, E.T. (Cork, 1959), pp. 218-221. Its relevance is uncertain, but one should not dismiss it out of hand, as P. Winter does (*On the Trial of Jesus*, p. 91).

/26/ On more and less severe beatings in Roman penal law cf. A. N. Sherwin-White, *Roman Society and Roman Law in the NT*, pp. 27 f.

/27/ Philo, *Flaccus* 36 ff.

/28/ M. *Sanhedrin* 7.5.

/29/ A. N. Sherwin-White, *Roman Society and Roman Law in the NT*, p. 47.

/30/ Philo, *Flaccus* 40.

/31/ Justin, *First Apology* 35.6.

/32/ Gospel of Peter, 7.

/33/ *On the Trial of Jesus*, p. 56. In the next paragraph he adds that this 'is immediately contradicted by the ensuing narrative' (p. 57).

/34/ Cf. V. Tzaferis, 'Jewish Tombs at and near Giv^cat ha-Mivtar, Jerusalem', *IEJ* 20 (1970), pp. 18 ff.; J. Naveh, 'The Ossuary Inscription from Giv^cat ha-Mivtar', *ibid.*, pp. 33 ff.; N. Haas, 'Anthropological Observations on the Skeletal Remains from Giv^cat ha-Mivtar', *ibid.*, pp. 38 ff.

/35/ A. N. Sherwin-White, *Roman Society and Roman Law in the NT*, p. 46; cf. T. Mommsen, *Römisches Strafrecht*, p. 240, n. 2.

# Targumic Transmission and Dominical Tradition

Bruce Chilton,
Department of Biblical Studies,
University of Sheffield,
Sheffield,    S1O 2TN.

"Targum" is not merely the appropriate designation for
certain documents; it implicitly refers to the process by
which those documents were produced.  This process (as well
as the fact that they are written in Aramaic) distinguishes
Targumim from other translations.  In these Aramaic paraphrases,
popular piety and rabbinic theology meet in a uniquely
informative way.  The synagogue was certainly the home of the
interpretation which led to the evolution of the documents
called Targumim.  The Hebrew Bible was too difficult in its
language, and often too obscure in its imagery, to be left
untranslated for the congregation.  The interpreter (meturgeman)
therefore rose to translate after the Hebrew reading, and a
passage in the Babylonian Talmud (Megillah 21b) indicates that
such interpretation was so popular that some congregations
desired to hear more than one targumic rendering of the same
Hebrew passage /1/.  Some of the translations were so firmly
fixed in folk memory that rabbis, we are told, consulted with
speakers of Aramaic to recover the proper phrasing in their
versions /2/.

With the mention of rabbis, we are brought to the second
and equally crucial element in the process of targumic
formation: it is obvious that the evolution of synagogue practice
alone cannot explain the existence of written, authoritative
Targums.  The usage of centuries produced a measure of
consolidation and common custom, but the step from rendering
those passages which happen to have been read in public worship
to translating an entire corpus was a considerable one.  The
passage cited from tractate Megillah shows that some variety
in practice was countenanced by the rabbis for good, pastoral
reasons; it also displays the rabbinic concern for and
involvement with targumic tradition.  The rabbis proscribed
some renderings and accepted others, handed on complete targumic
versions in the names of certain rabbis, and claimed Onqelos as

"our Targum" /3/.  The rabbinic influence on the actual content
of Onqelos has been established in a recent monograph by Moses
Aberbach and Bernard Grossfeld /4/.  The evidence quite
clearly indicates, then, that while Targums might be characterized
as "popular paraphrases" in respect of their liturgical
function /5/, substantively they are products of a dialectical
relationship between synagogue and academy.  Put in another,
perhaps overly simplified way, Targums are popular in origin
but scholarly in their presentation.

     Once Targums are understood in this fashion, their
importance for the student of early Judaism becomes obvious.
Mishnah, Midrash and Talmud evidence, in the main, intramural
rabbinic discussion.  Targums provide us with some insight into
how those discussions found expression (and qualification) in a
more public, less expert context, i.e., in the worship of the
faithful.  We may say this without being so rash as to imagine
that the standard rabbinic translations were everywhere or
consistently accepted, or that there was an exclusive norm
among the rabbis themselves.  The large number of extant Targums
militates against the propriety of such a supposition.  The
Targums better represent a process than an ideal, and the
process is distinct from, even though related to, that which
produced Mishnah, Midrash and Talmud /6/.

     Inasmuch as the reader of the New Testament is by
definition a student of early Judaism, the recent explosion
in Targum studies is to be welcomed even if it is somewhat
daunting to those who attempt to keep abreast of the
literature /7/.  But despite, or perhaps because of, the
diligence of many skilled scholars, the dating of Targums
remains a matter of dispute.  This is a cause for concern,
because our understanding of when a Targum, as we know it, was
in circulation determines how we use it (and whether we use it)
in exegeting the New Testament.  Were Jesus and Paul, for
example, familiar with the Targums we can read today, or are the
Targums actually products of rabbinic retrenchment in the
post-Yavneh period and therefore designed in part to refute
Christian claims?

     The evidence of the Targums themselves and of other
rabbinic literature is notoriously ambiguous in this regard.
The Pseudo-Jonathan Pentateuch Targum, for example, alludes to
the majesty of John Hyrcanus on one hand, and mentions
relatives of Mohammed on the other /8/.  We read in Talmud

that Jonathan ben Uzziel, a disciple of Hillel, composed the
Prophets Targum which bears his name, but he is described as
a follower of Haggai, Zechariah and Malachi /9/; as if just to
compound the confusion, renderings of Prophetic passages which
are clearly related to readings in the Targum Jonathan are
transmitted in the name of Joseph bar Hiyya, the fourth century
sage of Pumbedita /10/. An attempt has been made to cut through
the Gordian knot by asserting that the failure of a Targum to
abide by mishnaic regulations proves that it is pre-mishnaic /11/.
The Targums do sometimes render passages in a way forbidden by
the rabbis and interpret what the rabbis said should not be
translated at all /12/, but does this evidence justify an early
dating? The divergence from Mishnah might be explained in terms
of the dissimilar purposes of targum and mishnah, or by the
influence of non-rabbinic, popular, but not necessarily
primitive opinion, or by divisions within rabbinic discussion
about which we may or may not be informed. All such divergences
prove only what we already know, that Targums are the products of
a distinctive process: the Targums can no more be measured by
mishnah alone than synodical proceedings could be said to furnish
an adequate criterion for dating parochial sermons.

Research into the language of the Targums has proceeded
at an intense level during this century, so one might have hoped
that it would shed some light on their date and provenience.
If so, the expectation has not been met; in order to explain
the situation as briefly as possible, an almost schematic
introduction to the work of the major contributors in this
field will be offered.

Towards the end of the last century, Zacharias Frankel
developed a view of the linguistic relationship between Onqelos,
the official Babylonian Targum, and Pseudo-Jonathan, styled the
"Jerusalem" or "Palestinian" Targum since, it was supposed, it
did not derive from Babylonia. Frankel noticed that Onqelos
and Pseudo-Jonathan sometimes agreed in using words not found
in the later Targums to the Hagiographa, while at other times
Pseudo-Jonathan parted company with Onqelos and employed the
usage of later centuries /13/. Largely following Frankel,
Gustav Dalman added that the defective orthography of
Pseudo-Jonathan reflected the common speech of Galilean and
Babylonian Aramaic from the fourth to the seventh century. The
language of Onqelos was characterized as "scholarly" and "artful",
a "Hebraized Aramaic" /14/, but more primitive than that of
Pseudo-Jonathan.

Paul Kahle and his famous student, Matthew Black,
presented an alternative reconstruction.  Kahle's study of the
Cairo Geniza material (dated to a period between the seventh
and the eleventh century) led him to conclude "that Onkelos
was without importance in Palestine, indeed, that it had not
even existed there till it was introduced from Babylonia, and
then scarcely before 1000 A.D." /15/.  For earlier renderings,
he thought, one had to look to the Fragment Targum, Pseudo-
Jonathan and the Geniza Fragments.  The obvious difficulty here
is that the documentation of these sources is relatively late:
the textual attestation of Pseudo-Jonathan and the Cairo Geniza
finds is post-Islamic, and that of the Fragment Targum is
medieval /16/.  To account for such evidence a Palestinian
Targum in what Black calls its "fluid state" has been postulated
as the matrix of what is alleged to be primitive material in the
later Targums /17/.  So far as the testimony of the documents
discussed can take us, this source is little more than a cipher;
earlier attestation to the "Palestinian Targum" was necessary
to make the hypothesis viable and thereby to overturn the
analysis of Frankel and Dalman.

In 1956 Alejandros Díez Macho publicly identified the
Vatican manuscript he had been working on for some years as an
early representative of the Palestinian Targum.  Since it
belong to the collection of the Library of Neophytes, he named
it Codex Neophyti I.  That this new and important discovery
further evidences non-Babylonian targumic renderings is a
matter of consensus.  But, while admitting that Neophyti's
Aramaic is that of seventh and eighth century manuscripts,
Díez Macho asserts that substantively his text is pre-mishnaic
in content /18/.  We have already observed that anti- or
non-mishnaic is not to be equated with pre-mishnaic, and one
of Díez Macho's most important followers, Martin McNamara, has
not always agreed with the early dating /19/.  Doubt has also
been cast on Díez Macho's claims linguistically, in that the
language of the Targum presents signs of Greek influence which
is so strong as to raise suspicions about the provenience of the
translation, and textually, in that the manuscript is the
victim of poor scribal handling /20/.  In sum, while the
importance of this sixteenth century document is not to be
minimized, neither will it serve as the vindication of Kahle's
thesis.  The recent investigation of Qumran Aramaic, pioneered
by Joseph Fitzmyer, suggests that the language of Onqelos
stands closest to the literary dialect of the first century /21/.
Díez Macho's rejoinder, that the Qumran finds employ a literary

Aramaic contaminated by the spoken Aramaic better attested in
the Palestinian Targum /22/, remains to be substantiated.

The circular path of recent discussion of the language of
the Targums reminds one, if not of the tower of Babel, then of
a plateau of discordant opinions from which continued ascent
is difficult. Nor should it be thought that this discussion,
even should it lead to agreement, would definitively settle the
literary question of the relationship between the Pentateuch
Targums. As Díez Macho reminds us, "the content might be older
than the language" /23/. In the end, it appears premature
to base Targumic exegesis - especially in respect of the New
Testament - on any single theory of how the Aramaic language
evolved: there seem to be more variables than any of them can
comfortably accommodate.

It has nonetheless proved possible to isolate heuristically
certain Targumic passages which antecede the New Testament.
This possibility has long been recognized, as selected examples
from only the recent literature will show. T.W. Manson
demonstrated that the form of Jesus' citation from Isaiah as
reported in Mark 4.12 is closer to what we read in the Isaiah
Targum than it is to the Masoretic or Septuagintal versions of
that book /24/. Among the many similar instances adduced by
Martin McNamara in his two tradition critical treatments of the
relationship between the New Testament and the Targums, Pseudo-
Jonathan on Leviticus 22.28 is quite striking in respect of
Luke 6.36: /25/.

My children, children of Israel, as our Father is
merciful in heaven, so shall you be merciful on
earth.

Investigations of this kind, whether or not all their
conclusions are accepted, have indicated that some of the
material which we can read in extant Targums - whatever their
dates of compilation - was known and used by those who contributed to the formation of the New Testament. When a Targumic
passage parallels or appears to provide the logical antecedent
to a New Testament passage, the natural inference is that the
Targum in question informs us of the basis on which the New
Testament tradents were operating. I have argued elsewhere
briefly and at length that such an inference is reasonable in
respect of the phrase, often attested in the Targums, "kingdom
of God" or "kingdom of the LORD" /26/. Since the phrase is

most frequently found in the Isaiah Targum (24.23; 31.4; 40.9;
52.7), I have devoted a study to that Targum in particular in
which I posit some fifteen instances in which sayings of Jesus
appear to reflect Targumic diction and themes /27/. For
the present purpose, perhaps a single instance will suffice
by way of example. In terms of Matthew 7.2 and Mark 4.24, the
following statement, found in Targum Isaiah 27.8, is surely
of note:

> With the measure with which you were measuring they
> will measure you ...

In evaluating all such work, it must be borne in mind that it
does not establish the date of any Targum as a whole, and there
is no realistic prospect that the tradition critical approach
can succeed in this regard: the Targums as a whole are too
disparate in the material they preserve and too dissimilar to
the New Testament and to Mishnah, Midrash and Talmud for every
Targumic pericope to be dated relative to those documents. The
point is worth emphasizing, because there is a tendency to assume
the antiquity of Targumic readings. The most notable example of
the tendency is recent discussion of the understanding of
Genesis 22 in the New Testament. Because some Targums present
Isaac as dying on Moriah in a way which was efficacious for
Israel, we are encouraged by such scholars as Geza Vermes and
Roger le Déaut to assume that the Aqedah influenced New
Testament soteriology. The fact is, however, that the Aqedah is
not mentioned in the New Testament, and some evidence indicates
that the rabbis actually embellished Genesis 22 and referred to
their haggadah at Passover time in order to reply to Christian
claims about the Passion /28/.

     In the recent monograph mentioned above, I have attempted
to apply a modified form of redaction criticism to the Isaiah
Targum in an attempt to determine its theology, provenience and
date. The results of my analysis are yet to be criticized, and
therefore do not qualify for treatment with the more tried and
tested approaches discussed above, but I hope that the
perspective and general conclusion of my method are at least
worthy of mention. Recognizing that historical allusions and
literary parallels might guide us to an understanding of the
date and provenience of a given passage or motif in a Targum,
and that language (if it were an established criterion) would
help us to suggest the time and place of the final compilation
of the document as a whole, we know that Targums as such are

not farragos of tradition or de novo compositions, but specimens
of extended exegesis.  To discover the provenience and date of
a Targum one must ask, first, what exegetical terms and phrases
are so frequently used as to constitute characteristic
conventions, and then, how do these conventions relate to
historical circumstances, to the New Testament and rabbinic
literature?  Such conventions, when repeatedly used in a given
Targum, would have provided the ordering principle of
traditional interpretations and for the inclusion of subsequent
insights.  This exegetical framework belongs to the esse of a
Targum: without it, targumic readings are only a pot pourri,
while with it the later addition of material does not constitute
a recension, only an addendum.  An analysis of some fifteen
characteristic terms and phrases in the Isaiah Targum reveals
a theology of messianic vindication centered on the return of
dispersed Israel and the re-establishment of cultic integrity.
This theology coheres with the cherished desire of the
Babylonian rabbinate in the Tannaitic period "to avenge the
sanctuary and make possible its restoration" in the words of
Jacob Neusner /29/.  Very recent treatments of the language of
the Prophetic Targum and its cousin, Onqelos, have tended
towards a corroborative finding /30/, though for the reasons
discussed earlier it would be wrong to see therein a proof
of the thesis.

The somewhat inconclusive results of intensive Targum
study perhaps explains why students of the New Testament have
been less than enthusiastic about referring to these documents
in their exegeses.  But if research has not yet shown when
precisely the Targums were compiled, the "why" and "how" of
their formation have become increasingly clear.  They were
designed to hand on and interpret the Law, Prophets, and
Writings.  In principle, they were oral: the meturgeman was
forbidden to look at a text as he translated, lest there be any
confusion between the paraphrase and the written canon in the
mind of the congregation /31/.  Whatever the practice in the
synagogue, the Targums did come to be fixed in writing, and
that froze their wording in a moment of their development in a
way which has permitted posterity to consider their formation.
The Hebrew text is the primary datum of all Targums, to which
they consistently do justice /32/, but they also deviate from
that written tradition for the sake of clarity or exposition /33/.
The workings of the process are particularly apparent in the
case of Pentateuchal Targums, where we can compare several
renderings of the same Hebrew corpus.  Among these Targums

(especially those styled Palestinian) we have verbatim
agreements and marked deviations; Martin McNamara has rightly
observed, "we do have a synoptic problem" /34/.

The more famous synoptic problem in the New Testament
presents an obvious possible analogy, and all the more so as
at least a restricted period of oral transmission must be
postulated in respect of dominical tradition.  J.M. Rist's
recent study resuscitates the oral gospel hypothesis to explain
the relationship between Matthew and Mark /35/, but just what
was this oral gospel like?  Various models have been suggested.
Form criticism gave us pericopae - discrete pearls threaded on
a redactional string by the Evangelists, and each pearl a
community formation over (at best) a dominical piece of sand /36/.
Thorleif Boman has attacked this model, showing quite
convincingly from the orally developed literature of many
cultures that we must think rather of longer, continuous epics
at the point of origin which were woven together in the course
of time /37/.  The evident weakness in Boman's analogy is that
the gospel of Jesus was not preached in some anthropological
abstract, but - in the first instance - in a specifically Jewish
culture.  Birger Gerhardsson has shown how much might be learned
from that fact and has used the Mishnah as a model for
understanding the development of the New Testament.  But
Morton Smith has rightly complained against Gerhardsson that,
in addition to being quite late, Mishnah is too specialist, to
the point of being sui generis, to be of direct relevance in
understanding the formation of the New Testament /38/.  Targums,
however, provide a possible analogy for four reasons, (1) they
are oral in one sense and written in another, (2) they are
specifically Jewish, (3) they are designed for popular consumption,
(4) they manifest a synoptic relationship.

As a test case, to assess the possible analogy further, I
propose to compare the Synoptic Temptation with the Poem of the
Four Nights in the Palestinian Targums.  These passages are
chosen because they are each self-contained and because both are
constructed from Old Testament citations and allusions.  (N.b.,
the Poem refers to more than Exodus 12.42, of which it is the
rendering).  It is to be stressed that any literary dependence
between the Targums and the Synoptic Gospels forms no part of
our argument; their qualitative difference in subject matter
immediately precludes such an implication.  Moreover, the Aqedah
reference in the Poem seems quite late, as I have argued
elsewhere /39/.  We are attending to the simple task of asking

if the structure of these passages and the alterations which
occur through their transmissions might justify the claim that
Synoptic tradition is cognate with Targumic tradition.

A consideration of the Poem as found in the Fragment
Targum will show the structural importance of Old Testament
references, of which the most major are identified in brackets:

It is a night to be observed and set aside for redemption
before the LORD when he brought forth the sons of Israel,
freed from the land of Egypt. Because four nights are
written in the book of memorials.

[The "watching" of the LORD and of Israel is already
mentioned in Exodus 12.42 MT.]

The first night, when the LORD's memra was revealed upon
the world to create it, when the world was without form
and void and darkness was spread on the face of the deep,
and the LORD's memra illuminated and enlightened; he
called it the first night.

[Genesis 1.1-5, quite obviously, paraphrased, one might
note (given that "memra" may be translated as "word"),
in a manner reminiscent of the Johannine prologue.]

The second night, when the LORD's memra was revealed upon
Abraham between the parts. Abraham was a hundred years
old and Sarah was ninety years old, to establish what
scripture says, is Abraham, a hundred years old, able to
beget, and is Sarah, ninety years old, able to bear?
Was not Isaac our father thirty-seven years old at the
time he was offered on the altar? The heavens descended
and came down and Isaac saw their perfections and his
eyes were dimmed from the heights, and he called it the
second night.

[The second night is identified with various moments in
salvation history, arranged in a sequential pattern:
Abraham's covenant sacrifice (Genesis 15.17), the removal
of the obstacle to the covenant promise (Genesis 17.17),
and the confirmation of the promise in respect of Isaac
(Genesis 22.1-18 cf. 27.1).]

The third night, when the LORD's memra was revealed upon
the Egyptians at the dividing of the night; his right hand

killed the firstborn of the Egyptians and his right hand
spared the firstborn of Israel, to establish what scripture
says, Israel is my firstborn son, and he called it the
third night.

[Primarily, this refers to Exodus 12.29, cf. vv.12,13,23,
27 and 4.22.]

The fourth night, when the end of the age is accomplished
to be redeemed, the bands of wickedness destroyed and the
iron yokes broken. Moses comes from the desert, but the
king messiah from above. One leads in the head of the cloud,
and the other leads in the head of the cloud, and the LORD's
memra leads them both, and they will go together.

This is the night of passover before the LORD, to be
observed and set aside by the sons of Israel in their
generations.

[Eventually, we get back to Exodus 12.42, but the
Moses-messiah eschatology is not biblical in the sense
that the references included in the texts attached to
the first three nights are.]

While the Neophyti Poem does deviate from this version, its most
striking feature is its similarity to the Poem as we have cited
it /40/.

The Fragment Targum's Poem obviously differs signally from
the Matthean Temptation. The Targum opens and closes with a
reference to the Hebrew text it renders, while Matthew refers
first to the temptation by the devil (4.1) and finally to the
support of the angels (4.11). Structurally, Matthew presents a
three-tiered dialogue or repartee between biblical passages as
spoken by the principals, while the Targum straightforwardly
offers the reader biblical exposition on the four nights. But
two significant similarities should be observed at the outset.
First, in each, a clear associative chain links the citations.
The LORD's memra is a primary agency in each Targumic
explication of the nights. The Matthean interplay of citations
centers on the proper place of the Son in relation to God.
Second, the climactic point in both (in the Targum, the Moses-
messiah haggadah, in Matthew, the devil's invitation to apostasy)
is not a direct biblical citation, but is immediately followed
by one. The structural patterns of these two very different

passages are therefore distinctive, and yet they are similar
enough to hint at the possibility that they were transmitted
in much the same way.

When we turn to Luke's Temptation, we see another structural
similarity to the Targumic Poem: Luke opens and closes (4.2,13)
with a reference to the devil's tempting, which he treats as
if it were his "text".  The Lukan order, however, insures that
the pattern of a climactic departure from scripture is broken.
But this may not be used as evidence that Luke here disrupts
any analogy to Targumic transmission.  On the contrary,
variations in order are well known to students of the Targums,
and two instances can be cited in respect of the Poem: (1) in
Neophyti, which generally follows the Fragment Targum more
closely than Luke follows Matthew, the reference to Exodus 4.22
("his firstborn son is Israel"), which the Fragment Targum
cites in the context of the third night, is attached in the
margin to the second night, (2) the ancient Exodus midrash,
Mekhilta de R. Simeon b. Johai, actually presents a poem of
three nights, omitting the messianic fourth night /41/.  The
Lukan alteration appears median between the slighter change of
Neophyti (margin) and the radical excision of the Mekhilta
(which also, of course, omits the departure from direct
scriptural reference altogether).

The Markan compression of the Temptation into two verses
(1.12,13) is so stark as to suggest to some scholars that it
does not come from the same stable as the "Q" account /42/.
But the relation of Mark to Matthew and Luke in this matter is
perhaps more explicable when we compare the following version
of the Poem, from Targum Pseudo-Jonathan, to those of the
Fragment Targum and Neophyti:

Four nights are written in the book of memorials before
the Lord of the world.  The first night, when he was
revealed to create the world; the second night, when he
was revealed upon Abraham; the third night, when he was
revealed against Egypt, his left hand killing all the
firstborn of Egypt and his right hand sparing the
firstborn of Israel; the fourth night, when he will be
revealed to redeem the people of the house of Israel
from among the nations ... /43/

It is true that the version in Pseudo-Jonathan at least
maintains the four night structure, while Mark does not do any

justice to the three specific temptations, and that there is
little new in Pseudo-Jonathan as compared to the Fragment
Targum and Neophyti, while the beasts mentioned by Mark
constitute an odd deviation from Matthew and Luke. But having
said that, the fact remains that the scriptural references in
the Poem as found in Pseudo-Jonathan are so attenuated as to
be nearly non-existent, the second night passage lacks a
reference to Isaac and the fourth night passage is no longer
messianic. The analogy to Mark in relation to his colleagues
is certainly not exact, but it is also not entirely uninstructive.

Literal agreement and frustrating variety in diction pose
a major difficulty to theories of documentary dependence. Why
should Mark follow his scroll of Matthew verbatim (or vice versa)
in one passage and pick up a different scroll when he comes to
write another? Even if it is credible that the Evangelists
had libraries at their disposal, why should an author use a
predecessor's material when writing up a passage and then,
before he gets to the end, suddenly go his own way by adding,
deleting, abbreviating, expanding, conflating, separating
and/or changing its context? "Literal agreement" is still the
battle cry of those who argue literary dependence, but the
latter is not a necessary inference from the former /44/. The
relationship between the Fragment Targum and Neophyti already
suggests that documents which were oral in origin - and were
always so in principle - might agree literally. But the
phenomenon in the Synoptic Gospels for which we are seeking
an analogy is agreement and variety together; for this purpose,
we may leave Mark and Pseudo-Jonathan aside, because both
documents present the passages in question in such a relatively
compressed form that they are idiosyncratic from the point of
view of the words they employ. We are therefore left to
compare Matthew and Luke on the one hand with the Fragment
Targum and Neophyti on the other.

The present inquiry does not require that we observe all
the variations manifest in the two sets of documents. We will
restrict ourselves to selecting a sample of substantive
deviations between Matthew and Luke, and then see whether or
not analogous deviations can be found between the Fragment
Targum and Neophyti. Because we use one of a pair of documents
as our starting point for collation, we will speak of its
partner as "changing" or "adding" or "omitting" words, but
such language is only used as a convenience in order to describe
the linguistic relations at issue, not as an assertion of

literary or oral priority. The deviations between Matthew and
Luke selected for analysis are as follows:

1. Luke 4.1 (cf. Matthew 4.1) adds "Full of the holy
spirit he returned from the Jordan".

2. Luke 4.2 (cf. Matthew 4.2) adds "And he ate nothing
in those days and when they were ended he hungered".

3. Luke 4.3 (cf. Matthew 4.3) changes "the tempter" to
"the devil" and "these stones" (nominative) to "this
stone" (dative).

4. Luke 4.4 (cf. Matthew 4.4) omits "but by every word
proceeding from God's mouth".

5. Luke 4.5,6 (cf. Matthew 4.8,9) adds "in a moment of
time" and "for it is given to me and to whom I wish to
give it".

6. Luke 4.13 (cf. Matthew 4.11) omits "And behold
angels came and ministered to him".

As will be seen, each of the deviations selected is
distinctive from the others, so we are not considering a mere
multiplication of the same sort of variant. Each deviation will
be described briefly, and a Targumic analogy posited.

*Deviation 1* is of a narrative order, linking the Lukan
Temptation to the Baptism (3.21,22). The resumptive clause is
appropriate, serving to take the story line up again after the
long, parenthetical genealogy (3.23-38).

*Analogy 1:* the Fragment Targum adds "between the parts" to the
beginning of the second night passage. This serves to specify
Genesis 15.17 as the relevant allusion. Of course, this is
not as substantial an addition as Luke's, the purpose is to fix
the second night exegetically, rather than geographically or
chronologically, and it may be argued that Neophyti implies the
allusion already. Nonetheless, the fact remains that, at the
beginning of a passage, the Fragment Targum augments the
narrative content relative to Neophyti.

*Deviation 2* is also narrative, but its purpose is to explain the
course of events more fully than Matthew's "afterward he

hungered" does.

*Analogy 2:* where, in the first night passage, the Fragment
Targum reads "the LORD's memra illuminated and enlightened",
Neophyti has "the LORD's memra was light", thereby explicating
the scene in terms of Genesis 1.3.  (Alternatively, the
Fragment Targum might be considered to fill out a bare
scriptural reference in more narrative terms).  Again, the
Targumic addition is less fulsome than Luke's, and it
explicates the Poem in respect of scripture, not event.
But it must be borne in mind that the Meturgeman's text was
the written word, while the Evangelist's "text" was Jesus,
and that the Poem is less susceptible of narrative embellishment
than is a haggadic story.

*Deviation 3* is a simple case of preferred idioms used of the
same referent.

*Analogy 3:* in each of the three cases (in the first, second and
third night texts) where Neophyti speaks of the LORD being
revealed, the Fragment Targum meticulously refers to the LORD's
"memra".  Similarly, in the prologue and epilogue to the Poem,
Neophyti says the night is remembered "to the name of the LORD",
while the Fragment Targum simply has "before the LORD".

*Deviation 4* instances an abbreviated citation of a biblical
passage, and it is interesting that Luke's comparative lacuna
is filled in many manuscripts /45/.

*Analogy 4:*  the Poem in Pseudo-Jonathan actually presents the
nearest such instance, but it has already been pointed out
that Neophyti omits the reference to Genesis 15.17 (see Analogy
1).  Without "between the parts" the second night might be
thought of as referring simply to Genesis 17 and 18.  The
sphere of ideas remains the same, but the precise allusions do
vary somewhat between the Fragment Targum and Neophyti.

*Deviation 5* is again essentially narrative, but it performs a
dramatic function in emphasizing the devil's power.

*Analogy 5:*  in the fourth night passage, the Fragment Targum
explicitly refers to the messiah, but Neophyti does not.  While
Moses and messiah appear on clouds in the Fragment Targum,
Moses and the (so far unidentified) figure in Neophyti lead the
flock /46/.  This complex of variants is more important than

may at first appear, because Neophyti then has the second figure
speak as "I", presumably an allusion to God himself.  This
adjustment in reference is a more extreme development than the
change from Matthew to Luke, but the Fragment Targum does
present a more balanced portrayal of the dramatis personae.

*Deviation 6* is the sole alteration in Luke which constitutes
a significant omission.

*Analogy 6:* as has already been mentioned (see Analogy 5),
Neophyti simply deletes "and the king messiah from above" from
the fourth night text.

     At several points we have already had to acknowledge that
the analogies posited are defective.  Where it is a question of
narrative deviation (see 1, 2, 5), the Gospels appeared to
embellish the Temptation, while the Targums in two out of three
of those cases (1, 2) merely added a biblical reference or made
the reference more explicit.  The difference in procedure may
tell us more about the distinction between Targum and Euanggelion
in respect of purpose than about any qualitative difference in
the manner in which they were transmitted.  Analogies 1 and 2 are,
it is true, rather more restrained than Deviations 1 and 2, but
the evidence we have considered prevents us from saying that
Targumic transmission was more conservative than Evangelical
transmission.  Deviation-Analogy 5 would overturn such a
generalization: the Targumic variation in defining the second
figure in the fourth night passage is more radical than the
Evangelical shift in emphasis on the devil's power.  The extent
of the change in the Targumic text is further indicated by the
fact that the same text presents the closest analogy to
Deviation 6, where Luke drops an important element of the
Temptation.  Deviation-Analogy 4 is also not very exact,
curiously because the Gospels of Matthew and Luke are more
extensive and precise in their biblical citation than the Targums
in question are at this particular point.  Deviation-Analogy 3
is unquestionably the best of the lot, and it is surely of
interest to the student of the Gospels that these Targums present
a pattern of distinct but practically synonymous expression -
the very linguistic relationship which lies at the heart of the
Synoptic Problem.

     When the dictional agreement and disagreement between the
Targumic Poems are considered in comparison with the Synoptic
Temptation, and one bears in mind how similar the Poem appears

to the Temptation in its structure and variations of order and
size, the possibility does emerge that the Gospels may have
taken shape according to a process cognate with that which
produced the Targums. The example analysis suggests that the
possibility might be used as a hypothesis for treating more
material of different types. Both the Temptation and the Poem
are basically sui generis within the documents within which
they appear; a representative sampling from the major strata of
the Gospels and the Targums would have to be dealt with in this
way, and similar results to those achieved in the present study
obtained, before the hypothesis here suggested could justifiably
be called a thesis /47/. Nonetheless, we do have before us a
possibility which might warrant such further research.

For those seeking the appropriate focus for future
research, the analysis here conducted offers certain warnings.
Quite obviously, nothing we have observed in the Temptation as
compared to the Poem should incline us to describe the Gospels
as a species of Targum /48/. On the contrary, our consideration
of dictional disagreements which are narrative (Deviations 1, 2,
5) plainly showed that these embellishments on the story line,
specifying Jesus' attitude and position in the proceedings and
the power of the devil he faced, were of a different order from
the exegetical notes and haggadic digressions added in the
Fragment Targum and Neophyti. The goal of Targums is to
provide an understanding of a written text, while Gospels are
designed to explain the significance of a person. The "text"
of the Evangelists was Jesus, and as soon as we have said that,
we realize that it is meaningless to say the Gospels are
Targumic in form, even though they occasionally cite Targumic
renderings /49/. Nor is the distinction between Targum and
Gospel merely formal: each form is congruent with the purpose
of its genre, and the Targums interpret a text as consistently
as the Gospels interpret a person. It follows that the
processes which produced Targums and Gospels should not be
confused, because the controlling influence on one process is
textual while the controlling influence on the other is
personal. For this reason, I speak of the two processes as
being "cognate" rather than "identical", and of the similarities
between the two as "analogies", not "parallels".

If these processes are cognate, then the Targums give us a
handle for grasping the interplay between tradition and
interpretation in the Gospels. When the meturgeman rose in
the synagogue to translate, his duty was twofold: (1) he had to

do justice to the biblical text in Hebrew which he was to render
in Aramaic, but (2) he was also obliged to look away from any
text, to face the congregation and in so doing to explain what
had been read in terms the congregation could appropriate.  At
times these two ends could seem to be in tension, as for
example in the case of the question of how Exodus 24.10 should
be rendered.  The Hebrew text is: "and they saw the God of
Israel".  This was impossible in the contemporary understanding,
so perhaps one should say "and they saw the angel of the God of
Israel".  R. Judah condemned both renderings in his famous and
paradoxical dictum (Kiddushin 49a) /50/:

> If one translates a verse literally, he is a liar;
> if he adds thereto, he is a blasphemer and a libeller.

In the same Talmudic passage, Onqelos ("our Targum") is
authorised as normative: "Then what is meant by translation?
Our translation".  And Onqelos solves the problem /51/:

> and they saw the glory of the God of Israel.

"Glory" is not an addition in the sense that "angel" is,
because God is not replaced with another figure; at the same
time, the lie that God is visible to men is not perpetrated.
The authority of a Targum resides in its care for tradition
(sc. the text and the efforts of earlier translators), but not
only in that; the other constituent of its authority is its
adequacy as a statement about the God referred to in the text.

Such interplay between tradition and redaction is easily
instanced in the Gospels.  The portrayal of Jesus which we see
in them is definitely conditioned by the traditions about him
which were available, but these traditions are selected and
shaped in the course of transmission (both at the traditional
and the redactional levels) /52/.  A single example will
perhaps suffice to illustrate.  In the controversy centered
on the man with a withered hand (Matthew 12.9-14; Mark 3.1-6;
Luke 6.6-11), Jesus confronts his opponents with a saying
(about doing good on the sabbath; vv. 12, 4, 9 respectively)
and an action (the healing; vv. 13, 5, 10).  The attitude of
the opponents is clear: they wish to find a reason to accuse
Jesus (vv. 10, 2, 7).  But what was the attitude of Jesus
himself?  In what seems an early characterization of his
attitude /53/, Mark 3.5 presents Jesus "looking  round at them
with anger, grieved at their hardness of heart".  Luke eschews

this affective language: Jesus merely fixes them with a stare
("looking round at them all") and performs the healing which
causes *them* to be "filled with fury" (6.10,11). Matthew has
no reference to emotion on either side in the two verses in
question (12.13,14), but pursues his characteristic tendency of
letting dialogue alone tell the tale /54/. Slight changes of
diction, such as we have seen in the Temptation passages and
their Targumic analogies, manifest distinctive emphases in the
portrayal of Jesus. The Markan Christ is consumed with the
acute emotions which almost force him to behave as he does /55/;
the Lukan Lord is the master of the situations that confront
him /56/; the Matthean Son is best characterized by the words
and deeds he himself provides as teaching /57/. The Church
which authorized these portraits of Jesus, and many others, by
including them in its canon attested not only to their value as
tradition, but to their efficacy as interpretations which
illuminated Jesus' person for believers /58/. The integrity of
such tradition was not a straightjacket which forced Gospel
tradents into merely mechanical transmission; the paramount
concern was rather for the significance of tradition for faith,
so that explication was as much a part of the authority of these
books as their incorporation of previous data.

"Oral tradition" is widely posited as the medium of gospel
transmission between the resurrection and our written Gospels,
largely on the faute de mieux argument that something of the
kind must have taken place during that period. The insecurity
felt by many at the notion that the facts about Jesus should
have been handed down in this fashion is inevitable, despite
the familiarity we all have with the howlers to which the
written word is liable, since "writing" and "accuracy" are so
closely allied in our culture. Birger Gerhardsson's
contribution has reminded us that this was not the case in the
New Testament period, and unease has been somewhat allayed.
By way of summary, we might contrast our findings with those
of the Gerhardsson thesis. He has suggested that mishnaic
transmission, in which the opinions of various rabbis were
recorded with a view to their relevance in legal controversies,
might be a model for understanding the pre-written history of
our Gospels. As mentioned above, Morton Smith has reminded us
that the Mishnah is simply too late (in comparison with the New
Testament) to supply us with a reliable model for Jewish oral
tradition in the first century. And we must stress again that
the Mishnah is essentially a tool for rabbinic discussion, not
a catechetical document for popular use. These objections

seriously vitiate the Gerhardsson thesis, and they must be
answered before it is appealed to as a support for the
authenticity of the Gospel tradition as a whole.  Further, we
might point out that Jesus' disciples obviously did not
transmit his sayings as those of the rabbis in Mishnah.
Mishnah presents a collection of sayings from various sages /59/,
but the early Christians never handed on dominical logia as
if their significance lay in their relationship to the
assertions of others.  From the collector who first brought
together the sayings which we know from the Synoptic Gospels
to the Coptic *Gospel according to Thomas,* what Jesus had to
say was seen to have divine authorization.  Indeed, Christians
ultimately went so far as to take the audacious step (from a
conservatively religious point of view) of adding something
they called the New Testament to Tanach.  They saw the words
and deeds of Jesus as having a status equivalent to that of
Moses and the prophets.  With this in mind, I see nothing
inappropriate in the claim that the disciples might have used
Targumic methods to transmit the words and deeds of Jesus.
They were certainly important enough to them to merit such
treatment, and our observation of synoptic analogies between
the Palestinian Targums and the first three Gospels suggests
that they may actually have received such treatment /60/.  Of
course (once again) we must always bear in mind that Targums
are essentially Aramaic paraphrases of Hebrew texts, while the
Gospels are expositions of Jesus' life, death and resurrection
which only occasionally (and largely inferentially) translate
Semitic locutions.  The evidence permits of no confusion
between Targums and Gospels, but it also intimates that the
latter were handed down by the use of procedures which were
developed in connection with the former.  Our suggestion is not
that the Gospels are Targums, but that the Gospels took shape
in much the same way that Targums did.  We have already seen
that the extant Palestinian Targums may be quite late, but the
process of Targum formation is agreed to be primitive in origin.
Also, the linguistic and substantive continuity between the
Palestinian Targums with which we have been concerned suggests
that they stem from about the same period, so that the synoptic
relationship between these texts need not have taken any longer
to develop than the synoptic relationship between the first
three Gospels.  Just as the present suggestion is not as
sensitive as Gerhardsson's when the question of dating is
raised, so it fares better when we recall that, unlike Mishnah,
the Targums belonged to the people in the synagogues as well as
to the experts in the academy.  The disciples of Jesus, as

synagogue participants, would have had first hand knowledge
of this sacred oral tradition: that knowledge, it seems, was
an important resource to them as they tried to transmit the
words and deeds of Jesus.

Their choice of a medium, no doubt more reflexive than
deliberate, evidences their apparently immediate appreciation
that the words and deeds of Jesus were of the order of the
words and deeds of the God of Tanach, and were accordingly to
be handed down by a method akin to that used by the meturgeman.
Tradition and interpretation were the proper means of making
what God had once done comprehensible, and were now embraced
and developed to announce what it was that God had done in
Jesus.


*NOTES*

/1/   "Our Rabbis taught: As regards the Torah, one reads and
one translates, and in no case must one read and two translate.
As regards the Prophets, one reads and two may translate.  As
regards the Hallel and the Megillah, even ten may read [and
ten may translate].  What is the reason?  Since the people like
it, they pay attention and hear".  The translation is that of
M. Simon in the I. Epstein edition, *The Babylonian Talmud*,
published by Soncino Press.
/2/   Gustav Dalman, *Grammatik des jüdisch-palästinischen
Aramäisch* (Leipzig: Hinrichs, 1905) 12 (citing *Genesis Rabbah*
79).
/3/   Kiddushin 49a, which is discussed below (cf. note 50).
/4/   *Targum Onqelos on Genesis 49: Translation and Analytic
Commentary:* SBL Aramaic Studies 1 (Missoula: Scholars Press,
1976).
/5/   Cf. Martin McNamara, *Targum and Testament. Aramaic
Paraphrases of the Hebrew Bible: A Light on the New Testament*
(Shannon: Irish University Press, 1972) 12, on the Palestinian
Targum, "Being a paraphrase rather than a translation proper,
this targum ... gives us a good idea of the religious
concepts current when it was composed".
/6/   Cf. John Bowker, *The Targums and Rabbinic Literature*
(Cambridge: CUP, 1969) and Roger LeDéaut, *Introduction à la
littérature targumique* (Rome: Pontifical Biblical Institute,
1966).
/7/   In which endeavour there are two indispensable aids:

the two volume contribution of Bernard Grossfeld, *A Bibliography of Targum Literature:* Bibliographica Judaica 3, 8 (New York: Ktav, 1972, 1977) and *The Newsletter for Targumic and Cognate Studies* (produced at Victoria College, Toronto).

/8/  At Deuteronomy 33.11, Pseudo-Jonathan adds, "and let there not be for those that hate Johanan the high priest a foot to stand on"; cf. McNamara, *The New Testament and the Palestinian Targum to the Pentateuch* (Rome: Pontifical Biblical Institute, 1966) 114-117. As McNamara also mentions (p.61), Genesis 21.21 in Pseudo-Jonathan refers to Ayisha and Fatima, the wife and daughter of Mohammed.

/9/  Megillah 3a: "The Targum of the Prophets was composed by Jonathan ben Uzziel under the guidance of Haggai, Zechariah and Malachi ...". This passage is discussed in a forthcoming monograph, dealing with the theological tendencies of the Isaiah Targum.

/10/  Joseph's translation of Isaiah 5.17 as reported in Pesahim 68a is strikingly similar to the Targumic rendering, but at times (e.g., in Sanhedrin 94b) Joseph refers to renderings of the Prophetic book in Aramaic as already extent. See the monograph cited in note 9 for further discussion and many more examples.

/11/  This procedure is instanced in the previous literature and refuted by A.D. York in "The Dating of Targumic Literature" *Journal for the Study of Judaism* 5 (1974) 49-62. York's position derives from the classic warning voiced in an article in Hebrew by Ch. Albeck entitled "The Apocryphal Halakhah in the Palestinian Targums and the Aggadah" in: J.L. Fishman (ed.), *Jubilee Volume to Dr. Benjamin Menashe Lewin* (Jerusalem: 1940) 93-104.

/12/  Pseudo-Jonathan at Leviticus 18.21 refers to intercourse with Gentiles, a reference censured in Mishnah Megillah 4.9; Mishnah Megillah 4.10 forbids the interpretation of Genesis 35.22, which is translated in all printed Targums. These examples are provided by McNamara, *New Testament* (cited in note 8) 46-51.

/13/  *Zu dem Targum der Propheten:* Jahresbericht des jüdisch-theologisches Seminars (Breslau: Schletter, 1872) 13-16 (place names are treated on 25-28).

/14/  *Op. cit.* (n.2), 60, 61 and 10, 13, 40-42.

/15/  So M. Black, "Aramaic Studies and the Language of Jesus" in: M. Black and G. Fohrer (eds.), *In Memoriam Paul Kahle:* BZAW 103 (Berlin: Töpelmann, 1968) 17-28, 18. Within the Kahle school, the major works are Kahle's own *The Cairo Geniza* (Oxford: Blackwell, 1959$^2$) and Black's *An Aramaic Approach to*

*The Gospels and Acts* (Oxford: Clarendon, 1967[3]).

/16/  Cf. Étan Levine, "Some Characteristics of Pseudo-Jonathan to Genesis" *Augustinianum* 11 (1971) 89-103; M.C. Doubles, "Indications of Antiquity in the Orthography and Morphology of the Fragment Targum" in: Black and Fohrer (n.15), 79-89; McNamara, *Targum* (n.5) 183.

/17/  *Op. cit.* (n.15) 19.

/18/  He has recently produced a lucid résumé of his position in "Le Targum palestinien" in: J.É. Ménard (ed.), *Exégèse Biblique et Judaïsme* (Strasbourg: Faculté de Théologie catholique, 1973) 17-77, cf. 36, 38f.  The article is also available in *Recherches de science religieuse* 47 (1973) 169-231.

/19/  Compare *New Testament* (n.8) 62-63 and *Targum* (n.5) 12, 186.

/20/  See G.J. Cowling, "New Light on the New Testament? The significance of the Palestinian Targum" *Theological Students' Fellowship Bulletin* 51 (1968) 6-14 and Klaus Koch, "Messias und Sündenvergebung in Jesaja 53 - Targum.  Ein Beitrag zu der Praxis der aramäischen Bibelübersetzung" *Journal of Semitic Studies* 3 (1972) 117-148, 118, 119 (that is, n.5).

/21/  Cf. *The Genesis Apocryphon of Qumran Cave I*: Biblica et Orientalia 18 (Rome: Pontifical Biblical Institute, 1966, 1971[2]) 17-34; Stephen A. Kaufman, "The Job Targum from Qumran" *Journal of the American Oriental Society* 93 (1973) 317-327; A. Tal, *The Language of the Targum of the Former Prophets and Its Position within the Aramaic Dialects* (Hebrew): Texts and Studies in the Hebrew Language and Related Subjects (Tel-Aviv: Tel-Aviv University, 1975).

/22/  Art. cit. (n.18) 27.

/23/  Art. cit. (n.18) 35.

/24/  *The Teaching of Jesus.  Studies of its Form and Content* (Cambridge: CUP, 1931) 77-80.

/25/  *New Testament* (n.8) 133-138 or *Targum* (n.5) 118.

/26/  "Regnum Dei Deus Est" *Scottish Journal of Theology* 31 (1978) 261-270 and *God in Strength.  Jesus' announcement of the Kingdom*: Studien zum Neuen Testament und seiner Umwelt (Monographien) 1 (Freistadt: Plöchl, 1979).

/27/  This was originally part of the monograph cited in n.9, but it will probably be published separately.

/28/  Cf. P.R. Davies and B.D. Chilton, "The Aqedah: a revised tradition history" *Catholic Biblical Quarterly* 40 (1978) 514-546.

/29/  *The History of the Jews in Babylonia* I: Studia Post-Biblica (Leiden: Brill, 1965) 67.

/30/  Cf. the work of Kaufman and Tal, cited in n.21.

/31/  Megillah 32a.

/32/  As Koch, art. cit. (n.20) has shown in particular.

/33/  See the introductory comments of J.F. Stenning in *Targum to Isaiah* (Oxford: Clarendon, 1949).

/34/  *Targum*  (n.5) 168.

/35/  *On the independence of Matthew and Mark*: SNTMS 32 (Cambridge: CUP, 1978).

/36/  For a convenient summary of the views of K.L. Schmidt and his successors, see W.G. Kümmel, *The New Testament: The History of the Investigation of Its Problems* (London: SCM, 1973) 327-338.

/37/  *Die Jesus-Überlieferung im Lichte der neuern Volkskunde* (Göttingen: Vandenhoeck and Ruprecht, 1967).

/38/  Gerhardsson, *Memory and Manuscript. Oral Tradition and Written Transmission in Rabbinic Judaism and Early Christianity*: Acta Seminarii Neotestamentici Upsaliensis (Lund: Gleerup, 1961); Smith, "A Comparison of Early Christian and Early Rabbinic Tradition" *Journal of Biblical Literature* 82 (1963) 169-176.

/39/  "Isaac and the second night: a   consideration" *Biblica* (forthcoming).

/40/  Unfortunately, Moses Ginsburger does not offer this passage in *Das Fragmententhargum* (Berlin: Calvary, 1899), but cf. Bishop Walton's Polyglot (London: 1655-1657), LeDeaut's *La nuit pascale*: Analecta Biblica 22 (Rome: Pontifical Biblical Institute, 1963) and J.W. Etheridge's translation (New York: Ktav, 1968) for the text here postulated.

In the case of Neophyti I, we offer the following version on the basis of Díez Macho's editio princeps (Madrid: Consejo Superior de Investigaciones científicas, 1970):

> It is a night to be observed and set aside for redemption to the name of the LORD in the time he brought forth the sons of Israel, freed from the land of Egypt. Indeed, four nights are written in the book of memorials.
> The first night, when the LORD was revealed upon the world to create it, and the world was without form and void and darkness was spread on the face of the deep, and the LORD's memra was light and enlightened; he called it the first night.
> The second night, when the LORD was revealed upon Abraham, a hundred years old, and Sarah his wife, ninety years old, to establish was scripture says, will Abraham, a hundred years old, beget, and will Sarah his wife, ninety years old, bear? And Isaac was thirty-seven years old when he was offered on the altar. The heavens descended and came down and Isaac saw their perfections, and he called it the second night.

> The third night, when the LORD was revealed upon the
> Egyptians at the dividing of the night; his hand
> killed the firstborn of the Egyptians and his right
> hand shielded the firstborn of Israel, to establish
> what scripture says, Israel is my firstborn son, and
> he called it the third night.
> The fourth night, when the end of the age is
> accomplished to be redeemed, the iron yokes broken
> and the generations of wickedness destroyed. Moses
> comes up from the desert. One leads in the head of
> the flock, and his memra leads them both, and I and
> they lead together.
> This is the night of passover to the name of the LORD,
> to be observed and set aside for redemption by all
> Israel in their generations.

The translations of the Fragment Targum and Neophyti here
presented are designed to give the reader opportunity to
compare more deviations than are discussed below.

/41/  LeDeaut, *La nuit* (n.40) 151 (n.50).

/42/  See, e.g., the commentaries of Vincent Taylor (London:
Macmillan, 1952) and C.E.B. Cranfield (Cambridge: CUP, 1959).

/43/  Cf. M. Ginsburger, *Pseudo-Jonathan* (Berlin: Calvary, 1903).

/44/  W.R. Farmer has been quick to call attention to the
"Lachmann fallacy", which Lachmann himself did not perpetrate,
but his logical acumen was not exercised by this more basic
specimen of legerdemain. Cf. *The Synoptic Problem. A Critical
Analysis* (London: Collier-Macmillan, 1964 and Dillsboro:
Western North Carolina Press, 1976).

/45/  The text here used is Kurt Aland's eighth edition of
*Synopsis Quattuor Evangeliorum* (Stuttgart: Württembergische
Bibelanstalt, 1967).

/46/  The difference in Aramaic is between $^c$anana and $^c$ana, as
Díez Macho points in the editio princeps (n.40) 78 n.10.
What the editor and translators missed is that the "I" ('ana)
reading of Neophyti represents a consistent application of the
same basic word play. This suggests that the deletion of the
clause about the messiah was not accidental.

/47/  Moreover, a comparison with the (prima facie less similar)
synoptic relationships in other rabbinic literature would be
necessary. My preliminary conclusion is based on a reading
of Jacob Neusner, *Eliezer ben Hyrcanus: The Tradition and the
Man: Studies in Judaism of Late Antiquity* 3, 4 (Leiden: Brill,
1973). I am happy to report that Morton Smith was inclined
to the same view, art.cit. (n.38) 173 n.9. Smith also agrees
that the "Sitz im Leben" of the Gospels "seems to have been

the synagogue, not the school", so he would logically find the present suggestion congenial.

/48/ Mutatis mutandis, on formal grounds doubt must also be cast on the attempt to understand the Gospels as a species of midrash, cf., for instance, Michael Goulder, *Midrash and Lection in Matthew* (London: SPCK, 1974).

/49/ This has been recognized by researchers from J.R. Harris ("Traces of Targumism in the New Testament" *Expository Times* 32 (1920-1921) 373-376) to Martin McNamara, who has wisely cautioned, "Pan-Targumism is no more a solution than Pan-Babylonianism, Pan-Hellenism or any of the other 'Pan's' which at one time or another have been put forward as explanations of the New Testament" (*Targum* (n.5) 169).

/50/ See the text and notes provided by M. Freedman in the Epstein edition (n.1), and McNamara's discussion in *New Testament* (n.8) 41.

/51/ And, according to McNamara (*loc. cit.*), "all Tgs to Ex 24,10".

/52/ The distinction between the two which I have attempted to explore elsewhere is not the focus of attention here. Cf. "An evangelical and critical approach to the sayings of Jesus" *Themelios* 3 (1978) 78-85; *God in Strength* (n.26); "The Transfiguration: dominical assurance and apostolic vision" *New Testament Studies* (forthcoming) and the other contributions to the Gospels Research Project.

/53/ As Taylor (n.42) observes, but Markan priority need not be assumed for the observation of divergence which is the present task.

/54/ Cf. H.J. Held, "Matthew as Interpreter of the Miracle Stories" in: G. Bornkamm, G. Barth, H.J. Held, *Tradition and Interpretation in Matthew* (London: SCM, 1963) 165-299.

/55/ Taylor (n.42) cites the evidence of other passages.

/56/ Cf. I.H. Marshall, *Luke: Historian and Theologian* (Devon: Paternoster, 1970).

/57/ Cf. J.D. Kingsbury, *Matthew: Structure, Christology, Kingdom* (London: SPCK, 1976).

/58/ Cf. R.M. Grant, *A Short History of the Interpretation of the Bible* (London: Collier-Macmillan, 1972).

/59/ Cf. B.T. Viviano, *Study as Worship. Aboth and the New Testament:* Studies in Judaism in Late Antiquity (Brill: Leiden, 1978).

/60/ But research into such analogies must obviously continue. Two articles of this nature (in respect of Josephus and Luke) by F.G. Downing are scheduled for publication in *Journal for the Study of the New Testament*.

# The Bodily Resurrection of Jesus /1/

William Lane Craig
Schellingstrasse 3/3
Universität München

There are probably few events in the gospels for which the historical evidence is more compelling than for the resurrection of Jesus. Historical-critical studies during the second half of this century, increasingly freed from the lingering Deistical presuppositions that largely determined in advance the results of resurrection research during the previous 150 years, have reversed the current of scepticism concerning the historical resurrection, such that the trend among scholars in recent years has been acceptance of the historical credibility of Jesus's resurrection.

Nevertheless, there is still one aspect of the resurrection that a great number of scholars simply cannot bring themselves to embrace: that Jesus was raised from the dead *physically*. The physicalism of the gospels' portrayal of Jesus's resurrection body accounts, I think, more than any other single factor for critical scepticism concerning the historicity of the gospel narratives of the bodily resurrection of Jesus. Undoubtedly the prime example of this is Hans Grass's classic *Ostergeschehen und Osterberichte*. /2/ Inveighing against the 'massiven Realismus' of the gospel narratives, Grass brushes aside the appearance stories as thoroughly legendary and brings every critical argument he can summon against the empty tomb. Not that Grass would construe the resurrection, at least overtly, merely in terms of the survival of Jesus's soul; he affirms a bodily resurrection, but the body is 'spiritual' in nature, as by the apostle Paul, not physical. Because the relation between the old, physical body and the new, spiritual body is *totaliter-aliter*, the resurrection entails, not an emptying of the tomb, but the creation of a new body. Because the body is spiritual, the appearances of Christ were in the form of heavenly visions caused by God in the minds of those chosen to receive them.

    It is difficult to exaggerate the extent of Grass's
influence.  Though few have been willing to join him in denying
the empty tomb, since the evidence inclines in the opposite
direction, one not infrequently finds statements that because
the resurrection body does not depend upon the old body, we are
not compelled to believe in the empty tomb.  And it is everywhere asserted, even by those who staunchly defend the empty
tomb, that the spiritual nature of the resurrection body
precludes physical appearances such as are narrated in the
gospels.  John Alsup remarks that '. . . no other work has been
so widely used or of such singular importance for the interpretation of the gospel accounts. . . as Grass'. . . .'/3/  But,
Alsup protests, Grass's insistence that the heavenly vision
type of appearance underlies the physical appearances of the
gospels 'is predicated upon the impossibility of the material
realism of that latter form as an acceptable answer to the
"what happened" question. . . . Grass superimposes this
criterion over the gospel appearance accounts and judges them
by their conformity or divergence from it.'/4/  As a result,
'. . . the contemporary spectrum of research on the gospel
resurrection appearances displays a proclivity to the last
century (and Celsus of the second century) in large measure
under the influence of Grass' approach.  In a sense the gospel
stories appear to be something of an embarrassment; their
"realism" is offensive.'/5/

    What legitimate basis can be given to such a viewpoint?
Those who deny the physical resurrection body of Jesus have
developed a line of reasoning that has become pretty much
stock-in-trade:

        The New Testament church does not agree about the
    nature of Christ's resurrected body.  Material in Luke and
    John perhaps suggest this body to be corporeal in nature.[43]
    Paul, on the other hand, clearly argues that the body is a
    spiritual body.  If any historical memory resides in the
    accounts of Paul's conversion in Acts, he must not have
    understood the appearance of Christ to have been a
    corporeal appearance.  Most critics identify this
    conversion with the event referred to in I Cor. 15:8:
    'Last of all, as to one untimely born, he appeared also to
    me.'[44]  The arguments in verses 47-50 of this chapter for
    the identity between Christ's body and the spiritual body
    of the resurrection indicate that for the Apostle his Lord
    rose from the dead in a spiritual body.  Most importantly,

Paul has equated the appearance of Christ to him with the appearances to the other apostles. The resurrected Christ, as he was manifested to the church is thus a spiritual body. . . .

[43]Luke 24.39-43; John 20.26-38. There are, of course, contradictory elements in the stories which imply the body is more than physical.
[44]. . ./6/

We can formulate this reasoning as follows:

1. Paul's information is at least *prima facie* more reliable than the gospels.
   a. For he stands in closer temporal and personal proximity to the original events.
2. Paul's information, in contrast to the gospels, indicates Jesus possessed a purely spiritual resurrection body.
   a. First Argument:
      (1) Paul equated the appearance of Jesus to him with the appearances of Jesus to the disciples.
      (2) The appearance of Jesus to Paul was a non-physical appearance.
      (3) Therefore, the appearances of Jesus to the disciples were non-physical appearances.
   b. Second Argument:
      (1) Paul equated Jesus's resurrection body with our future resurrection bodies.
      (2) Our future resurrection bodies will be spiritual bodies.
      (3) Therefore, Jesus's resurrection body was a spiritual body.
3. Therefore, Jesus possessed a purely spiritual resurrection body.

In this way the gospel accounts of the physical resurrection may be dismissed as legendary.

Now it is my conviction that this reasoning cannot bear the weight placed upon it by those who would reject the physical resurrection. I shall not in this essay contest the first premiss. But I wish to take sharp issue with the second. Neither of the two supporting arguments, it seems to be, is sound; on the contrary, they embody serious misconceptions.

With regard to the first supporting argument, concerning
the appearance of Jesus to Paul, it seems to me that both
premisses (1) and (2) are highly questionable. Taking the
premisses in reverse order, what is the evidence for  (2) *The
appearance of Jesus to Paul was a non-physical appearance?*
Usually appeal is made to the accounts of this incident in Acts,
where, it is said, the appearance is to be understood as a
visionary experience (Acts 9.1-19; 22.3-16; 26.9-23). As a
matter of fact, however, the appearance in Acts, while involving
visionary elements, cannot without further ado be characterized
as purely visionary, since in all three accounts it is
accompanied by extra-mental phenomena, namely, the light and
the voice, which were experienced by Paul's companions.  Grass
dismisses these as due to Luke's objectifying tendencies./7/
This is, however, very doubtful, since Luke does not want to
objectify the *post*-ascension visions of Jesus; it is the *pre*-
ascension appearances whose extra-mental reality Luke emphasizes.  Had Luke had no tradition that included Paul's
companions, then we should have another vision like Stephen's,
lacking extra-mental phenomena.  And secondly, if Luke had
invented the extra-mental aspects of the appearance to Paul, we
should have expected him to be more consistent and not to
construct such discrepancies as that Paul's companions heard
and did not hear the voice.  These inconsistencies suggest that
the extra-mental phenomena were part of Luke's various
traditions.

Grass further maintains that Luke had before him a
tradition of Paul's experience that could not be assimilated to
the more physical appearances of Christ to the disciples and
that therefore the tradition is reliable; the extra-mental
aspects are the result of mythical or legendary influences./8/
But one could argue that precisely the opposite is true:  that
because the appearance to Paul is a post-ascension experience
Luke is forced to construe it as a heavenly vision, since Jesus
has physically ascended.  Grass's anthropomorphic parallels
from Greek mythology (Homer *Illiad* α 158; idem *Odyssey* π. v.
161; Apollonius *Argonauts* 4. 852) bear little resemblance to
Paul's experience; a genealogical tie between them is most
unlikely.  Thus, no appeal to the Acts accounts of the
appearance to Paul can legitimately be made as proof that that
appearance was purely visionary in nature.

Paul himself gives us no firm clue as to the nature of
Christ's appearance to him.  But it is interesting to note that

when Paul speaks of his 'visions and revelations of the Lord' (II Cor 12.1-7) he does *not* include Jesus's appearance to him. Paul and the early Christian community as a whole were familiar with religious visions and sharply differentiated between these and an appearance of the risen Lord./9/  But what was the difference?  Grass asserts that the only difference was in *content*:  in an appearance the exalted Christ is seen./10/  But surely there must have been religious visions of the exalted Christ, too.  Both Stephen's vision and the book of Revelation show that claims to visions of the exalted Christ which were not resurrection appearances were made in the church.  Nor can it be said that the distinctive element in an appearance was the commissioning, for appearances were known which lacked this element (the Emmaus disciples, the 500 brethren).  It seems to me that the most natural answer is that an appearance involved extra-mental phenomena, something's *actually* appearing, whereas a vision, even if caused by God, was purely in the mind.  If this is correct, then Paul, in claiming for himself an *appearance* of Christ as opposed to a *vision* of Christ, is asserting to have seen something, not merely in the mind, but actually 'out there' in the real world.  For all we know from Paul, this appearance could conceivably have been as physical as those portrayed in the gospels; and it is not impossible that Luke then 'spiritualized' the appearance out of the necessity of his pre- and post-ascension scheme!  At any rate, it would be futile to attempt to prove that either Acts or Paul supports a purely visionary appearance to the apostle on the Damascus road.

But suppose this is altogether wrong.  Suppose the appearance to Paul was purely visionary.  What grounds are there for believing premiss (1), *Paul equated the appearance of Jesus to him with the appearance of Jesus to the disciples?* Usually appeal is made to the fact that Paul places himself in the list of witnesses of the appearances; hence, the other appearances  must have also been visionary appearances like his own.  This, however, does not seem to follow.  First, in placing himself in the list of witnesses, Paul does not imply that the foregoing appearances were the same *sort* of appearance as the one to him.  He is not concerned here with the *how* of the appearances, but with *who* appeared.  He wants to list witnesses of the risen Christ, and the mode of the appearance is entirely incidental.  But second, in placing himself in the list, Paul is not trying to put the appearances to the others on a plane with his own; rather he is trying to level up his own experience to the objectivity and reality of the others.

Paul's detractors doubted or denied his apostleship (I Cor 9.
1-2; II Cor 11.5; 12.11) and his having seen Christ would be an
important argument in his favor (Gal 1.1, 11-12, 15-16; I Cor 9.
1-2; 15.8-9). His opponents might tend to dismiss Paul's
experience as a mere subjective vision, not a real appearance,
and so Paul is anxious to include himself with the other
apostles as a recipient of a genuine, objective appearance of
the risen Lord. By putting himself in the list, Paul is saying
that what *he* saw was every bit as much a real appearance of
Jesus as what *they* saw. In fact, one could conceivably argue
that Paul's adding himself to the list is actually a case of
special pleading! At any rate, it is a *non sequiter* to infer
that because Paul includes himself in the list of witnesses, all
the other appearances must be of the same mode as the appearance
to Paul.

Hence, the first argument against Jesus's physical resurrection seems doubly unsound. Not only does the evidence run
against a purely visionary appearance to Paul, but there is no
indication that Paul equated the mode of the appearance of Jesus
to himself with the mode of the appearances to the other
disciples.

Let us turn then to the second supporting argument for a
purely spiritual resurrection body of Jesus: the argument from
Paul's term σῶμα πνευματικόν. Premiss (1), *Paul equated Jesus's
resurrection body with our future resurrection bodies*, is surely
correct (Phil 3.21; I Cor 15.20; Col 1.18). But the truth of
premiss (2), *our future resurrection bodies will be spiritual
bodies*, depends upon how one defines its terms. Therefore,
before we look more closely at Paul's discussion of the resurrection body in I Cor 15.35-57, a word ought to be said about
Paul's anthropological terms σῶμα, σάρξ, and ψυχή.

The most important term in the second half of I Cor 15 is
σῶμα./11/ During the nineteenth century under the influence of
idealism, theologians interpreted the σῶμα as the form of a
thing and the σάρξ as its substance./12/ In this way they
could avoid the objectionable notion of a physical resurrection,
for it was the form that was raised from the dead endowed with
a new spiritual substance. Hence, in the old commentaries one
finds that the σῶμα πνευματικόν was conceived to be a body made
out of *himmlischer Lichtsubstanz*. This understanding has now
been all but abandoned./13/ The view of σῶμα as merely form
and σάρξ as its substance cannot be exegetically sustained;

σῶμα *is* the body, form and substance. This does not mean,
however, that twentieth century theologians take σῶμα to mean
the physical body. Rather under the influence of existentialism,
particularly as adopted by Bultmann, they take σῶμα, when used
theologically, as the whole person conceived abstractly in
existentialist categories of self-understanding. Thus, σῶμα
does not equal the physical body, but the person, and hence, a
bodily resurrection means, not a resurrection of the physical
body, but of the person. In this way the doctrine of physical
resurrection is avoided as adroitly as it was in the days of
philosophical idealism. It is the burden of Gundry's study to
show that this understanding is drastically wrong. Even if his
exegesis suffers at times from over-kill,/14/ Gundry succeeds
admirably in carrying his main point: that σῶμα is never used
in the New Testament to denote the whole person in isolation
from his physical body, but is much more used to denote the
physical body itself or the man with special emphasis on the
physical body. Gundry's conclusion is worth quoting:

> The *sōma* denotes the physical body, roughly synonymous
> with 'flesh' in the neutral sense. It forms that part of
> man in and through which he lives and acts in the world.
> It becomes the base of operations for sin in the unbeliever,
> for the Holy Spirit in the believer. Barring prior
> occurence of the Parousia, the *sōma* will die. That is the
> lingering effect of sin even in the believer. But it will
> also be resurrected. That is its ultimate end, a major
> proof of its worth and necessity to wholeness of human
> being, and the reason for its sanctification now./15/

The importance of this conclusion cannot be over-
emphasized. Too long we have been told that for Paul σῶμα is
the ego, the 'I' of a man. Like a dash of cold water, Gundry's
study brings us back to the genuine anthropological consciousness of first century man. The notion of body as the 'I' is a
perversion of the biblical meaning of σῶμα: Robert Jewett
asserts, 'Bultmann has turned σῶμα into its virtual opposite:
a symbol for that structure of individual existence which is
essentially non-physical.'/16/ Hence, existentialist treatments
of σῶμα, as much as idealist treatments, have been a positive
impediment to accurate historical-critical exegesis of I Cor 15
and have sacrificed theology to a philosophical fashion that is
already passé./17/ To say that σῶμα refers primarily to the
physical body is not to say that the word cannot be used as
*synecdoche* to refer to the whole man by reference to a part.

'The *sōma* may represent the whole person simply because the *sōma*
lives in union with the soul/spirit. But *sōma* does not *mean*
"whole person," because its use is designed to call attention to
the physical object which is the body of the person rather than
the whole personality.'/18/ Nor does this preclude metaphorical
use of the word, as in the 'body of Christ' for the church; for
it is a *physical* metaphor: the church is not the 'I' of Christ.
When we turn to I Cor 15 and inquire about the nature of the
resurrection body, therefore, we shall be inquiring about a *body*,
not about an ego, an 'I', or a 'person' abstractly conceived
apart from the body.

I have already alluded to Paul's use of σάρξ, and it will
not be necessary to say much here. Theologians are familiar
with σάρξ as the evil proclivity within man. This touches
sensitive nerves in German theology because the Creed in German
states that I believe in the resurrection of the *Fleisch*, not of
the *body* as in the English translation. Hence, many theologians
are rightly anxious to disassociate themselves from any doctrine
that the flesh as a morally evil principle will be resurrected.
But they seem prone to overlook the fact that Paul often uses
σάρξ in a non-moral sense simply to mean the physical flesh or
body. In this morally neutral sense the resurrection of the
flesh = resurrection of the body. Now in I Cor 15 Paul is
clearly speaking of σάρξ in a physical, morally neutral sense,
for he speaks of the flesh of birds, animals, and fish, which
would be absurd in any moral sense. Hence, understood in a
physical sense, the doctrine of the resurrection of the flesh
is morally unobjectionable.

Finally a brief word on the third term ψυχή: Paul does not
teach a consistent dualism of σῶμα–ψυχή, but often uses πνεῦμα
and other terms to designate the immaterial element of man. In
fact in the adjectival form, ψυχικός has a meaning that does not
connote immateriality at all, but rather the natural character
of a thing in contradistinction to the supernatural character of
God's Spirit. Thus in I Cor 2.14–3.3 Paul differentiates three
types of men: the ἄνθρωπός ψυχικός or natural man apart from
God's Spirit; the ἄνθρωπός πνευματικός or spiritual man who is
led and empowered by God's Spirit; and the ἄνθρωπός σαρκινός or
carnal man who, though possessing the Spirit of God (I Cor 12.
13), is nevertheless still under the sway of the σάρξ or evil
principle in human nature. This makes it evident that for Paul
ψυχικός did not have the connotations which we today associate
with 'soul.'

With these terms in mind we now turn to Paul's discussion
in I Cor 15.35-37. He begins by asking two polemical questions:
How are the dead raised? With what kind of body do they come?
(v 35; cf. II Bar 49.2-3). Paul's opponents seemed to have been
unable to accept the resurrection because the resurrection of a
material body was either inconceivable or offensive to their
Greek minds (cf. Bultmann's 'resuscitation of a corpse'). Paul's
answer steers a careful course between the crasser forms of the
Pharisaic doctrine of resurrection, in which the raised will,
for example, each beget a thousand children and eat the flesh of
Leviathan, and the Platonistic doctrine of the immortality of
the soul apart from the body. Paul will contend that the
resurrection body will be radically different from this natural
body, but that it will nevertheless be a *body*—Paul contemplates
no release of the soul from the prison house of the body. Paul's
answer is that the resurrection body will be a marvellous transformation of our present body, making it suitable for existence
in the age to come—a doctrine not unusual in the Judaism of
Paul's day and remarkably similar to that of the contemporary
II Bar 50-51, which should be read in conjunction with Paul's
argument./19/ It is highly instructive, particularly if we
accept that the author of Luke-Acts was an associate of Paul,
that Luke specifically identifies Paul's doctrine of the
resurrection with that of the Pharisees (Acts 23.6; cf. 24.14;
16.6, 21-23).

In the first paragraph, vv 36-41, Paul searches for
analogies to the resurrection of the dead (v 42). The first
analogy is the analogy of the seed. The point of the analogy
is simply to draw attention to how different the plant is from
the seed that is buried in the ground (cf. Matt 13.31-32 for
Jesus's use of a similar analogy in another context). It is a
good analogy for Paul's purposes, for the sowing of the seed and
its death are reminiscent of the burial of the dead man (vv 42-
44). To criticize Paul's analogy from the standpoint of modern
botany—saying, for example, that a seed does not really die—
presses the analogy too far. Similarly some commentators
criticize Paul's analogy because he lacked the modern botanical
notion that a particular type of seed yields a particular type
of plant; Paul thought God alone determined what plant should
spring up from *any* seed that was sown (v 38). But this is
quite unreasonable, as though Paul could think that a date-palm
would conceivably spring from a grain of corn! He specifically
says that God gives 'each kind of seed its own body' (v 38),
which harks back to the Genesis account of creation according

to kinds (Gen 1.11). At any rate this loses the whole point of
the analogy: that from the mere seed God produces a wonderfully
different plant.

Paul then appeals to the analogy of different sorts of
flesh again in order to prove that if we recognize differences
even in the physical world then the resurrection body could also
be different from our present body. Paul's analogy may have in
mind the creation account, but I think the Jewish distinction
between clean and unclean food is closer (cf. Lev 11; animals:
1-8; fish: 9-12; birds: 13-19; insects: 20-23; swarming
things: 29-30)./20/ So I do not think σάρξ here is precisely
identical with σῶμα. Not only would that reduce Paul's argument
to the rather banal assertion that men have different bodies
from fish, but it would also entail the false statement that all
animals have the same kind of body. Rather in the present
connection, σάρξ means essentially 'meat' or 'organic matter.'
The old commentaries were therefore wrong in defining σάρξ *tout
simple* as 'substance,' for inorganic matter would not be σάρξ;
Paul would never speak of the flesh of a stone. To say that the
resurrection body has therefore a different kind of flesh than
the present body probably presses the analogy too far; all Paul
wants to show is that as there are differences among mundane
things, analogously the supernatural resurrection body could
also differ from the present body.

The third analogy is that of terrestrial and celestial
bodies (vv 40-41). There can be no doubt from v 41 that Paul
means astronomical bodies, not angels. Again the point of the
analogy is the same: there are radical differences among
bodies in the physical world, so why should not the body in the
world to come differ from the present body? Paul's analogy is
particularly apt in this case because as the heavenly bodies
exceed terrestrial bodies in glory, so does the resurrection
body the natural body (v 43; cf. Phil 3.21)./21/ The δόξα of
the heavenly bodies is their brightness, which varies; there is
no trace here of *Lichtsubstanz*. When applied to the resurrection body, however, δόξα seems to be honor (v 43). Paul has
thus prepared the way for his doctrine of the world to come by
three analogies from the present world. All of them show how
things can be radically different from other things of the same
kind; similarly a σῶμα πνευματικόν will be seen to be radically
different from a σῶμα ψυχικόν. Moreover, Paul's analogies form
an ascending scale from plant to animal to terrestrial bodies
to celestial bodies; the next type of body to be mentioned will

be the most wonderful and exalted of all.

From vv 42-50 Paul spells out his doctrine of the σῶμα πνευματικόν. The body that is to be differs from the present body in that it will be imperishable, glorious, powerful, and spiritual; whereas the present body is perishable, dishonourable, weak, and physical (vv 42-44). These are the four essential differences between the present body and the resurrection body. What do they tell us about the nature of the resurrection body?

First, it is sown ἐν φθορᾷ, but it is raised ἐν ἀφθαρσίᾳ. These terms tell us clearly that Paul is not talking about egos, or 'I's,' but about bodies, for (1) the σπείρεται-ἐγείρεται has primary reference to the burial and raising up of a dead man's body, not the 'person' in abstraction from the body; and (2) only the body can be described as perishable (II Cor 4.16), for man's spirit survives death (II Cor 5.1-5; cf. Rom 8.10; Phil 1.23). Rather the disjunction under discussion concerns the radical change that will take place in our *bodies*: Paul teaches personal bodily immortality, not immortality of the soul alone (cf. vv 53-54). Strange as this may seem, the Christian teaching (or at least Paul's) is not that our souls will live forever, but that we will have bodies in the after-life.

Second, it is sown ἐν ἀτιμίᾳ, but it is raised ἐν δόξῃ. Our present bodies are wracked by sin, are bodies of death, groaning with the whole creation to be set free from sin and decay; we long, says Paul, for the redemption of our bodies (II Cor 5.4; Rom 8.19-24). This body, dishonored through sin and death, will be transformed by Christ to be like his glorious body (Phil 3.21). In a spiritual sense we already have an anticipation of this glory insofar as we are conformed inwardly to the image of Christ and are sanctified by his Spirit (II Cor 3.18), but Paul teaches that the body will not simply fall away like a useless husk, but will be transformed to partake of this glory also.

Third, it is sown ἐν ἀσθενίᾳ, but it will be raised ἐν δυνάμει. How well Paul knew of weakness! Afflicted with a bodily malediction which was offensive to others and a burden to those around him, Paul found in his weakness the power of Christ (Gal 4.13-14; II Cor 12.7-10). And on his poor body which had been stoned, beaten, and scourged for the sake of the gospel, Paul bore the marks of Christ, so much so that he dared

to write '. . . in my flesh I complete what is lacking in
Christ's afflictions. . .' (Col 1.24). Just as Christ 'was
crucified in weakness, but lives by the power of God' (II Cor
13.4) so Paul longed to know the power of the resurrection and
looked forward to the day when he, too, would receive the
resurrection body (II Cor 5.1-4; Phil 3.10-11).

     Fourth, it is sown a σῶμα ψυχικόν, but it is raised a σῶμα
πνευματικόν. By a σῶμα ψυχικόν Paul clearly does not mean a
body made out of ψυχή. Rather just as Paul frequently uses
σαρκικός to indicate, not the physical composition of a thing,
but its orientation, its dominating principle, so ψυχικός also
indicates, not a composition, but an orientation. In the New
Testament ψυχικός always has a negative connotation (I Cor 2.14;
Jas 3.15; Jude 19); that which is ψυχικός partakes of the
character and direction of natural human nature. Hence, the
emphasis in σῶμα ψυχικόν is not that the body is *physical*, but
that is is *natural*. Accordingly, σῶμα ψυχικόν ought rightly to
be translated 'natural body;' it means our present human body.
This is the body that will be sown. But it is raised a σῶμα
πνευματικόν. And just as σῶμα ψυχικόν does not mean a body made
out of ψυχή, neither does σῶμα πνευματικόν mean a body made out
of πνεῦμα. If σῶμα πνευματικόν indicated a body made out of
spirit, then its opposite would not be a σῶμα ψυχικόν, but a
σῶμα σάρκινον. For Paul ψυχή and πνεῦμα are not substances out
of which bodies are made, but dominating principles by which
bodies are directed. Virtually every modern commentator agrees
on this point: Paul is not talking about a rarefied body made
out of spirit or ether; he means a body under the lordship and
direction of God's Spirit. The present body is ψυχικόν insofar
as the ψυχή is its dominating principle (cf. ἄνθρωπός ψυχικός--
I Cor 2.14). The body which is to be will be πνευματικόν, not
in the sense of a spiritual substance, but insofar as the πνεῦμα
will be its dominating principle (cf. ἄνθρωπός πνευματικός--
I Cor 2.15). They do not differ *qua* σῶμα; rather they differ
*qua* orientation. Thus, philological analysis leads, in
Clavier's words, to the conclusion that '. . . le "corps
pneumatique" est, en substance, le même corps, ce corps de
chair, mais controlé par l'esprit, comme le fut le corps de
Jésus-Christ.'/22/ The contrast is not between physical body /
non-physical body, but between naturally oriented body /
spiritually oriented body. Hence, I think it very unfortunate
that the term σῶμα πνευματικόν has been usually translated
'spiritual body,' for this tends to be very misleading, as
Héring explains:

En français toutefois la traduction littérale *corps
spirituel* risque de créer les pires malentendus.  Car la
plupart des lecteurs de langue française, étant plus ou
moins consciemment cartésiens, céderont à la tendence
d'identifier le spirituel avec l'inétendu et naturellement
aussi avec l'im-matériel, ce qui va à l'encontre des idées
pauliniennes et crée de plus une *contradictio in adjecto*;
car que serait un corps sans étendue ni matière?/23/

Héring therefore suggests that it is better to translate σῶμα
πνευματικόν as the opposite of natural body (σῶμα ψυχικόν) as
*supernatural* body.  Although this has the disadvantage of
ignoring the connotation of πνευματικός as 'Spirit-dominated,'
it avoids the inevitable misunderstandings engendered by
'spiritual body.'  As Héring rightly comments, this latter term,
understood substantively, is practically a self-contradiction.
By the same token, 'physical body' is really a tautology.  Thus,
natural body/supernatural body is a better rendering of Paul's
meaning here.

Having described the four differences between the present
body and the resurrection body, Paul elaborates the doctrine of
the two Adams.  His statement that the first Adam was εἰς ψυχὴν
ζωσᾶν and the second εἰς πνεῦμα ζφοποιοῦν (v 45) must be understood in light of the foregoing discussion.  Just as Paul does
not mean Adam was a disembodied soul, neither does he mean
Christ turned into a disembodied spirit.  That would contradict
the doctrine of the resurrection of the σῶμα.  Rather these
terms refer once again to the natural body made at creation and
the supernatural body produced by the resurrection (cf. v 43b).
First we have our natural bodies here on earth as possessed by
Adam, then we shall have our supernatural bodies in the age to
come as possessed by Jesus (vv 46, 49; cf. vv 20-23).  The fact
that materiality is not the issue here is made clear in v 47:

ὁ πρῶτος ἄνϑρωπος ἐκ γῆς χοϊκός
ὁ δεύτερος ἄνϑρωπος ἐξ οὐρανοῦ

There is something conspicuously missing in this parallel
between τὸ ψυχικόν and τὸ πνευματικόν (v 46):  the first Adam is
*from* the earth, *made* of dust; the second Adam is *from* heaven,
but *made of*--?/24/  Clearly Paul recoils from saying the second
Adam is made of heavenly substance.  The contrast between the
two Adams is their origin, not their substance.  Thus, the
doctrine of the two Adams confirms the philological analysis.

Then comes a phrase that has caused great difficulties to
many: 'I tell you this, brethren, flesh and blood cannot
inherit the kingdom of God, nor does the perishable inherit the
imperishable' (v 50.) Does not this clearly indicate that the
resurrection body will be immaterial? Jeremias has tried to
escape this conclusion by arguing that 'flesh and blood' refers
to those alive at the Parousia, while the 'perishable' refers
to the dead in Christ; Paul means that neither living nor dead
*as they are* can inherit God's kingdom, but must be transformed
(v 51)./25/  This however, is unlikely, for it requires that
v 50 go with v 51. But not only does v 50 appear to be a
summary statement of the foregoing paragraph, but v 51 introduces a new paragraph and a new thought, as is indicated by the
introductory words, 'Lo! I tell you a mystery!' and by the fact
that something new and previously unknown is about to be
communicated. Neither need one adopt the expedient of
Bornhäuser that Paul means flesh and blood will decay in the
grave, but the bones will be raised./26/ This falsely assumes
Paul is here speaking of anatomy. Rather commentators are
agreed that 'flesh and blood' is a typical Semitic expression
denoting the frail human nature./27/ It emphasizes our feeble
mortality over against God; hence, the second half of v 50 is
Paul's elaboration in other words of exactly the same thought.
The fact that the verb is in the singular may also suggest that
Paul is not talking of physical aspects of the body, but about
a conceptual unity: 'flesh and blood *is* not able to inherit
. . . .' Elsewhere Paul also employs the expression 'flesh and
blood' to mean simply 'people' or 'mortal creatures' (Gal 1.16;
Eph 6.12). Therefore, Paul is not talking about anatomy here;
rather he means that mortal human beings cannot enter into God's
eternal kingdom; therefore, they must become imperishable (cf.
v 53). This imperishability does not connote immateriality or
unextendedness; on the contrary, Paul's doctrine of the world
to come is that our resurrection bodies will be part of, so to
speak, a resurrected creation (Rom 8.18-23). The universe will
be delivered from sin and decay, not materiality, and our bodies
will be part of that universe.

In the following paragraph, Paul tells how this will be
done. When he says 'We shall not all sleep, but we shall all be
changed' (v 51), it is not clear whether he means by 'all'
either Christians in general or Christians alive at his time
(cf. I Thess 4.15, 17). But in either case, two things are
clear: (1) Paul held that the transformation would take place
instantaneously at the moment of the resurrection (v. 52).

In this he differs sharply from II Bar 50-51 which holds that
the resurrection yields the old bodies again which are transformed only after the judgement./28/ Paul's doctrine is that we
are raised imperishable and glorified.  (2) For Paul the resurrection is a *transformation*, not an *exchange*.  Klappert draws
the distinctions nicely:

> Es geht also in der Auferstehung nach Paulus weder 1. um
> eine Wiederbelebung, d.h. um eine Neuschöpfung aus (!) dem
> Alten, noch 2. um eine Schöpfung aus dem Nichts, d.h. um
> eine Neuschöpfung anstelle (!) des Alten, sondern 3. um
> eine radikale Verwandlung des sterblichen Leibes, d.h. um
> eine Neuschöpfung an (!) dem Alten./29/

In the resurrection the 'ego' of a man does not trade bodies.
Rather the natural body is miraculously transformed into a
supernatural body.  The metaphor of the sowing and raising of
the body points to this.  In fact, the very concept of resurrection implies this, for in an exchange of bodies there would
be nothing that would be raised.  When Paul says, 'We shall *all*
be changed,' he means the bodies of both the *dead* and the *living*
alike.  Paul's doctrine is that at the Parousia, the dead will
rise from their graves transformed and that those who are still
alive will also be transformed (vv 51-52; I Thess 4.16-17).
The concept of an exchange of bodies is a peculiarly modern
notion.  For the Jews the resurrection of the dead concerned the
remains in the grave, which they conceived to be the bones./30/
According to their understanding, while the flesh decayed, the
bones endured.  It was the bones, therefore, that were the
primary subject of the resurrection.  In this hope, the Jews
carefully collected the bones of the dead into ossuaries after
the flesh had decomposed.  Only in a case in which the bones
were destroyed, as with the Jewish martyrs, did God's creating
a resurrection body *ex nihilo* come into question.  It is
instructive that on the question of the resurrection, Jesus
sided with the Pharisees.  He held that the tomb is the place
where the bones repose and that the dead in the tombs would be
raised (Matt 23.27; John 5.28).  It is important to remember,
too, that Paul was a Pharisee and that Luke identifies his
doctrine of the resurrection with that of the Pharisees.  Paul's
language is thoroughly Pharisaic, and it is unlikely that he
should employ the same terminology with an entirely different
meaning.  This means that when Paul says the dead will be raised
imperishable, he means the dead *in the graves*.  As a first
century Jew and Pharisee he could have understood the

expression in no other way.

Thus, Grass is simply wrong when he characterizes the resurrection as an exchange, a re-creation, and not a transformation./31/ He mistakenly appeals to v 50; his statement that Paul has no interest in the emptying of the graves ignores the clear statements of I Thess 4.16 (which in light of v 14, which probably refers, according to the current Jewish idea, to the souls of the departed, can only have reference to the bodies in the graves); I Cor 15.42-44, 52. He attempts to strengthen his case by arguing that the relation of the old world to the new is one of annihilation to re-creation and this is analogous to the relation of the old body to the new. But Grass's texts are chiefly non-Pauline (Heb 1.10-12; Mk 13.31; Rev 6.14; 20.11; 21.1; II Pet 3.10). As we have seen, Paul's view is a transformation of creation (Rom 8.18-23; cf. I Cor 7.31). According to Paul it is *this* creation and *this* body which will delivered from bondage to sin and decay. Paul, therefore, believed that the bodies of those alive at the Parousia would be changed, not discarded or annihilated, and that the remains (the bones?) of the dead bodies would likewise be transformed.

But this at once raises the puzzling question: what happens to those Christians who die before the Parousia? Are they simply extinguished until the day of resurrection? The clue to Paul's answer may be found in II Cor 5.1-10. Here the earthly tent = σῶμα ψυχικόν, and the building from God = σῶμα πνευματικόν. When do we receive the heavenly dwelling? The language of v 4 is irresistably reminiscent of I Cor 15.53-54, which we saw referred to the Parousia. This makes it evident that the heavenly dwelling is not received immediately upon death, but at the Parousia. It is unbelievable that had Paul changed his mind on the dead's receiving their resurrection bodies at the Parousia, he would not have told the Corinthians, but continued to use precisely the same language. If the body were received immediately upon death, there would be no reason for the fear of nakedness, and v 8 would become unintelligible. In short this would mean that Paul abandoned the doctrine of the resurrection of the dead; but his later letters show he continued to hold to it.

In I Cor 15 Paul did not speak of a state of nakedness; the mortal simply "put on" (ἐνδύσασθαι) the immortal. But in II Cor 5 he speaks of the fear of being unclothed and the preference to be further clothed (ἐπενδύσασθαι), as by top-clothing. It is evident that Paul is here describing losing the earthly body as being stripped and hence naked. He would rather not quit the body, but simply be transformed at the Parousia without experiencing the nakedness of death. In this sense, putting on the new body is like putting on top-clothing; namely, one need not undress first. Taken in isolation, this might be thought to imply that the resurrection is an exchange of bodies, not a transformation; but this presses the metaphor too hard. Paul is not trying to be technical, as is evident from his use of the ordinary ἐνδυσάμενοι in v 3; and the notion of 'putting on' is not inconsistent with the concept of transformation, as I Cor 15.53-54 makes clear. Indeed, the 'putting on' consists precisely in being transformed. Neither the ἔχομεν nor the αἰώνιον of v 1 indicates that the new body already exists; rather they express the certitude of future possession and the subsequent eternal duration of the new body. The idea that the new body exists already in heaven is an impossible notion, for the idea of an unanimated σῶμα πνευματικόν, stored up in heaven until the Parousia, is a contradiction in terms, since πνεῦμα is the essence and source of life itself. Rather from I Cor 15 we understand that the heavenly dwelling is created at the Parousia through a transformation of the earthly tent, a point concealed by Paul's intentional contrast between the two in v 1, but hinted at in v 4 (cf. also Rom 8.10-11, 18-23). What Paul wants to express by the metaphor is that he would rather live to the Parousia and be changed than die and be naked prior to being raised.

The nakedness is thus the nakedness of an individual's soul or spirit apart from the body, a common description in Hellenistic literature. This is confirmed in vv 6-9 where Paul contrasts being at home in the body and being at home with the Lord as mutually exclusive conditions. Paul is saying that while we are in this natural body we sigh, not because we want to leave the body through death and exist as a disembodied soul, but because we want to be transformed into a supernatural body without the necessity of passing through the intermediate state. But despite the unsettling prospect of such an intermediate state, Paul still thinks it better to be away from the body and with the Lord (v 8). Christ makes all the difference; for Paul the souls of the departed are not shut up in caves or caskets until the end time as in Jewish apocalyptic, nor do they 'sleep'; rather they go to be with Jesus and experience a conscious, blissful communion with him (cf. Phil 1.21, 23) until he returns to earth (I Thess 4.14). This overrides the dread of nakedness.

Paul's doctrine of the nature of the resurrection body now becomes clear. When a Christian dies, his conscious spirit or soul goes to be with Christ until the Parousia, while his body lies in the grave. When Christ returns, in a single instant the remains of the natural body are transformed into a powerful, glorious, and imperishable supernatural body under the complete lordship and direction of the Spirit, and the soul of the departed is simultaneously reunited with the body, and the man is raised to everlasting life. Then those who are alive will be similarly transformed, the old body miraculously changed into the new without excess, and all believers will go to be with the Lord.

This doctrine teaches us much about Paul's conception of the resurrection body of Christ. In no sense did Paul conceive Christ's resurrection body to be immaterial or unextended. The notion of an immaterial, unextended body seems to be a self-contradiction; the nearest thing to it would be a shade in Sheol, and this was certainly not Paul's conception of Christ's glorious resurrection body! The only phrases in Paul's discussion that could lend themselves to a 'dematerializing' of Christ's body are 'σῶμα πνευματικόν' and 'flesh and blood can not inherit the kingdom of God.' But virtually all modern commentators agree that these expressions have nothing to do with substantiality or anatomy, as we have seen. Rather the first speaks of the orientation of the resurrection body, while the second refers to the mortality and feebleness of the natural body in contrast to God.

So it is very difficult to understand how theologians can persist in describing Christ's resurrection body in terms of an invisible, intangible spirit; there seems to be a great lacuna here between exegesis and theology. I can only agree with O'Collins when he asserts in this context, 'Platonism may be hardier than we suspect.'/32/ With all the best will in the world, it is extremely difficult to see what is the difference between an immaterial, unextended, spiritual 'body' and the immortality of the soul. And this again is certainly not Paul's doctrine! Therefore, the second supporting argument for Jesus's having a purely spiritual resurrection body also fails.

We have seen, therefore, that the traditions of the appearance of Jesus to Paul do not describe that event as a

purely visionary experience; on the contrary extra-mental
accompaniments were involved. Paul gives no firm clue as to
the nature of that appearance; from his doctrine of the nature
of the resurrection body, it could theoretically have been as
physical as any gospel appearance. And Paul does insist that
it was an *appearance*, not a vision. Luke regarded the mode of
Jesus's appearance to Paul as unique because it was a post-
ascension encounter. Paul himself gives no hint that he
considered the appearance to him to be in any way normative for
the other appearances or determinative for a doctrine of the
resurrection body. On the contrary, Paul also recognized that
the appearance to him was an anomaly and was exercized to bring
it up to the level of objectivity and reality of the other
appearances. Furthermore, Paul conceived of the resurrection
body as a powerful, glorious, imperishable, Spirit-directed
*body*, created through a transformation of the earthly body or
the remains thereof, and made to inhabit the new universe in
the eschaton. The upshot of all this is the startling
conclusion that *Paul's doctrine of the resurrection body is
potentially more physical than that of the gospels, and if
Christ's resurrection body is to be conceived in any less than
a physical way, that qualification must come from the side of
the gospels, not of Paul.*

So although many theologians try to play off the 'massiven
Realismus' of the gospels against a Pauline doctrine of a
spiritual resurrection body, such reasoning rests on a fundamental and drastic misunderstanding of Paul's doctrine. One
cannot but suspect that the real reason for scholarly
scepticism concerning the historicity of the gospel appearances
is that, as Bultmann openly stated, this is offensive to
'modern man,' and that Paul has been made an unwilling
accomplice in critics' attempts to find reasons to support a
conclusion already dictated by *a priori* philosophical
assumptions. But Paul will not allow himself to be put to this
use; a careful exegesis of Pauline doctrine fully supports a
physical resurrection body. And, it must be said, this was how
first century Christians apparently understood him, for the
letters of Clement and Ignatius prove early wide acceptance of
the doctrine of physical resurrection in first century churches,
including the very churches where Paul himself had taught. The
ground is thus cut from beneath those scholars who object to
the historicity of the gospel resurrection narratives because
of their physicalism.

But more than that:  given the temporal and personal
proximity of Paul to the original witnesses of the resurrection
appearances, the historicity of the bodily resurrection of
Jesus can scarcely be denied.  For the physicalism of the
gospels cannot now be explained away as a late legendary or
theological development; on the contrary, what we see from Paul
is that it was there from the beginning.  And if it was there
from the beginning, then it must have been historically well-
founded--otherwise, one is at a loss how to explain that the
earliest witnesses should believe in it.  Though it is
constantly repeated that the physicalism of the gospels is an
antidocetic apologetic, scarcely a single piece of evidence is
ever produced in favor of this assertion--and mere assertion is
not proof.  We have seen that both Paul's personal contact and
temporal proximity with the original disciples precludes a late
development of the notion of physical resurrection, which is
implied by the anti-docetic hypothesis.  And Paul's doctrine
can hardly be explained away as an anti-docetic apologetic, for
it was the crass materialism of the Jewish doctrine of resurrection that Paul's Corinthian opponents probably gagged at (I Cor
15.35), so that Paul found it necessary to emphasize the transformation of the earthly body into a supernatural body.  An
anti-docetic apologetic would have been counter-productive.
Hence, the evidence of Paul precludes that the physical resurrection was an apologetic development of the gospels aimed at
Docetism.

But this consideration aside, there are other reasons to
think that in the gospel narratives Docetism is not in view:
(1) For a Jew the very term 'resurrection' entailed a physical
resurrection of the dead man in the tomb.  The notion of a
'spiritual resurrection' was not merely unknown; it was a
contradiction in terms.  Therefore, in saying that Jesus was
raised and appeared, the early believers must have understood
this in physical terms.  It was Docetism which was the response
to this physicalism, not the other way around.  The physical
resurrection is thus primitive and prior, Docetism being the
later reaction of theological and philosophical reflection.
(2) Moreover, had purely 'spiritual appearances' been original,
then it is difficult to see how physical appearances could have
developed.  For  (a) the offense of Docetism would then be
removed, since the Christians, too, believed in purely
spiritual appearances, and  (b) the doctrine of physical appearances would have been counter-productive as an apologetic, both
to Jews and pagans; to Jews because they did not accept an

individual resurrection within history and to pagans because
their belief in the immortality of the soul could not
accommodate the crudity of physical resurrection.  The church
would therefore have retained its purely spiritual appearances.
(3) Besides, Docetism was mainly aimed at denying the reality
of the incarnation of Christ (I John 4.2-3; III John 7), not the
physical resurrection.  Docetists were not so interested in
denying the physical resurrection as in denying that the divine
Son  perished on the cross; hence, some held the Spirit
deserted the human Jesus at the crucifixion, leaving the human
Jesus to die and be physically raised (Irenaeus *Against
Heresies* 1. 26. 1).  An anti-docetic apologetic aimed at proving
a physical resurrection therefore misses the point entirely.
(4) The demonstrations of corporeality and continuity in the
gospels, as well as the other physical appearances, were not
redactional additions of Luke or John, as is evident from a
comparison of Luke 24.36-43 with John 20.19-23 (it is thus
incorrect to speak, for example, of 'Luke's apologetic against
Gnosticism'), but were part of the traditions received by the
evangelists.  Docetism, however, was a later theological
development, attested in John's letters.  Therefore, the gospel
accounts of the physical resurrection tend to ante-date the
rise and threat of Docetism.  In fact, not even all later
Gnostics denied the physical resurrection (cf. Gospel of Philip,
Letter of James, and Epistle of Rheginus).  It is interesting
that in the ending added to Mark there is actually a switch
from material proofs of the resurrection to verbal rebuke by
Jesus for the disciples' unbelief.  (5) The demonstrations
themselves do not evince the rigorousness of an apologetic
against Docetism.  In both Luke and John it is not said that
either the disciples or Thomas actually accepted Jesus's
invitation to touch him and prove that he was not a Spirit.
Contrast the statements of Ignatius that the disciples did
physically touch Jesus (Ignatius *Ad Smyrnaeans* 3.2; cf. *Epistula
Apostolorum* 11-12).  As Schnackenburg has said, if an anti-
docetic apology were involved in the gospel accounts, more
would have to have been done than Jesus's merely *showing* the
wounds./33/  (6) The incidental, off-hand character of the
physical resurrection in most of the accounts shows that the
physicalism was a natural assumption or presupposition of the
accounts, not an apologetic point consciously being made.  For
example, the women's grasping Jesus's feet is not a polemical
point, but just their response of worship.  Similarly, Jesus
says, 'Do not hold me,' though Mary is not explicitly said to
have done so; this is no conscious effort to prove a physical

resurrection. The appearances on the mountain and by the Sea
of Tiberias just naturally presuppose a physical Jesus; no
points are trying to be scored against Docetism. Together
these considerations strongly suggest that the physical appearances were not an apologetic to Docetism, but always part of
the church's tradition; there is no good reason to doubt that
Jesus did, in fact, show his disciples that he had been
physically raised.

And it must be said that despite the disdain of some
theologians for the gospels' conception of the nature of the
resurrection body, it is nonetheless true that like Paul the
evangelists steer a careful course between gross materialism
and the immortality of the soul. On the one hand, every gospel
appearance of Jesus that is narrated is a physical appearance.
/34/ The gospels' unanimity on this score is very impressive,
especially in view of the fact that the appearance stories
represent largely independent traditions; they confirm Paul's
doctrine that it is the earthly body that is resurrected. On
the other hand, the gospels insist that Jesus's resurrection
was not simply the resuscitation of a corpse. Lazarus would
die again some day, but Jesus rose to everlasting life (Matt 28.
18-20; Luke 24.26; John 20.17). And his resurrection body was
possessed of powers that no normal human body possesses. Thus,
in Matthew when the angel opens the tomb, Jesus does not come
forth; rather he is already gone. Similarly, in Luke when the
Emmaus disciples recognize him at bread-breaking he disappears.
The same afternoon Jesus appears to Peter, miles away in
Jerusalem. When the Emmaus disciples finally join the
disciples in Jerusalem that evening, Jesus suddenly appears in
their midst. John says the doors were shut, but Jesus stood
among them. A week later Jesus did the same thing. Very often
commentators make the error of stating that Jesus came through
the closed doors, but neither John nor Luke says this. Rather
Jesus simply appeared in the room; contrast the pagan myths of
gods entering rooms like fog through the keyhole (Homer *Odyssey*
6. 19-20; *Homeric Hymns* 3. 145)! According to the gospels,
Jesus in his resurrection body had the ability to appear and
vanish at will, without regard to spatial limitations.

Many scholars have stumbled at Luke's 'a spirit has not
flesh and bones as you see that I have,' claiming this is a direct
contradiction to Paul. In fact, Paul speaks of 'flesh and
blood' not 'flesh and bones.' Is the difference significant?
It certainly is! 'Flesh and blood,' as we have seen, is a

Semitic expression for mortal human nature and has nothing to
do with anatomy.  Paul agrees with Luke on the physicality of
the resurrection body.  But furthermore, neither is 'flesh and
bones' meant to be an anatomical description.  Rather, proceeding from the Jewish idea that it is the bones that are preserved
and raised (Gen R 28.3; Lev R 18.1; Eccl R 12.5), the expression
connotes the physical reality of Jesus's resurrection.
Michaelis writes,

> Wenn nach Lukas ein Geist weder Fleisch noch Knochen
> hat, der Auferstandene aber kein Geist ist, so besagt das
> nicht, dass der Auferstandene, mit der paulinischen
> Terminologie zu reden, kein "pneumatisches (verklärtes,
> himmlisches) Soma," sondern ein "psychisches (natürliches,
> irdisches) Soma" habe.  Mit Fleisch und Knochen in der
> lukanischen Aussage ist vielmehr (wie zugeben werden muss,
> in einem kräftigen Ausdruck, den Paulus aber nicht
> unbedingt als "lästerlich" empfunden haben müsste) das
> ausgedrückt, was Paulus mit dem Begriff "Soma" (Leib,
> Leiblichkeit) ausdrückt.  Durch den Hinweis auf Fleisch
> und Knochen soll nicht der pneumatische Charakter dieses
> Soma bestritten, sondern die Realität des Somatischen
> bezeugt werden.  Auch Lukas steht, wie sich zudem aus der
> Gesamtheit der bei ihm sich findenen Hinweise ergibt (vgl.
> 24.13ff; Apg. 1.3), unter den Voraussetzung, dass es sich
> bei den Erscheinungen nur um Begegnungen mit dem Auf-
> erstandenen in seiner verklärten Leiblichkeit handeln
> kann./35/

The point of Jesus's utterance is to assure the disciples that
this is a real resurrection, in the proper, Jewish sense of
that word, not an appearance of a bodiless πνεῦμα.  Though it
stresses corporeality, its primary emphasis is not on the
constituents of the body.  Thus, neither Paul nor Luke are
talking about anatomy, and both agree on the physicality *and*
the supernaturalness of Jesus's resurrection body.

In conclusion, we have seen that the critical argument
designed to drive a wedge between Paul and the gospels is
fallacious.  Neither the argument from the appearance to Paul
nor the argument from Paul's doctrine of the resurrection body
serves to set Paul against the gospels.  Quite the opposite, we
have seen that Paul's evidence serves to confirm the gospels'
narratives of Jesus's bodily resurrection and that their
physicalism is probably historically well-founded, that is to

say, Jesus did rise bodily from the dead and appear physically
to the disciples.  And finally we have seen that the gospels
present like Paul a balanced view of the nature of Jesus's
resurrection body.  On the one hand, Jesus has a body--he is not
a disembodied soul.  For the gospels and Paul alike the
incarnation is an enduring state, not limited to the 30 some
years of Jesus's earthly life.  On the other hand, Jesus's body
is a supernatural body.  We must keep firmly in mind that for
the gospels as well as Paul, Jesus rises glorified from the
grave.  The gospels and Paul agree that the appearances of Jesus
ceased and that physically he has left this universe for an
indeterminate time.  During his physical absence he is present
through the Holy Spirit who functions in his stead.  But some-
day he will personally return to judge mankind and to establish
his reign over all creation.


NOTES


/1/ This research was made possible through a
generous grant from the Alexander von Humboldt Foundation and
was conducted at the Universität München and Cambridge
University.  The full results of this research will appear in
two forthcoming volumes, *The Historical Argument for the
Resurrection of Jesus: Its Rise, Decline, and Contribution* and
*The Historicity of the Resurrection of Jesus.*

/2/ Hans Grass, *Ostergeschehen und Osterberichte* (4th
ed.; Göttingen: Vandenhoeck & Ruprecht, 1970).

/3/ John E. Alsup, *The Post-Resurrection Appearance
Stories of the Gospel-Tradition* (Stuttgart: Calwer Verlag,
1975), 32.

/4/ Ibid., 34.

/5/ Ibid., 54.

/6/ Robin Scroggs, *The Last Adam* (Oxford: Basil
Blackwell, 1966), 92-3.

/7/ Grass, *Ostergeschehen*, 222.

/8/ Ibid., 219-20.

/9/ See ibid., 189-207.

/10/ Ibid., 229-32.

/11/ The outstanding work on this concept, which I follow here, is Robert H. Gundry, Sōma *in Biblical Theology* (Cambridge: Cambridge University Press, 1976).

/12/ C. Holsten, *Zum Evangelium des Paulus und des Petrus* (Rostock: Stiller, 1868); Hermann Lüdemann, *Die Anthropologie des Apostels Paulus und ihre Stellung innerhalb seiner Heilslehre* (Kiel: Universitätsverlag, 1872); remarkably so also Hans Conzelmann, *Der erste Brief an die Korinther* (KEKNT 5; Göttingen: Vandenhoeck & Ruprecht, 1969), 335.

/13/ See the six point refutation in Gundry, Sōma, 161-2.

/14/ See ibid., 122, 141. Most of Gundry's texts do not support dualism, but merely aspectivalism; but when he adduces texts that clearly contemplate the separation of soul or spirit and body at death, then his argument for dualism is strong and persuasive.

/15/ Gundry, Sōma, 50.

/16/ Robert Jewett, *Paul's Anthropological Terms* (AGAJY 10; Leiden: E.J. Brill, 1971), 211.

/17/ Gundry, Sōma, 167.

/18/ Ibid., 80.

/19/ Paul's teaching is essentially the Jewish doctrine of glorified bodies, according to Johannes Weiss, *Der erste Korintherbrief* (9th ed.; KEKNT 5; Göttingen: Vandenhoeck & Ruprecht, 1910), 345; W.D. Davies, *Paul and Rabbinic Judaism* (2d ed; London: SPCK, 1965), 305-8; Ulrich Wilckens, *Auferstehung* (Stuttgart and Berlin: Kreuz Verlag,' 1970), 128-31; Joseph L. Smith, 'Resurrection Faith Today,' *TS* 30 (1969): 406.

/20/ On the different types of flesh, see Tractate

Chullin 8. 1, where the author explains that one cannot cook
flesh in milk, unless it is the flesh of fish or of grass-
hoppers; fowl may be set on the table with cheese, but not
eaten with it.  See also Davies, *Paul*, 306.

/21/ Cf. II Bar 51.1-10 where the glory of the
righteous seems to be a literal brightness like the stars'.
For Paul the glory of the righteous seems to mean majesty,
honor, exaltation, etc., not so much physical radiance, which
is a mere analog.  See Joseph Coppens, 'La glorification
céleste du Christ dans la théologie neotestamentaire et
l'attente de Jésus,' in *Resurrexit* (ed. Édouard Dhanis; Rome:
Editrice Libreria Vaticana, 1974), 37-40.

/22/ H. Clavier, 'Breves remarques sur la notion de
σῶμα πνευματικόν,' in *The Background of the New Testament and
Its Eschatology* (ed. W. D. Davies and D. Daube; Cambridge:
Cambridge University Press, 1956), 361.  Despite the philological evidence, Clavier goes for a substantival understanding
of spiritual body on two grounds:  (1) in the seed/plant
analogy, the plant is not numerically identical with the seed,
and  (2) I Cor 15.50.  The first reason is astounding, for the
plant certainly is numerically identical with the seed!
Pressing the analogy this far supports the continuity of the
resurrection body with the earthly body.  Clavier sadly
misunderstands v 50, as evident from his remark that Paul should
have mentioned bones along with flesh and blood.

/23/ Jean Héring, *La première épître de saint Paul aux
Corinthiens* (2d ed., CNT 7; Neuchatel, Switzerland: Delachaux
et Niestlé, 1959), 147.

/24/ Or alternatively, the first Adam is made of the
dust of the earth; the second Adam is from heaven.  The first
speaks of constitution, the second of origin.  See also *TWNT*,
s.v. 'πνεῦμα,' by Kleinknecht, *et.al.*

/25/ Joachim Jeremias, '"Flesh and Blood Cannot
Inherit the Kingdom of God" (I Cor. XV. 50),' *NTS* 2 (1955-6):
151-9.

/26/ Karl Bornhäuser, *Die Gebeine der Toten* (BFCT 26;
Gütersloh: C. Bertelsmann, 1921), 37.

/27/ It is found in Matt 16.17; Gal 1.16; Eph 6.12;

Heb 2.14; see also Sir 14.18 and the references in Hermann L. Strack and Paul Billerbeck, eds., *Kommentar zum Neuen Testament aus Talmud und Midrasch* (5th ed., 6 vols.; München: C. H. Beck, 1969), 1: 730-1, 753. The Semitic word pair σάρξ καὶ αἷμα is first attested in Ecclesiasticus 14.18; 17.31 and occurs frequently in Rabbinic texts, especially Rabbinic parables, as בשר ודם.

/28/ According to Baruch the old bodies are raised for the purpose of recognition, that the living may know that the dead have been raised. But for Paul, believers, like Christ, emerge glorified from the grave.

/29/ Berthold Klappert, 'Einleitung,' in *Diskussion um Kreuz und Auferstehung* (ed. idem; Wuppertal: Aussaat Verlag, 1971), 15.

/30/ See Bornhäuser, *Gebeine*; C. F. Evans, *Resurrection in the New Testament* (SBT 2/12; London: SCM, 1970), 108; Walther Grundmann, *Das Evangelium nach Lukas* (8th ed., THKNT 3; Berlin: Evangelische Verlagsanstalt, 1978), 451.

/31/ Grass, *Ostergeschehen*, 154.

/32/ Gerald O'Collins, *The Easter Jesus* (London: Darton, Longman & Todd, 1973), 94.

/33/ Rudolf Schnackenburg, *Das Johannesevangelium* (3 vols., 2d ed., HTKNT 4; Freiburg: Herder, 1976), 3: 383. This goes for both the appearance to the Twelve and to Thomas, he argues.

/34/ Although some critics have wanted to construe Matthew's mountaintop appearance as a heavenly vision similar to Paul's, this attempt seems futile. Matthew clearly considered Jesus's appearance to be physical, as is evident from his appearance to the women (Matt 28.9, 10) and his commissioning of the disciples. Even in the appearance itself, there are signs of physicality: the disciples' worshipping Jesus recalls the act of the women in v 9 and does not suit well a heavenly appearance; and Jesus's coming toward the disciples (προσελθών) seems to indicate decisively a physical appearance.

/35/ Wilhelm Michaelis, *Die Erscheinungen der*

*Auferstandenen* (Basel: Heinrich Majer, 1944), 96.

# The Gospels and Jewish Tradition: Twenty Years After Gerhardsson

Peter H. Davids
Trinity Episcopal School for Ministry, 311 Eleventh St.,
Ambridge, PA, 15003, USA

The relationship of synoptic material to Judaism in
general and particularly to the exegetical and transmissional
features of rabbinic Judaism has become an increasingly
interesting question over the past couple of decades.  The goal
of this paper is not to solve any of the issues, but, using the
material provided by Birger Gerhardsson as a framework, to
explore where the issues are and what the solutions appear to
be to date.  As such it should be more a stimulus to further
research than a final answer on its own.

Over the past ages the more or less peaceful shores of
Europe have been suddenly disturbed from time to time by
incursions from the North, the Viking raiders striking fear
into the heart of European culture.  While the raiders usually
returned to their homelands, the places they struck were never
quite the same -- not just the skeletons of their raid remained,
but also some new ideas and perhaps some progeny, continuing
their effect long afterwards.

This brief analogy more or less fits the works of the
Scandanavian school of Engnell, Riesenfeld, and Gerhardsson
(sometimes called the Uppsala school).  The first 'strike' of
these raiders at the secure fortress of form-criticism was
Harald Riesenfeld's 'The Gospel Tradition and Its Beginnings:
A Study in the Limits of 'Formgeschichte'', first presented at
the Oxford International Conference on the Four Gospels in 1957.
/1/  The next incursion was that of Birger Gerhardsson with
Memory and Manuscript /2/  followed by his response to his
critics in Tradition and Transmission in Early Christianity /3/.
It appeared at this point in time that the invasion had been
repulsed, but in fact Prof. Gerhardsson was quietly extending
his work into the synoptic gospels, an area which received only
scant mention in his first work. /4/ During the interim,
however, other voices began to be raised over the issues which
Riesenfeld and Gerhardsson had dared to mention. /5/  Recently

Gerhardsson has struck again with a short work growing out of a
seminar in Germany in 1976. /6/  The persistent questionings
will not go away, so it is necessary to come to terms with them.

Unfortunately the issues raised by these men are so
immense that they point to several extensive programs of
research.  Thus we are here simply delineating issues and
pointing to the direction of debate or consensus as it has
appeared over roughly the past twenty years.

## Pharisees and Rabbis

Gerhardsson began his work by describing the place of oral
tradition in rabbinic transmission.  That is, he discusses the
role of the tannaim as the professional memorizers and means
of oral publication within early rabbinic circles:  the
tradition as well as the decisions of rabbinic authorities,
either as expansions of or corrections to (including deletions)
the tradition, were passed along to future rabbis by this
professional class.  Gerhardsson's contribution on this level
comes in describing the transmission process of the tannaitic
period in detail in English, for this description has so far
received scholarly consent. /7/ There is little debate that
from the time of Akiba on mishnaic material was transmitted
primarily in oral form by means of a deliberate and careful
process of oral publication focused institutionally in the
rabbinic academy and professionally in the tanna.  While the
public transmission depended upon oral recitation using a
variety of mnemonic devices, written notes ('scrolls of
secrets') were often used in private to assist. /8/ The whole
process was as intentional as the written transmission of the
scriptures, although in the case of the oral law deliberate
alteration by constituted authorities was possible.

Disagreement begins, however, as soon as one argues that
this process of transmission began before Akiba, particularly
when the claim is that it began before AD 70.  Two issues must
be settled:  (1) what were the proto-rabbis before Johanan b.
Zakkai went to Jamnia (we naturally consider him also a proto-
rabbi, since he was a Galilean contemporary of Jesus) ?  (2)
How much change was introduced by the upheaval of AD 66-70 and
the consequent coming to power of the rabbinic sages under
Gamaliel II  ?

The second issue in particular has been hotly debated

since J. Neusner has been writing. /9/ His <u>Rabbinic Traditions</u> <u>about the Pharisees before 70</u> /10/ , as well as his later works on the same topic, /11/ have introduced form-criticism into the discipline of rabbinic studies. This means that for Neusner the form of a given rabbinic pericope, the people mentioned in it, and the people who comment upon it (and their separation from it in time) are determinative for dating a tradition (assuming that forms do not alter through later redaction). Thus content is explicitly rejected as a major factor in dating. Since the form and identifiable names in many of the 371 traditions about the <u>perushim</u> fit a Jamnian <u>Sitz-im-Leben</u>, Neusner believes that Jamnia is the place of origin of the identifiable tradition and that any claims to knowledge about the pre-70 <u>perushim</u> or <u>zugoth</u> (pairs) must be received with a scepticism verging on agnosticism. Naturally he cannot accept Gerhardsson's claim on the basis of Old Testament, intertestamental, and Greek parallels to be able to retroject the teaching methods (not the content) of the early rabbis back into the pre-70 period. /12/

Neusner and his pupils have come under severe criticism by many of the Jewish scholars of this generation, who argue that his form-critical methodology distorts the data of the text and that the shifts in political fortune and formal methodology in the Jamnia period were not nearly so extensive as Neusner believes. /13/ Even those who lack Neusner's near-total scepticism, however, do not maintain an uncritical attitude towards the text:
    'The rabbinic literature, therefore, must be judged on its
    merits, with careful analysis given to each halakah, not
    on the basis of form-criticism alone, but on the basis of
    how the halakah matches the historical context, whose name
    it is attached to, and whether it appears plausible as a
    saying by that person at that time within that historical
    context. /14/
The question, then, is whether only a detailed knowledge of rabbinic history (as opposed to a formal analysis of the text) can provide the data to dispute the authenticity of a given text. The Jewish scholars to whom we refer would answer in the affirmative, stating that considerations of form, including the bias of the redactor, may change the shape of the tradition, but have little effect on its basic content. The traditions in the mishnaic collections of AD 100 to 200, then, might provide accurate information about the sages of 200 BC to AD 70: while the form in which some of the traditions have been preserved may be later than the traditions, the changes introduced after

AD 70 are detectable by proper historical methodology and need
not have altered the essential meaning of the traditions. /15/

The discussion between these two positions has yet to go
on long enough for a scholarly consensus (which might be a
mediating position) to appear. This lack of agreement is
especially unfortunate since every scholar dealing with rabbinic
materials will ipso facto take some position on these issues,
whether he realizes it or not. Thus it is important for us to
make our working hypothesis clear. Neusner has indeed shown
that any naive confidence in rabbinic texts is unwarranted. He
has further provided us with indispensible data and valuable
arguments on individual texts. But he has yet to prove his
position of radical scepticism about the pre-70 period, for
form and content are not necessarily related issues and the
break in AD 70 has not so far been proven to have been so sharp
that the leaders in the proto-rabbinic movement suddenly changed
doctrine or methodology when they came to power. This simply
means that we can have at least a modicum of confidence in
those elements of the tradition for which at least some
evidence exists at an earlier era or which cohere with the
historical situation of the earlier era as best we can
reconstruct it.

While rejecting the degree of Neusner's scepticism,
however, we are still far from either settling the first issue
or endorsing Gerhardsson's interpretation of the data.
Gerhardsson, for example, has argued that there was a
continuing transmission of oral halakah in Pharisaic circles
(i.e. proto-rabbinic groups) beginning before the time of
Christ. /16/ The literature which he collects indicates that
while one may question many of the details as being
retrojections of post-70 idealizations he is correct not only
for the proto-rabbis, but also for other Jewish groups in at
least three particulars. First, virtually all teaching-
learning situations in the ancient world required some
memorization of the sayings and traditions of the teacher (or
of his text). Thus one would expect this phenomenon to be
common in teaching situations in Israel. Second, even much of
the literature of the Old Testament (e.g. the prophetic oracles)
and the wisdom sayings of the intertestamental period were
probably originally transmitted orally. One would not expect
oral transmission to suddenly disappear. Thus even without the
institution of the tanna (assuming the office was purely a
post-70 phenomenon), if Hillel and Shammai existed and had

disciples, these men certainly learned and passed on the sayings
of their teacher. /17/ Third, even Neusner notes some mnemonic
structures in the pre-70 material, as well as some continuity
in interest between that and the Jamnia period. /18/ This data
adds to the impression that oral transmission did occur before
70 and that on at least some topics the transition to power
after 70 made no radical difference.

While we cannot doubt the existence of oral transmission
of what came to rabbinic halakoth before AD 70, Prof.
Gerhardsson has underemphasized at least two features of the
early tradition: (1) the role of written transmission, and (2)
the lack of control over both oral and written transmission.
As far as the first feature is concerned, although many of the
works of the Old Testament and intertestamental period were
originally oral, we have nevertheless received them in written
form. Furthermore, some groups contemporary with the New
Testament had no hesitation in composing their works as written
documents (e.g. the apocalypticists and the sectaries of Qumran)
/19/ Memory played a large part in the education and
transmission of tradition in all of these groups, but it was
the memorization of written texts (e.g. 1Q Sa I, 4-8).
Gerhardsson, on the other hand, while admitting that notes and
'scrolls of secrets' were used in proto-rabbinic circles, /20/
assumes that the later rejection of written transmission (b.
Erubin 54b, b. Gittin 60b) must also have been characteristic
of the earlier period. There is no evidence for this
assumption. There may well have been a natural preference for
the living voice of the wise teacher, but not the exclusive
stress on memory, which may in fact be a later reaction to
Roman persecution (i.e. the living book, the tanna would be
harder for Romans to discover and investigate than a written
book). /21/ The proto-rabbis in all likelihood used more
written materials than their descendents. /22/

As to the second feature, there is evidence that there was
much less formal control on the tradition than Gerhardsson
imagines. /23/ On the one hand, the text of scripture was
nowhere near as standardized in the first century as
Gerhardsson supposed, although the process of stabilization
had begun and would be completed by the end of the century.
/24/ On the other hand, the oral tradition was also in some
disarray. The disputes between the schools of Shammai and
Hillel (e.g. m. Eduyoth 1) show one part of this lack of
unity: the final unification of the rabbinic tradition did not

come until after Akiba. /25/ The tradition itself raises other
issues related to the question of whether some of the divergent
traditions have not been suppressed. Why are so few names
preserved from this period ? Why do Gamaliel the Elder and
Simon b. Gamaliel appear outside the chain of tradition in m.
Aboth 2:8 ? Surely parts of a much more varied tradition have
been suppressed by the triumph of Johanan b. Zakkai and later
of Akiba (although we should also consider the role of Gamaliel
II). /26/ The idea that the Great Sanhedrin was a doctrinal
authority in any but the loosest sense (i.e. since it was a
court it influenced positively or negatively any group involved
in the affairs of the country) is mythical.

Furthermore, we have still only considered the variety
within the known proto-rabbinic circles in Judaism before AD 70.
These groups were certainly not alone and may not even have been
influential in the life of the country. We know of the
existence of at least the Sadducees and the sectaries of Qumran.
Doubtless many other groups also existed. The concept of a
given normative Judaism of the New Testament period in the
sense in which Moore established the term is now dead.

As one aspect of the above, note that we have not
identified the proto-rabbinic teachers as Pharisees (perushim),
for there is certainly a great deal of well-grounded dispute
over who the perushim or φαρισαίοι really were. Rivkin
identifies them as 'a class of audacious revolutionaries' who
were responsible for establishing the Hasmoneans and changing
the nature of Judaism. /27/ To Neusner they were a
philosophical school within Judaism which went from political
involvement to pietistic quietism (under Hillel) and back to
political involvement (under Johanan b. Zakkai). /28/ Zeitlin,
however, sees them as a much more diffuse group, not a sect per
se. /29/ All of these identifications, as well as the
contributions of others, /30/ have one factor in common: they
identify the φαρισαίοι of Josephus and the gospels with the
proto-rabbinic movement, including at least some of the
Talmudic perushim, sopherim, and hakamim within that category.

This identification, however, is not as clear as has been
assumed, particularly when the gospels are admitted as evidence.
/31/ Of the φαρισαίοι mentioned in Josephus and the gospels,
only Gamaliel the Elder is also included by rabbinic sources
among the proto-rabbis (m. Aboth 1:16, Acts 5:34, where he is
identified as a Pharisee who is also a νομοδιδάσκαλος). While

it is clear that the rabbis were aware that some of their
ancestors were called pejoratively perushim, it is also clear
that the rabbinic tradition basically criticises the perushim
for some of the same things for which the gospels criticise the
Pharisees. Thus the rabbinic sources do not clearly identify
the proto-rabbis or sages (hakamim) with the perushim, although
there was at least some overlap in the two terms so that both
could apply to at least one or two individuals. /32/

We have, then, a right to question a too-easy
identification of the Pharisees with the proto-rabbis. The
absence of virtually every known proto-rabbi from the gospel
records may not be accidental. It is this data which leads
Sigal to conclude that the Pharisees are ' a complex,incohate
mass of pietists and separatists' which would include people
like those in Qumran and pietistic hasidim, among others. /33/
Thus one must be very cautious in using the references to the
Pharisees in the gospels to describe proto-rabbis. In some
cases proto-rabbis are probably included in the term, but in
many cases it may indicate groups with whom they disagreed or
it may simply group together a conglomeration of strange
bedfellows because of their agreement on a certain point. Only
rabbinic sources can help us differentiate the passages which
might include proto-rabbis. This argument means, of course,
that the proto-rabbis (except Gamaliel the Elder, whom Aboth
separates somewhat from the 'pure' line) may not have been
especially influential in pre-70 Judaism.

Given what has already been said, how can one evaluate the
transmission of the tradition within the proto-rabbinic
movement in particular and Judaism in general during the New
Testament period ? First, we must agree with Prof. Gerhardsson
that there was some transmission of oral tradition. It would
have been an exceptional period in Jewish history indeed if
this were not the case. We further agree that the teachings
of great sages (e.g. a Hillel) were learned by heart and held
to be fundamentally important in the circles of their disciples
(although not necessarily with the name of the teacher being
attached to the tradition as was later the case).

Second, we agree with Gerhardsson that the scriptures were
memorized as part of normal elementary schooling, partially as
part of the process of learning to read, partially as a result
of continual reading aloud, and partially as a deliberate goal
of the educative process, whether in Hebrew or Greek education.

In Palestine this memorization was true not only of the
scripture per se, but also of whatever other books were
important to the community doing the education (e.g. at Qumran
at least 1Q S and similar texts were learned).

Third, the mnemonic and exegetical forms used in the later
periods of Jewish literature were alive and well in the New
Testament period.  The midrash style, for example, may be
traced back to 165 BC, if not earlier.  /34/ Mnemonic forms have
frequently been identified in rabbinic sayings purporting to
come from the earlier sages, some of which even Neusner feels
are early.  Thus we must agree with Gerhardsson that the data,
including Neusner's data, points to the continued use of
educational, exegetical, and homiletical styles across the
cataclysm of AD 70.

Fourth, we have found it necessary to modify Gerhardsson's
thesis in that the transmission of early traditions was not
necessarily oral nor carefully controlled.  Certainly there was
a wide use of notebooks and perhaps even written mishnah
collections during the New Testament period.  Many Jewish groups
were transmitting their traditions in writing.  /35/ But the
texts so transmitted, although perhaps uniformly controlled in
some cases (e.g. the priestly aristocracy probably controlled
the ritual traditions of the temple most carefully), were in
many cases multiform, being altered and redacted by various
individuals since there was no central authority in power.  /36/
Only an examination of the relevant documents can produce the
data needed to decide in a given case the nature and date of the
tradition.  For some groups (e.g. the Sadducees) this job will
be impossible due to our lack of information.  Even traditions
claiming to come from the proto-rabbis will in many cases be
difficult to date exactly.  /37/

### Gospels and Rabbis

Having surveyed the first part of Gerhardsson's work and
remembering that the Scandanavian scholars have written with an
eye to the application of the material to the gospels, we turn
to the question of what the implications of this programme of
research might be for gospel origins ?  Again, we can only do an
overview of the results of the last twenty years.

The classical form- and redaction-critical approach to the
formation of the gospels has posited:  (1) a community which was

not interested in the life and teachings of Jesus of Nazareth
per se, (2) an expectation of an immediate parousia followed by
a shift in thought due to parousia delay, (3) an experience of
the risen Lord so immediate that his word through the prophet
was often read back into stories of the life of Jesus, (4) an
extended oral period during which the gospel materials were
transmitted as folk literature rather than as controlled
traditions, (5) a freedom in the community to expand and alter
traditions to fit its own Sitz-im-Leben, and (6) a final
conscious editorial process in which one or more editors in one
or more stages reduced the oral tradition to writing and
produced a careful theological product, a gospel, bearing his
own stamp.

In contrast to this 'unchastened' form-critical picture
(admittedly limited and sketchy for reasons of space)
Gerhardsson, not without appreciation for form-critical
contributions, has posited the following:  (1) Jesus,
functioning as a rabbi and deliberately training his disciples,
(2) the disciples memorizing his teaching according to the
normal educational practice of their day, (3) the
post-resurrection apostolic group forming a self-conscious
rabbinate which controlled and passed on the tradition to other
tradents, (4) this same Jerusalem circle widening the tradition
by use of haggadic and other midrashic techniques to exposit its
inner meaming, (5) the church continuing to prefer oral
tradition to written until the second century, and (6) gospel
books being gradually formed as notebooks used to aid memory
were collated into full gospels and finally replacing the oral
word they were first designed merely to supplement. /38/

While these pictures differ, we must not exaggerate the
this difference, for Gerhardsson is not arguing for total
historical accuracy or lack of redactional activity in the
gospels.  As Haacker and Michel write, 'Man darf diese Theorie
der Entstehung und Formung der Jesustradition nich
missverstehen als konservativen Verzicht auf historische Kritik.
Selbstverständlich rechnet Gerhardsson mit Umformungen und
Neubildungen von Jesustraditionen durch die nachösterliche
Gemeinde.' /39/  This note must be taken seriously, for too often
the critics of the Uppsala school have precisely this
misunderstanding, as do many conservatives who would like to
force Gerhardsson into support of their uncritical work.

We shall approach the examination of the contribution

of Gerhardsson's point-of-view in three stages:  (1) Jesus as a
teacher, (2) the church as the transmitter, and (3) the written
word as the end of the tradition.  First, Gerhardsson's picture
of Jesus' teaching activity is certainly to a large extent
accurate.  The synoptic gospels use διδάσκαλος 40 times and
ῥαββεί 8 times to describe Jesus. /40/ Jesus in the tradition
often has the outward trappings of a teacher of that period:  he
is surrounded by a group of disciples who live with him and
serve him, he has an inner circle of 'advanced students' to whom
he explains his deeper teaching, he teaches privately in houses
and publicly in synagogues and in the open.  One may indeed
question whether ῥαββεί was in any sense a formal title at this
date, /41/ one may argue whether Jesus' teaching was truly
rabbinic or more on the model of Qumran's Teacher of
Righteousness, /42/ Ben Sira's sage (Sirach 51: 23-30), or a
prophetic-apocalytic seer, but unless the picture of Jesus in
the gospels is totally false in one of its most basic aspects,
Jesus was recognized in his day as some type of a teacher. /43/

Since Jesus was a teacher with a group of disciples, it
would be foolish to argue that he transmitted no tradition
(which one might loosely call halakah) to them.  They certainly
learned information about the Kingdom from him, and their
lifestyle was regulated by his direction.  Furthermore, there
is a firm tradition in the gospels that Jesus used his disciples
to transmit his teaching to others during his lifetime (Mk. 6:
7-13, Lk. 9:1-6 , 10:1-16, Matt. 9:36-10:15).  Here again is
evidence for the self-consciousness of the didactic process and
the deliberate formation of a pre-Easter Jesus teaching
tradition. /44/ His controversies with other groups, without
which the crucifixion could hardly be explained, would add
another element to our picture of the Sitz-im-Leben of the
pre-Easter tradition.

Given that we have both a tradition that Jesus taught and
a setting for the formation of the early tradition, one can
attempt to recover the content of this tradition in two ways
beyond the criteria of coherence and historical 'fit'.  First,
one can work from Greek back into Aramaic to see if obviously
primitive forms appear.  Each major study has in fact discovered
a quantity of the mnemonic forms which must have characterized
such a tradition:  parallelism, rhythmic sayings, alliteration,
assonance, etc. /45/ Other didactic passages contain expressions
which can best be explained by an early Palestinian setting./46/
Gerhardsson has posited that the typical form of the teaching

of Jesus was the _mashal_, the parable, the pithy saying or
riddle. /47/  The discovery of these forms in the primitive
material is confirmation to him that Jesus did in fact transmit
traditions to his disciples.  Such simple sayings could easily
be memorized , suiting transmission, and in fact the gospels do
contain the tradition that this was Jesus' teaching style
(e.g. Mk. 4:33-34 and parallels).  Thus it is likely that
_mashalim_ formed a large portion of the teaching of Jesus and
will form the bedrock of the historically verifiable material
in that tradition.  Gerhardsson may also be right in arguing
that some of the larger units developed as the exposition of
the originally isolated saying or incident, a text being
illustrated by a story or an expansion much as gemara was later
added to mishnah. /48/

     Second, one can locate early material without necessarily
retranslating it into Aramaic by structural analysis, which
often points to units in the authentic Jesus-tradition much
larger than the _mashal_ which are similar to traditional units
in Jewish exegesis.  The most worked-on of these forms is the
midrash pattern. /49/ Where these patterns appear in the
gospels , they are evidence that the whole unit has been
transmitted together rather than developed piecemeal from an
initial saying. /50/  The presence of such exegetical material
in authentic Jesus-tradition is not in the least surprising,
for one could not conceive of a Jewish teacher who 'taught
in their synagogues' who did not refer to and comment upon the
Old Testament.  While some such cases could arise from the
Palestinian church's reading their own exegesis back into the
pre-Easter tradition, such an explanation if generalized would
leave the question open as to where the Palestinian church
received the ideas for its own understanding of scripture. It
is indeed likely that the church developed its pattern of
exegesis because of the way Jesus handled the scripture and
thus simply expanded upon the teaching she had received. /51/
While Prof. Gerhardsson has rightly stressed the place of the
_mashal_, he has missed the presence of these larger structures
in the Jesus-tradition.

     One of the problems of the Jesus-tradition is the variety
in the form of sayings; the synoptic gospels are simply not a
homogenous unity.  Since this fact impinges on his theory of
controlled transmission, Gerhardsson has handled the problem
in two ways:  (1) he appeals to the probability that Jesus said
similar things on several occasions, and (2) he points to the

fact that the Aramaic sayings probably suffered from a variety
of more or less paraphrastic translations into Greek (for even
translators of a 'holy word' may be 'traitors'). /52/ The
first of these points is a priori probable, but one cannot see
how it could be used as a tool in gospel criticism: how can
one separate differences due to point of origin from those due
to alteration during transmission, and how can one rule out the
complication that originally distinct traditions would tend to
assimilate to each other during the course of transmission ?

Gerhardsson's second point is also probable, for certainly
no official body produced an authorized Greek translation of
the teaching of Jesus. But here again one faces a complication
in the likelihood that in bilingual Palestine some of Jesus'
teaching was originally delivered in Greek. /53/ If this were
the case, it is important for two reasons: (1) as Gerhardsson
admits, /54/ Hellenistic Jews showed no reticence in using
writing to transmit traditions, and (2) if the same man gave
teaching in both Greek and Aramaic, even a pre-Easter
separation in thought between Aramaic-speaking and Hellenistic
communities becomes that much less likely. Both the use of
writing and the bilingual trandition would tend to produce a
far greater continuity in the tradition than early form-critics
were prone to admit.

The above moves us on to the second stage of our
consideration, namely, the church as the transmitter of the
Jesus-tradition. While it has often been claimed that the
early church had no interest in the historical Jesus, it
appears unlikely to us that the disciples of Jesus did not seek
to pass on a Jesus tradition from the earliest period. First,
the hypothesis of the radical nature of the parousia delay
appears unfounded, for even some of the admittedly genuine
parables of Jesus appear to have such a delay built into them.
/55/ Second, however excited the early Christians may have
been about the presence of the risen Christ, the teaching of
the earthly Jesus was surely the first place they went to
instruct new converts in how to live in the eschatological
community, as indicated by the content of the 'Q' material.
/56/ Third, the form of the earliest preaching included data
about the life of Jesus as 'a man approved by God' (Acts 2:22),
which would indicate that the narrative element in the Jesus-
tradition did not have much of a chance to grow before it
became a vital part of the kerygma and the instruction of new
converts. /57/ Gerhardsson, of course, recognizes this latter

fact, although he approaches it from the perspective of the rabbinic literature in which the rabbis pass on to their disciples traditions of both the deeds and words of their own masters (the deeds being acted halakah or perhaps haggadic expositions of a halakah).

Yet to argue that the Jesus-tradition was probably deliberately transmitted from the first is not to make the process as simple and uniform as Gerhardsson appears to assume. First, we have pointed out both in relation to Jewish traditions and in relation to the language of Jesus that there is no reason to assume that the early transmission was exclusively oral. The apostles may not have been studied in the Jewish law (so Acts 4:13), but due to the prevalence of education in Jewish communities many, if not most, of them must have been literate. /58/ We should not therefore be surprised if at least a minimal amount of the testimonia, narratives, and teaching which found their way into the gospels was recorded in writing before or soon after Easter. /59/

Second, while the presence of disciples of the earthly Jesus as leaders in the church in Jerusalem must have limited the variety allowed in the emerging gospel material, Gerhardsson is probably wrong in assuming that the apostolic college functioned like the later theorectical rabbinic Great Sanhedrin (as in Deut. 17:8ff.), officially controlling both the tradition and its expansion. /60/ Jerusalem and the body of apostles was important in the early church, for while Luke may have idealized his picture, that data of Acts 6, Acts 15, and even the speeches in Acts point to an underlying tradition from earlier Jewish sources. /61/ The narrative of Acts 1: 21-22 indicates that at least to some in the church the role of the apostles was not only that of a witness to the resurrection, but also that of a witness to the life and presumably the teaching of Jesus. It would be hard to believe that men with such a role did not by their presence exert some control upon the development of tradition. /62/

Confirmation of the picture in Acts comes from the fact that even Paul felt the power and authority of the Jerusalem church and the apostles. While Paul insists that his legitimacy as an apostle comes directly from Christ, he still reports that he found it necessary to go to Jerusalem at least twice and on one occasion to seek formal approval of his gospel from the apostles (Gal. 2:1-10). This would be most astounding

if Paul did not feel that the apostles had at least some type
of authority over the content of the tradition.  Thus although
Paul refuses to become dependent upon Jerusalem, he has the
highest respect for the role of the community as a stronghold
of pure doctrine and tradition. /63/

So long as the apostles existed, then, and particularly so
long as they existed in Jerusalem, the respect in which they
were held had the effect of dampening variation in the
tradition, but neither Acts, nor Paul, nor the data of the
gospels points to a unitary orally published tradition or to
formal control by the apostles over that tradition.  The story
of the earthly Jesus was widely used in the early church, even
Paul using it in his teaching and preaching, /64/ but the
tradition was hardly formally unified, even though there must
have been a limited number of recognized tradents. /65/ Luke,
for example, can speak of a knowledge not of one official line,
but of many compilations (Lk. 1:1-4).  He apparently did some
critical work on some passages in removing accretions in the
pre-Marcan form of the tradition, /66/ as well as combining
a number of different traditions.  The complex nature of the
tradition in 'Q' and Mark, not to mention Luke and Matthew,
cuts two ways, for it raises serious questions over the
assumption of a long oral period as posited by classic
form-criticism, but it also undercuts the idea of any official
control over the tradition as posited by Gerhardsson. /67/ The
tradition was not totally free from informal control so long
as there were eyewitnesses in respected positions, nor would
the community wish it so, for communities themselves do not
tend to be creative especially when it comes to their
foundation narrative, but the activity of the Spirit (which
Gerhardsson does not discuss) was too powerful for the
formation of an effective central controlling authority, which
meant that prophets and apostles had some room for creativity
in their handling of the tradition. /68/

Gerhardsson may well be right, however, in his belief
that much of the expansion of the tradition took place in
Jerusalem using exegetical processes analogous to those later
used in the Talmud. /69/ The supposition that narrative
material was treated with more freedom than teaching material
(analogous to haggada and halaka)  and that teaching material
was exposited in the context of the church situation to
produce a clear teaching for the church is not unlikely.  Such
careful editing and development by leaders in a community is

surely more logical than the free creation of sayings by a community to fit the situation, as well as more like similar situations known from anthropological research.

Turning to the last stage of our consideration, the written word as the end of the tradition, we note that Gerhardsson's argument for the preference of the oral word as the primary means of transferring the tradition has not found wide acceptance. Citing Papias (Eusebius, <u>H</u>. <u>E</u>. XXXIX, 13) and Irenaeus (<u>H</u>. <u>E</u>. V, 20), he argues for the primacy of the oral word. /70/ But the passages in question prove no more than a personal preference for oral communication of tradition, such as a modern student's delight in hearing a lecture by a noted professor, although he may later gladly refer to the same content in a journal article. Certainly Irenaeus is not reticent in writing down the traditions he has heard (<u>adv</u>. <u>Haereses</u> IV, 27, 1; IV, 31, 1; IV, 32, 1). /71/ Furthermore, Papias appears to be gathering a multitude of traditions from different sources, not tracing a unified tradition back to the single source in Jerusalem. Here again the data has been overstepped, for the presence of and delight in oral tradition (and its probable influence on the written text) has been made into the chief vehicle of the tradition.

In conclusion we can draw together what presently appears to be the lasting contribution of the Uppsala school to gospel study, remembering that in our criticisms we have been dealing with a pioneer who was breaking ground upon which others, including himself, have built.

(1) Gerhardsson was correct over against the form-critical school in looking at the gospel material, especially the didactic parts, as traditions deliberately taught by Jesus to the disciples and in part passed on by them before the passion. Further research, however, has shown that at an early date at least part of this process was in a written form (<u>i</u>.<u>e</u>. the Qumranic model was as much that of Jesus' milieu as the later rabbinic) and that the material was from the beginning partially in Greek.

(2) After Easter the early church did take an intense interest in the life and teaching of Jesus. Translation of Aramaic traditions into Greek must have been almost immediate in Jerusalem, where Hellenistic Jews were part of the early church. The presence of eyewitnesses of that life up until

the period when the written gospels were appearing, witnesses
who were in high church positions, must have had a strongly
conservative effect on the tradition (remembering that the
church as much as the rest of its society valued the authority
of elders). The church was clearly conscious that it was
passing on tradition, not creating new ex nihilo (cf. even Paul
in 1 Cor. 15:1ff., 11:23ff., which are some of the few places
where his arguments overlap gospel concerns). Yet this
transmission was also probably more in writing than Gerhardsson
allows. Furthermore, the apostolic band did not have the
amount of authority he posits. There was a holy word from the
one teacher, Jesus, but the job of the apostle was not simply
to pass the word on to students, to exegete the word, or to
decide cases upon it, although they certainly did some of this,
but to proclaim it to the world.

(3) The Jesus-tradition did expand during the course of
transmission, especially as Jesus' teaching was made more
clear. Rather less control was maintained over the narrative
element. While prophetic interpolation may have had a role to
play in the development of the tradition, exegetical processes
were probably the most important ones at work. The tradition
was also multiform and open to redaction from the beginning,
yet more of the larger structures than Gerhardsson admits
appear to have a Sitz-im-Leben Jesu.

The Uppsala school, then, has begun a process of
reexamining the way in which the gospel traditions were
transmitted in the light of contemporary Judaism. This process
needs continued research in many of the areas surveyed, but it
has already called into question some of the more sceptical
conclusions of form-criticism and continues to cry out for a
full-scale evaluation of that discipline using historical and
anthropological controls to sift its lasting contributions from
any unhistorical assumptions it may contain. /72/

. Notes

1. (London, 1957). Also in Studia Evangelia = TU 73
(1959), pp. 43-65 and The Gospel Tradition (Philadelphia, 1970),
pp. 1-29.

2. (Uppsala, 1961).

3. Coniectanea Neotestamentica XX (Lund, 1964). This work
principally answers Morton Smith's strongly worded attack, 'A
Comparison of Early Christian and Early Rabbinic Tradition',
JBL 82 (1963), pp. 169-176.

4. E.g. The Testing of God's Son (Lund, 1966), which
applied much of his theory to Matt. 4:1-11. Cf. 'The Parable of
the Sower and Its Interpretation', NTS 14 (1968), pp. 165-193;
'Geistiger Opferdienst nach Matth 6, 1-6,  16-21', Neues
Testament und Geschichte (Festschrift for O. Cullmann) (Zürich,
1972), pp. 69-77; 'The Seven Parables in Matthew XIII', NTS 19
(1972), pp. 16-37; 'Gottes Sohn als Diener Gottes', StTh 27
(1973), pp. 73-106; 'The Hermeneutic Programme in Matth 22:
35-40', Jews, Greeks, and Christians (Festschrift W. D. Davies)
(Leiden, 1976). We now also have studies by his students, e.g.
S. Westerholm, Jesus and Scribal Authority (Lund, 1978).

5. E.g. T. Boman, Die Jesus-Überlieferung im Lichte der
neueren Volkskunde (Göttingen,  1967), E. Güttgemanns, Offene
Fragen zur Formgeschichte des Evangeliums (München, 1970),
and J. Weingreen, From Bible to Mishna (Manchester, 1976).

6. Die Anfänge der Evangelientradition (Wuppertal, 1977).
The forward to this work was significantly written by K. Haaker
and O. Michel. This book has just been published in English
as The Origins of the Gospel Tradition (Philadelphia, 1979),
but we have yet to receive a copy and so cite the German
edition.

7. Gerhardsson, Memory and Manuscript, pp. 71-170.
Typical approval is that of A. Goldberg in BiOr 21 (1964), pp.
223-225: 'He has read widely, has fine discrimination and has
really written the best all-round presentation available in
any language, with the exception perhaps of Hebrew of the
nature, character and manner of transmission of the Jewish
Oral Law.' Cf.S. Lieberman, Hellenism in Jewish Palestine

(New York, 1950), pp. 83-99, and J. Neusner, Early Rabbinic
Judaism (Leiden, 1975), pp. 83-89, for similiar, if much briefer
treatments.

8. Cf. Weingreen, op. cit., pp. 76-81.

9. Much of Neusner's position is in essence an expansion
and development of that of his revered teacher M. Smith.
Compare Neusner's position with that of Smith, op. cit., pp.
169-171.

10. (Leiden, 1971).

11. From Politics to Piety: The Emergence of Pharisaic
Judaism (Englewood Cliffs, NJ, 1973) and Early Rabbinic Judaism
are his major recent contributions on this topic, although he
is such a prolific writer that a score of volumes could be
cited as relevant. E.g. his'Studies on the Problem of the
Tannaim in Babylonia' Proceedings of the American Academy for
Jewish Research 30 (1962), pp. 79ff. on the form of Jewish
education in Babylonia between AD 135 and 175, and 'History and
Purity in First-Century Judaism' History of Religions 18 (1978),
pp. 1-17, which shows that he has not altered his approach to
the texts in the last few years, as well as his monumental
studies on Johanan ben Zakkai and Eleazar ben Hyrcanus and his
multi-volume History of the Mishnaic Law of Purities and
History of the Mishnaic Law of Sacrifice.

12. From Politics to Piety, pp. 92-95; Early Rabbinic
Judaism, pp. 77-99. For similar reasons (i.e. because the
gospel pericopae and Josephus fit the apologetic situation of
the AD 70-90 period) he totally rejects the relevancy of New
Testament material. For further information on the
form-criticism of the rabbinic literature, see A. J. Saldarini,
'"Form Criticism" of Rabbinic Literature', JBL 96 (1977), pp.
257-274.

13. S. Zeitlin, 'Spurious Interpretations of Rabbinic
Sources in the Studies of Pharisees and Pharisaism', JQR 65
(1974-1975), pp. 127-135. While Zeitlin accuses Neusner of
being ignorant of the Talmud, as well as of errors and
distortions, there is also a strong mutual animosity between
Neusner and Israeli Talmudic scholars, e.g. E. E. Urbach, The
Sages: Their Concepts and Beliefs (Jerusalem, 1975), which
Neusner has attacked in lecture, on the question of historical

reliability and methodology.

14. P. Sigal, <u>The</u> <u>Halakah</u> <u>of</u> <u>Jesus</u> <u>of</u> <u>Nazareth</u> <u>according</u> <u>to the</u> <u>Gospel</u> <u>of</u> Matthew (Ph.D. dissertation, University of Pittsburgh, 1979), p. 54, <u>cf</u>. pp. 63-67.  We expect to see this work published, joining the other works of this scholar on the history of the Jews.

15. This is not to argue that the task is easy or the material from particularly the earlier part of this period is reliable, but that form and date of attestation are not sufficient grounds for rejecting the content of a tradition.

16. <u>Memory</u> <u>and</u> <u>Manuscript</u>, p. 72.; <u>Tradition</u> <u>and</u> <u>Transmission</u>, p. 15.  Here Gerhardsson calls upon the data amassed by scholars such as Nyberg, Mowinckel, Ringgren, Nielsen, Widengren, and Grunneweg.

17. Cf. Boman, <u>op</u>. <u>cit</u>., pp. 9-28, who points out that all traditional societies rely on accurate oral transmission of tradition.  Thus Israel would have been exceptional if it <u>did</u> <u>not</u> have some oral traditions of a character later called halakic and haggadic.

18. <u>Early</u> <u>Rabbinic</u> <u>Tradition</u>, pp. 73ff.  <u>Cf</u>.  pp. 58-62, where he argues that Eleazar b. Hyrcanus essentially continued and liberalized earlier 'Pharisaic' interests.  The prevalence of oral transmission in the pre-70 period has also been argued by J. M. Baumgarten, 'The Unwritten Law in the Pre-Rabbinic Period', JSJ 3 (1972), pp. 7-29.  He argues from both Josephus, Antiq.13,297 and Philo.

19. G. Widengren, 'Tradition and Literature in Early Judaism and in the Early Christian Church', Numen 10 (1963), pp.52-60.  Widengren also points to the role of written texts in the transmission of mystery religions and elsewhere in the ancient Near East.

20. <u>Memory</u> <u>and</u> <u>Manuscript</u>, pp. 160-163.

21. This explanation is at least as likely as Gerhardsson, <u>Memory</u> <u>and</u> <u>Manuscript</u>, pp. 22-27, who argues that the stress on oral tradition resulted from a power struggle with the Sadducees who did keep their halakah in written form in the temple.  His data on this point is simply not that persuasive.

22. Neusner, Early Rabbinic Judaism, pp. 90-99, agrees, although he rejects any sure knowledge of this period. For a more thorough argument, see Weingreen, op. cit., pp. 76-81.

23. Memory and Manuscript, pp. 38-40, 100-101, 246-249, 253. Gerhardsson argues for an essentially stabilized text in the first century, as well as for a centralized doctrinal authority (i.e. the Great Sanhedrin).

24. J. A. Sanders, 'Text and Canon: Concepts and Method', JBL 98 (1979), pp. 6-7, gives a succinct summary of the data and a bibliography of the most important works.

25. Cf. J. Bowker, The Targums and Rabbinic Literature (Cambridge, 1969), pp. 53-60. Along with Akiba's Mishnah one has that of Ishmael. In all likelihood earlier collections also existed. The final codification came only with Rabbi.

26. Cf. Sigal, op. cit., pp. 35-57, for a reconstruction of the history involved here.

27. E. Rivkin, A Hidden Revolution (Nashville, 1978), p. 28.

28. From Politics to Piety, p. 11.

29. S. Zeitlin, Studies in the Early History of Judaism (New York, 1973-1975), vol. 2, p. 295.

30. E.g. L. Finkelstein, The Pharisees: The Sociological Background of Their Faith (Philadelphia, 1962); T. Herford, The Pharisees (Boston, 1962).

31. The problem with the gospels is that they have not appeared to agree with the attitudes rabbinic material posits for the proto-rabbis. Since Christians have rediscovered rabbinic Judaism (i.e. from the period leading up to G. F. Moore's Judaism) both they and rabbinic scholars have generally tried one of three solutions to the apparent conflict: (1) some argue that Pharisaic-rabbinic thought shifted for some reason between the gospels and the Mishnah, (2) others reject the gospels as polemically inspired falsifications, and (3) still others limit the attacks in the gospels to only a part of the proto-rabbinic movement. We are suggesting here that this last solution was a move in the right direction.

32. _Cf_. the data presented and the conclusions drawn by J. Bowker, _Jesus and the Pharisees_ (Cambridge, 1973), pp. 1-38. This interpretation has been criticised by Zeitlin in 'Spurious Interpretations', pp. 122-127, but certainly Bowker was moving in the right direction in discovering a variety of meanings in the terms, even if he was not right in detail. So also E. Rivkin, 'Defining the Pharisees: The Tannaitic Sources', HUCA 40-41 (1969-1970), pp. 205-249.

33. Sigal, _op_. _cit_., p. 5. Sigal argues that the proto-rabbis were for the most part non-rigourist and therefore relatively accepting of Jesus as a teacher within the limits of accepted halakic variation (although they did not agree with him). _Cf_. E. P. Sanders, _Paul and Palestinian Judaism_ (Philadelphia, 1977), p. 62, who comments, 'The question of who the Pharisees were and of how they saw themselves _vis à vis_ the rest of Judaism appears quite wide open.'

34. _E.g_. J. Z. Lauterbach,'Midrash and Mishnah' in _Rabbinic Essays_ (Cincinatti, 1951); E. E. Ellis, _Prophecy and Hermeneutic in Early Christianity_ (Tübingen, 1978), pp. 189-208.

35. _Cf_.J. Kaplan, _The Redaction of the Babylonian Talmud_ (Jerusalem, 1979), pp. 261-288, who also argues for written transmission of tradition among rabbis.

36. As P. Sigal points out in another context in _New Directions in Judaism_ (New York, 1972), pp. 25-37, halakoth were changed, accidentally or deliberately, in ancient Judaism. One can also compare parallel accounts in rabbinic literature and discover alterations in name, detail, and application.

37. We have only dealt tangentally with another point, which is that Gerhardsson has over-stressed the rabbinic model in all of his work at the expense of an examination of wider models in Judaism (_e.g_. Qumran, wisdom traditions, and prophetic traditions). Unless the proto-rabbis were indeed a dominant force in the New Testament period, there is no reason to concentrate on their model of transmission above any other.

38. While _Memory and Manuscript_, pp. 193-335, is his most detailed argument of the theory as a whole, _Anfänge_, pp. 20-64, focuses much more directly on the gospels, and _Testing of God's Son_, especially pp. 71-83, shows how Gerhardsson is not simply

arguing for fidelity in transmission, but also for careful and
deliberate creation of haggadic midrash as an explanation of
the tradition.

39. Gerhardsson, Anfänge, p. 6 (Vorwort).

40. J. Donaldson, 'The Title Rabbi in the Gospels -- Some
Reflections on the Evidence of the Synoptics', JQR 63 (1972-
1973), p.289, points out that particularly the term διδάσκαλος
in Mark does not appear theologically motivated but simply
means that 'he outwardly conformed to the picture of a teacher
of his day.'

41. Cf. H. Shanks, 'Is the Title "Rabbi" Anachronistic in
the Gospels ?' JQR 53 (1963), pp. 337-345, and Donaldson, op.
cit., pp. 287-291. S. Zeitlin follows Shanks' article with a
reply (pp. 345-349), whereas Donaldson is summing up the
argument. Certainly 'rabbi' in its later technical sense was
not used in the time of Jesus, but Shanks does produce evidence
that it was used as a popular title for those who did in fact
teach.

42. Widengren, op. cit., p. 64.

43. Cf. G.Aulén, Jesus in Contemporary Historical Research
(Philadelphia, 1976), pp. 36-37.

44. One might call this a kerygmatic-halakic tradition,
since elements of both the later kerygma and Christian
'halakah' were present. See J. Jeremias, Neutestamentliche
Theologie (Güttersloh, 1973, ed. 2), pp. 122-229. Cf. H.
Schürmann, 'Die vorösterliche Anfänge der Logientradition',
Traditionsgeschichtliche Untersuchungen (Düsseldorf, 1968),
pp. 39-65. We are aware that the role of the twelve in
particular has been variously evaluated, but believe that the
evidence points to their existence as portrayed in the
synoptics. Cf. E. E. Ellis, The Gospel of Luke (London, 1974,
ed. 2), pp. 136-137, and I. H. Marshall, The Gospel of Luke
(Exeter, 1978), pp. 349-350. Even some who view the historical
position of the twelve in quite a different light, however,
see the group there represented as more or less faithful
transmitters of the Jesus-tradition, e.g. G. Theissen,
'Itinerant Radicalism' in The Bible and Liberation (Berkeley,
1976), pp. 84-93 (originally in German in ZTK 70 (1973), pp.
245-271).

45. J. Jeremias, op. cit., pp. 19-46; M. Black, An Aramaic Approach to the Gospels and Acts (Oxford, 1954, ed. 2); and of course C. F. Burney, The Poetry of Our Lord (Oxford, 1925); G. Dalman, Die Worte Jesu (Darmstadt, 1975), pp. 1-72.

46. Cf. Widengren, op. cit., pp. 65ff.

47. Gerhardsson, Anfänge, pp. 37-44.

48. This is the argument of his Testing of God's Son.

49. J. W. Doève, Jewish Hermeneutics in the Synoptic Gospels and Acts (Assen, 1954) and D. Daube, The New Testament and Rabbinic Judaism (London, 1954) are two of the seminal works.

50. E. E. Ellis, 'New Directions in Form Criticism' in Prophecy and Hermeneutic in Early Christianity (Tübingen, 1978), pp. 247-253. Prof. Ellis discusses Lk. 10:25-37 and Matt. 21: 33-44 as examples of the yelammedenu midrashic pattern. For other patterns see W. G. Braude, Pesikta Rabbati (New Haven, 1968), pp. 3-6.

51. Cf. R. N. Longenecker, Biblical Exegesis in the Apostolic Period (Grand Rapids, 1975), pp. 51-78, and Boman, op. cit., pp. 9-15, who argues that individuals, not groups, are creative in all situations examined by anthropologists. Notice there is no claim here that all use of the Old Testament in the gospels is dominical, but simply that some (perhaps much) of it is and that one key to dominical exegetical forms is the presence of sayings recognized as dominical in a larger exegetical context of which it is an integral part.

52. Anfänge, pp. 56ff.

53. I. H. Marshall, 'Palestinian and Hellenistic Christianity', NTS 19 (1972-1973), pp. 271-287; J. N. Sevenster, Do You Know Greek ? (Leiden, 1968); S. Lieberman, Greek in Jewish Palestine (New York, 1965, ed. 2), especially pp. 1-67; M. Hengel, Judaism and Hellenism (Philadelphia, 1974), vol. 1, pp. 58-106.

54. Tradition and Transmission, pp. 45-46. The point is well made by Ellis in 'New Directions', pp. 245-246.

55. S. S. Smalley, 'The Delay of the Parousia', JBL 83 (1964), pp. 41-54.

56. This fact is also indicated by the strong dependence upon the Jesus-tradition of such paraenetic works as James.

57. Naturally we refer to C. H. Dodd, The Apostolic Preaching and Its Developments (London, 1936) and According to the Scriptures (London, 1952), as well as B. Lindars, New Testament Apologetic (London, 1961).

58. Ellis, 'New Directions', p. 243.

59. The pre-Easter Sitz-im-Leben of such material was the mission of the twelve and the need to leave teaching behind as the itinerant band travelled. The post-Easter setting was the teaching needs of the growing church and especially the mission outside Jerusalem. The Hellenists of the Stephen group surely had reduced much of the Gospel to writing in Greek. Cf. Ellis, ibid., p. 244, and M. Hengel, 'Zwischen Jesus und Paulus', ZTK 72 (1975), pp. 151-206, especially p. 204.

60. Memory and Manuscript, pp. 214-225.

61. On these three citations in Acts see respectively, Hengel, 'Zwischen Jesus und Paulus', O. Linton, Das Problem der Urkirche (Uppsala, 1932), pp. 189ff., and J. W. Bowker, 'The Speeches in Acts', NTS 14 (1967-1968), pp. 96-111, also Ellis, Prophecy and Hermeneutic, pp. 198-208.

62. W. D. Davies, The Setting of the Sermon on the Mount (Cambridge, 1963), pp. 472-473.

63. We should add the collection for Jerusalem to our indications of Paul's respect for the mother church. Naturally Paul does not play his whole hand every time he writes. In Galatians it is useful to state that his divinely given apostelship later received Jerusalem's approval; in 2 Corinthians the same argument would have been devastating to his cause. Yet even in that work he never deprecates the apostles per se. Paul's attitude, then, is basically one of respect, although he shifts his openness in expressing it according to his audience. Cf. J. Drane, Paul: Libertine or Legalist ? (London, 1975) for which this unity and diversity form a major part of the theme.

64. G. N. Stanton, Jesus of Nazareth in New Testament Preaching (Cambridge, 1974), has clearly shown that there was an interest in the life and teaching of Jesus throughout the early church, including Paul. Paul has been maligned on this account partly through a misinterpretation of Gal. 1 and 2 Cor. 5:16 and partly through a focus on the epistles which views them, not as written to already-initiated believers, but as if they were replacements for the Gospel itself. This latter is to badly falsify Paul's thought by neglecting the difference between kerygma and later debate within the church.

65. So Boman, op. cit., pp. 11-15.

66. E.g. M. Hengel, 'Das Gleichnis von den Weingärtnern Mc 12, 1-12 im Lichte der Zenopapyri und der rabbinischen Gleichnisse', ZNW 59 (1968), pp. 1-39. Page 6 in particular points out how Luke and the Gospel of Thomas logion 64 remove pre-Marcan additions to the tradition.

67. Ellis, 'New Directions', p. 239.

68. Certainly the pneumatic character of early Christianity was quite fundamental. The Apocalypse, 1 Cor. 14: 37, 1 Thess. 4:15, and possibly 1 Cor. 7:10 refer to words of the exalted Jesus, a phenomenon with which Gerhardsson does not deal. It may also occur in Lk. 11:49-51 and frequently in the Johannine material. The analogy which we have drawn to rabbinic authority, however, must not blind us to the diversity among the rabbis until the period of Judah ha-Nasi; we can still detect this disunity despite the fact we have edited editions of the traditions.

69. Supra, note 43.

70. Memory and Manuscript, pp. 202-207.

71. Widengren, op. cit., pp. 72-75.

72. This process, of course, is already on-going, e.g. Güttgemanns, op. cit.

# Mark and the Teaching of Jesus

R.T. France
Tyndale House, Cambridge

Much recent study of the Gospel of Mark has
been preoccupied with the search for its purpose.
Different situations, adversaries or theological
hobby-horses have been postulated with a view to
explaining the <u>raison d'être</u> of what is generally
agreed to be a bold new type of writing. If Mark
created the genre 'gospel', it is assumed that he
did so for some purpose, and the search for that
purpose shows no sign of abating.

I venture to ask whether the question is not
perhaps misconceived. No doubt some documents are
written with a single clear purpose. Examples might
be a legal contract, a surveyor's report, or the
recording of a debate in Hansard. But would this be
true of anything which deserves the name of
literature? For novels, poems, histories,
biographies, anthologies, and even for text-books
and articles in learned journals, it is usually
impossible to determine a single aim, and it is
often a matter of debate which of a number of
suggested aims was the controlling one. Even the
author himself might have difficulty in resolving
the debate.

It is, then, unrealistic to elevate a
particular slant which may be discovered at certain
points in the gospel into the determining principle
by which all the contents of the book must be
judged. Most of us have a rather untidy assortment
of pet themes which are likely to emerge in anything
we write, but which could certainly not be described
as <u>the purpose</u> of our writing, or even be
systematised into a coherent 'theology' which
governs our thought and expression. The variety of
suggested purposes and themes which are currently on
offer in relation to the Gospel of Mark suggests
strongly that its author was no exception to this
pattern /1/.

Thus any attempt to evaluate Mark's gospel as
a source for our understanding of Christian origins
must beware of neglecting the minor themes. They
may be quite different from other more prominent
emphases, even scarcely compatible with them, but
they may nonetheless be real concerns of the
author, and are therefore relevant in assessing the
type of book he has left us.

In this paper I want to explore one such theme,
Mark's interest in Jesus as a teacher. I would not
want to claim that this is his main concern, that
the gospel was written primarily as a record of
Jesus' teaching. That would be self-evidently
false. But it has long been recognised that an
emphasis on Jesus' teaching activity is one of the
characteristics of Mark's editorial work, and this
must have implications both for his christology and
for our understanding of the way he has presented
the teaching of Jesus in his gospel.

We may start from the frequently stated dilemma
that the gospel which lays the strongest stress on
teaching as an activity of Jesus is also
comparatively thin in the amount of actual teaching
material which it contains. This latter point led
Bultmann, following Dibelius, to wonder why Mark
included any sayings-material at all: 'Since the
dominical sayings were originally collected for
instructional purposes, the reason for their
incorporation into the Gospel is not self-evident.'
He can only conclude that 'it would have been
unnatural in the long run to have kept the dominical
sayings out,' but they remain for him essentially
irrelevant to the plan of the gospel /2/.

But if Bultmann is right, why did Mark lay such
stress on Jesus as a teacher? What could the
concept have meant to him if he was not interested
in recording the actual teaching material? Was
'instruction' in fact so foreign to Mark's purpose
as he assumes?

I propose therefore to reexamine the essential
data. Is it in fact true that the quantity of

sayings-material recorded is an insignificant element in the plan of the gospel? How do the sayings recorded fit into the narrative context, and what may this tell us about their function in the gospel? What sort of sayings did Mark choose to include, and does this indicate anything about his purpose in recording them? What may we learn from this about his attitude to the sayings-tradition? Was he in fact concerned about preserving the teaching of Jesus as such, or has he felt at liberty to fill out in his own way an idealistic portrait of Jesus as the great Teacher?

I Mark's Emphasis on Jesus' Teaching Activity

It seems clear not only from the Christian gospels but also from Jewish tradition that Jesus of Nazareth was known as a teacher /3/. His teaching activity appears in all strata of the gospel traditions, and it seems certain that this represents a historical feature of the activity and the reputation of Jesus; indeed it would be cause for surprise if he were not so represented.

But it is particularly in the Gospel of Mark that this aspect of Jesus' activity is emphasised /4/. Vocabulary statistics are not the whole story, but they provide a useful lead into the subject. The verb διδάσκειν is used of the activity of Jesus 15 times in Mark, compared with 9 in Matthew and 15 in Luke; διδάσκαλε as a term of address to Jesus occurs 10 times in Mark, compared with 6 in Matthew and 11 in Luke ( and ῥαββί or ῥαββουνί 4 times in Mark compared with 2 in Matthew and none in Luke); the noun διδαχή is used to describe Jesus' characteristic activity 5 times in Mark, compared with 2 in Matthew and 1 in Luke. Given the relative lengths of the gospels these figures show a much heavier emphasis on this word-group in Mark /5/.

This emphasis is seen more clearly when it is noted that most of the uses of διδάσκειν and διδαχή in Mark are in summaries of Jesus' ministry or in the 'seams' which link or introduce pericopae /6/, i.e. that it is precisely in Mark's editorial

material rather than in the units received from
tradition that this emphasis occurs. In these uses
it is assumed, and sometimes made explicit /7/, that
teaching was Jesus' normal activity /8/. The title
διδάσκαλε is the most common form of address to Jesus
in Mark, and is used fairly indiscriminately by
disciples (4: 38; 9: 38; 10: 35; 13: 1; also ῥαββί
in 9:5; 11:21; 14:45), suppliants (9:17; also
ῥαββουνί in 10:51) and those posing questions, even
from hostile motives (10: 17,20; 12: 14,19,32). Two
further non-vocative uses (5:35; 14: 14) suggest
that it was a suitable description for Jesus as
others saw him /9/. All this indicates that the
description of Jesus as a teacher was both normal
and significant for Mark. In comparison with the
much reduced use of such terminology in Matthew and
Luke /10/ (including the quite conspicuous
avoidance of the title διδάσκαλε as a term of
address to Jesus by the disciples) we may fairly
classify this as a matter of special interest to
Mark. For him, teaching is 'das für Jesus typische
Handeln, das man so nicht vom Taüfer oder von der
Kirche aussagen könnte.' /11/

The relation of Mark's use of διδάσκειν to the
theme of proclamation (κηρύσσειν) is interesting in
this regard. κηρύσσειν appears in Mark only three
times with reference to the activity of Jesus, and
is sometimes regarded as virtually a synonym of
διδάσκειν /12/. But in Mark, in contrast, with
Matthew /13/, the two verbs do not occur in the same
context, and κηρύσσειν as a description of Jesus'
activity is restricted to the initial announcement
of the gospel in 1: 14,38f /14/. Thereafter the two
verbs are kept distinct, in that, with the sole
exception of 6: 30, only Jesus is said to teach,
whereas κηρύσσειν is used of others (John the
Baptist, disciples, and those who have been healed)
who preach about Jesus. There is apparently for
Mark something uniquely appropriate to Jesus in the
activity of διδάσκειν /15/.

Correlative to the portrayal of Jesus as a
teacher is that of his associates as μαθηταί (43
times in Mark). This is not the place to attempt an

adequate discussion of the meaning of discipleship
in Mark /16/. Certainly it would be wrong to
imagine that their relationship with Jesus was
merely that of learner to teacher. It was a total
relationship of casting in their lot with Jesus,
involving renunciation, taking up the cross,
devoting oneself to the service of others /17/. But
the term μαθητής implies also a 'learning' role,
parallel in some way to that of the talmid of a
rabbi, and the frequent portrayal of Jesus' teaching
as specifically directed to his disciples in Mark's
gospel indicates that he gave due weight also to
this aspect of discipleship. According to Mark the
Twelve /18/ were appointed in the first place 'to be
with him' (3: 14), and particularly in 8: 27 - 10:
52 they are frequently portrayed as being 'with him'
in order to be instructed. While διδάσκειν is
generally used of Jesus' public teaching, Mark also
uses it twice of the private instruction given to
the μαθηταί (8: 31; 9: 31), and lays considerable
emphasis on the privilege of the disciples as the
recipients of revelation and explanation not open
to others. It is their function not only to act
and proclaim, but also to see and to hear, to
understand and remember. (This at least must be
implied by the strange passage about the loaves in
8: 14-21.) They are the disciples of the teacher,
one of whose functions it will be to pass on his
teaching to others /19/. This repeated failure to
understand or to accept his teaching leads only to
further concentration on their private instruction
/20/. The Marcan Jesus is, then, a teacher who
reveals the hidden truth to his chosen disciples.

The private teaching of the disciples is,
however, only one part of Jesus' teaching ministry
according to Mark. He lays equal emphasis on the
wider range of Jesus' teaching. The 'crowd', who
are constantly present in the earlier part of the
gospel, are specifically said to be the objects of
his teaching (2: 13; 4: 1f; 6: 34; 7: 14; cf. also
10: 1), and this is true also in the ministry in
the temple in chapters 11-12 (11: 18; 12: 12,37).
Characteristic of Mark is the use of πᾶς ὁ or ὅλος ὁ
in indicating the wide response to Jesus' teaching

(1: 28,33,39; 2: 13; 4:1; 6: 33,55; 9: 15; 11:18;
cf. πάντοθεν, 1: 45; πολὺ πλῆθος, 3: 7f; and the many
references to the gathering of crowds round Jesus).

This response of the crowd to Jesus' teaching
is more specifically described by such verbs as
ἐκπλήσσεσθαι (1: 22; 6: 2; 11: 18; cf. also 10: 26
where the disciples are the subject) and (ἐκ)
θαμβεῖσθαι (1: 27; 9:15; cf. 10: 24, again with the
disciples as subject); and the reason for their
astonishment is said to be the ἐξουσία shown in
Jesus' teaching, an ἐξουσία sufficient to mark it
out as a διδαχὴ καινή (1: 22, 27). The direct and
irresistible authority of Jesus' teaching is
contrasted with that of the scribes (1: 22), and
throughout the gospel there is a high concentration
of what Vincent Taylor appropriately called
'pronouncement-stories', where a word from Jesus
settles an issue, leaving no room for dispute. This
authority inherent in Jesus' teaching is clearly of
christological importance to Mark, hence its
prominence in the programmatic episode with
the Galilean ministry is launched in 1: 21-28 /21/.
We must now therefore consider what role the idea of
Jesus as teacher plays in the Marcan christology.

II  Jesus as Teacher in Marcan Christology

We have seen good reason for regarding Jesus'
teaching function as a matter of some importance
for Mark, to the extent that E. Best can say that in
his editorial material 'Mark leaves us with the
impression that the main activity of Jesus was
teaching.' /22/

This special interest of Mark becomes clearer
in comparison with the use of didactic language by
Matthew and Luke /23/. Both of them of course share
Mark's understanding that Jesus was a teacher, and
retain some of Mark's uses of διδάσκειν in this
connection. Further uses of διδάσκειν appear in
Matthew's editorial summaries and link-passages (4:
23; 5: 2; 9: 35; 11: 1) and in those of Luke (4: 15;
5: 3; 13: 22; 19: 47; 21: 37). Both Matthew and
Luke substitute διδάσκειν for Mark's vaguer

περιπατεῖν to describe what Jesus was doing in the
temple in 11: 27, and Luke has further inserted
διδάσκειν in two passages from the triple tradition
(5: 17; 6: 6).  On the other hand, of Mark's 15 uses
of διδάσκειν of the activity of Jesus, only 4 are
reproduced in Matthew and 2 in Luke /24/, and
neither Matthew nor Luke reproduces Mark's repeated
ἐν τῇ διδαχῇ αὐτοῦ (4: 2; 12: 38).

All this suggests that Matthew and Luke, while
they had no quarrel with Mark's use of didactic
language to describe Jesus' activity, used this sort
of language in a comparatively colourless way in
setting the scene, but did not emphasise it as Mark
had done.  For Matthew in particular it was
apparently an inadequate term, so that he tends in
his editorial passages to add to it more positive
descriptions of Jesus as κηρύσσων and θεραπεύων (4:
23; 9: 35; 11: 1); twice he has θεραπεύειν in place
of a Marcan use of διδάσκειν (Mt. 14: 14 / Mk. 6:
34; Mt. 19: 2 / Mk. 10: 1).  Neither Matthew nor
Luke is prepared to reproduce διδάσκειν in
introducing the crucial christological revelations
of Mark 8: 31; 9: 31.  Even more significantly, the
striking and emphatic use of διδαχή in Mark 1: 22,27
in the context of an exorcism is defused by Matthew,
whose parallel to Mark 1: 22 is in the more
conventionally 'teaching' situation of the Sermon on
the Mount (7: 29; cf. 22: 33, again in a context of
academic debate in contrast with the Marcan
'parallel' at the cleansing of the temple, Mk. 11:
18), and who has no parallel to Mark 1: 27, while
Luke substitutes in 4: 36 the scarcely more
appropriate λόγος.  Thus διδάσκειν and διδαχή, which
in Mark denote a full-blooded and varied activity of
Jesus, are reduced in Matthew and Luke to a more
conventional use, correct enough as terms
descriptive of what Jesus spent his time doing, but
too prosaic to be applied to his distinctive
messianic function.

The use of διδάσκαλος in the three synoptic
gospels supports this impression.  Most of the uses
are in the vocative, as a term of address to Jesus,
and of these (including uses of ῥαββί and ῥαββουνί)

Mark has 14, Matthew 8 and Luke 11 (and once
addressed to John the Baptist, 3: 12). Luke in
particular, with 6 uses in his Sondergut (7: 40; 10:
25: 11: 45; 12: 13; 19: 39; 20: 39) and one in a
Marcan passage where Mark does not use it (21: 7),
clearly accepts that it is an appropriate form of
address to Jesus. But for that reason it is the
more striking that both Matthew and Luke are unable
to echo Mark's apparently indiscriminate use of this
form of address. The following Marcan uses are not
reproduced in either Matthew or Luke: Mark 4: 38;
9: 5 (ῥαββί); 9: 38; 10: 20; 10: 35; 10: 51
(ῥαββουνί); 11: 21 (ῥαββί); 12: 32; 13: 1. The
interesting thing about this list is that in 6 of
these 9 cases the speakers are disciples of Jesus
(and in the other cases suppliants or questioners
well disposed towards him). Where this vocative
address is not simply absent in Matthew's and Luke's
versions of these incidents, it is generally
replaced by a more definitely christological title,
κύριε (so Mt. 8: 25; 17: 4; 20: 33; Lk. 18: 41; also
Mt. 17: 15, where Luke retains διδάσκαλε) or, in
Luke, ἐπιστάτα (8: 24; 9: 33,49). Where διδάσκαλε is
reproduced by Matthew and Luke, it is spoken by
outsiders, and in contexts of debate rather than of
existential involvement (Mk. 10: 17, 12: 14,19).
The same pattern is maintained in the three
peculiarly Matthean uses (12: 38; 22: 36; in 8: 19
the speaker is a potential disciple only) and in the
seven peculiar to Luke listed above. (In Lk. 21: 7
the 'disciple' who addressed Jesus by this term in
Mk. 13: 1 has been replaced by an impersonal τινες
and 'they'.) It seems then that whereas for Mark
διδάσκαλε was a fit form of address to be used for
Jesus both by disciples and by outsiders, for
Matthew and Luke it is only the latter who can use
it, while the former must use more exalted and less
apparently academic titles.

Matthew goes even further than this, and seems
to regard the term as definitely unacceptable; for
him it is in general suitable only for Jesus'
enemies. Thus he retains the term in the cases
where Mark has it spoken by Jesus' opponents
(22: 16,24), and adds it on two other such

occasions (12: 38; 22: 36); he retains its use by
a potential disciple who failed to make the grade
(19: 16), and adds it in a similar case (8: 19).
But he also twice introduces the phrase ὁ διδάσκαλος
ὑμῶν as an accusing description of Jesus by the
Jewish authorities in dialogue with his disciples
(9: 11; 17: 24). Similarly he retains only one of
Mark's uses of ῥαββί (26: 49 = Mk. 14: 45), but the
speaker there is Judas Iscariot, and he adds
another, again by Judas (26: 25). It is therefore
hardly enough to describe 'teacher' language as
inadequate in Matthew's view - it is almost
derogatory /25/.

         In contrast with this reserve, Mark's free use
of the term stands out clearly. διδάσκαλε is the
most common form of address to Jesus in Mark, by
disciples as well as by others, and the use of ὁ
διδάσκαλος in 14: 14 as a designation for use in
identifying Jesus to one of his supporters suggests
that it may fairly be called a christological title
(cf. also 5: 35 for a similar use, though without
the identifying function). Its use as a form of
address in some contexts where teaching was not in
view would indicate this as well (4: 38; 9: 17; 9:
38; 10: 35; 13: 1) /26/.

         And whereas in Matthew and Luke its use is
largely restricted to contexts of academic
discussion, in Mark it is used by those in need of
practical help, of a supernatural kind (4: 38; 5:
35; 9: 17 /27/; 10: 51), or asking for a share in
Jesus' eschatological glory (10: 35). The Marcan
uses of ῥαββί in particular occur in settings of
numinous power (the transfiguration, the healing of
Bartimaeus, and the withering of the fig-tree). For
Mark, διδάσκαλος is far from being a merely polite
or academic title.

         This then raises the question of how for Mark
Jesus' teaching activity relates to the other
aspects of his mission, particularly his works of
power. The prophetic and messianic traits which no
doubt fuelled Matthew's conviction that διδάσκαλος
was too low a term for a truly Christian confession

of Jesus are prominent also in Mark's account of
Jesus, and yet he has no such hesitation over the
idea of Jesus as teacher. How then does he relate
these apparently contrasting elements in Jesus'
ministry, as a 'teacher' and yet as the dynamic
bringer of the kingdom of God?

That they are related, and not just placed
incongruously side by side, is indicated by the
pericope to which we have already referred as
programmatic for Jesus' ministry, 1: 21-28. Here
the narrative is of an exorcism, but it takes place
in the context of Jesus' teaching in the synagogue
(1: 21). His teaching produces astonishment because
of its ἐξουσία (1: 22), but then the exorcism
produces a similar astonishment, focused in a
mention of Jesus' διδαχὴ καινὴ κατ' ἐξουσίαν, this
ἐξουσία being further specified in terms of his
power over unclean spirits, Here, then, power in
exorcism and authority in teaching are quite
deliberately linked, to the extent that exorcism is
apparently identified as διδαχή, and the two
together create a total impression of an unheard-of
ἐξουσία.

Is the teaching then Jesus' primary function,
with the works of power as an authentication of the
teaching? Such a pattern is apparently intended in
the way the healing is introduced in 2: 1-12 /28/.
Indeed are the works themselves a form of teaching
/29/? Or, on the other hand, should the teaching be
regarded as itself a work of power, as in J.M.
Robinson's view that the debates and the exorcisms
are equally parts of the cosmic struggle in which he
finds the key to Mark's understanding of history
/30/? On such a view, Mark's account of Jesus'
teaching focuses on controversies because they are
'more congruous than any other type of teaching with
Mark's story, which is primarily one of power
through mighty works.'/31/ This view depends, of
course, on giving comparatively less weight to the
considerable amount of non-controversial teaching in
Mark.

What emerges from these contrasting emphases is

that teaching and action belong together.  It is
difficult to say to which Mark gave the greater
weight precisely because he did not in fact set them
over against one another, but regarded them as each
in its own right a part of the mission of Jesus, and
as contributing together to the fulfilment of his
messianic role. Either emphasis without the other
would have meant an imbalance in the inauguration of
the kingdom. A 'new teaching' was apparently to be
a part of the messianic age /32/, so that the
Messiah would be expected to accomplish his mission
in word as well as in deed, and this Mark shows
Jesus as doing. (The Marcan account of the first
feeding miracle may illustrate this conception,
where Jesus' response to the need of the crowd
consists both of teaching (6: 34) and of miraculous
feeding /33/.) The kingdom is established as much in
his teaching as in his works.

     This, then, is the christological basis for
Mark's special interest in Jesus as a teacher.  But
it has been observed that in the majority of cases
where Mark introduces the teaching of Jesus as an
aspect of his messianic ministry, it is the fact of
teaching only, not its content, which is mentioned.
Thus διδάσκειν is used without either direct object
or a ὅτι-clause to specify the content in 1: 21f; 2:
13; 4:1; 6: 2,6; 10: 1; 14: 49. Moreover, in 4:2 (ἐν
παραβολαῖς πολλά); 6: 34 (πολλά); 12: 14 (τὴν ὁδὸν
τοῦ Θεοῦ) the object is only very vaguely expressed.
K.H. Rengstorf regards this absolute use of the verb
as a striking characteristic of the gospels,
untypical of koinē Greek, which indicates a unique
total impression of Jesus as an authoritative
teacher /34/.  In fact the usage is not always
absolute.  For instance, 4:1f introduces a
considerable collection of actual sayings-material;
in 8: 31 and 9: 31 the content of the 'teaching' is
stated quite specifically as the passion
predictions; and in 11:17 and 12:35 again the verb
introduces specific sayings.  H. Riesenfeld therefore
argues for a deliberate distinction in this respect
between the generalised teaching activity of the
first part of the gospel and the teaching with
specified content in the (for him) contrasted second

part, in which <u>didachē</u> succeeds <u>kērugma</u> /35/.  But
the frequent absolute usage is nonetheless
remarkable.

      E. Schweizer concludes from Mark's emphasis on
Jesus' teaching activity without specifying the
content that it is in Jesus himself, not in what he
taught, that Mark located the authority.  It was in
the act of teaching with authority as well as in the
mighty works that he saw the irruption of the
kingdom of God into human affairs.  Mark's interest
was therefore in Jesus the teacher, not in his
teaching.  To emphasise the content of his teaching
was not only unnecessary, but a real hindrance to
true faith, substituting academic historical
reconstruction for existential commitment.  By
deliberately refraining from reporting the content
of the teaching, Mark was warning his readers off
from the peril of turning Jesus into an object for
historical research.  He is rather someone to be
encountered in his living authority /36/.

      This radical solution to the problem of why
Mark emphasises Jesus' teaching and yet records so
little of it has the attraction of proposing a
clearly defined theological orientation, and one
which is likely to have a wide appeal today in that
it makes Mark a boldly existentialist theologian
(though it leaves open Bultmann's question of why in
that case Mark recorded any sayings-material at all
/37/!)

      But does the text of the gospel in fact support
this radical rejection of the sayings-tradition?  Is
it in fact true that Mark was uninterested in (or
even hostile to) the preservation of the content of
Jesus' teaching?

      III   The Teaching Recorded by Mark

      In all that has been said so far we have
operated on the commonly stated assumption that the
Gospel of Mark contains little of the teaching of
Jesus.  It is time now to reexamine that assumption.

Such statements are normally made on the basis
of a comparison with Matthew and Luke.  In the light
of the Sermon on the Mount or the other collections
of Q and other teaching material in the longer
gospels, Mark appears short of teaching, and is
quickly labelled as a gospel of the deeds rather
than the words of Jesus.  But is this fair to Mark?
Ought not his intentions to be assessed rather on
the basis of what he has actually produced than on
the productions of others?  If we had no Matthew or
Luke, and could approach Mark with an open mind,
would we in fact conclude that he was uninterested
in the content of Jesus' teaching?  It is such an
approach that this section attempts.

1. The proportion of teaching material in the
   gospel as a whole.

To begin with a relatively straight-forward
statistic, 279 of the 661 verses of Mark contain
words of Jesus in direct speech.  Some 43 of these
'sayings' are merely questions incidental to a
narrative, or words of healing and the like, and
cannot fairly be classed as teaching /38/; but
against these must be set some 13 verses where the
content of Jesus' words is reported in indirect
speech /39/.  So some 40% of the verses of Mark
contain sayings of Jesus with some 'teaching'
content /40/, not to mention a further roughly 12%
which consists of the narrative contexts required to
introduce important sayings and dialogues (in
controversy and pronouncement-story pericopae)
where the teaching is the raison d'être of the
narrative.  When we take into consideration the
length of the passion narrative, in most of which
Jesus is conspicuously silent, and the long and
circumstantial accounts of some of the miracles, of
the death of John the Baptist, etc., this is a
considerably higher proportion than would be
suggested by the view that Mark was not interested
in giving the content of Jesus' teaching.  For
whatever motive, he has in fact devoted roughly half
his gospel to doing just that.

2. The place of the teaching material in the
   structure of the gospel.

We shall first consider how this teaching
material is distributed and integrated into the
narrative. A study along traditional form-critical
lines would not answer this question, for whether a
pericope is classed as parable, wisdom-saying, legal
teaching or whatever does not affect its role in the
structuring of the gospel as we have it. What I
have attempted instead is a rough division of the
sayings-material into three classes: A, sayings
incidental to the narrative, where the narrative is
apparently recorded for its own sake (this will
include not only questions and words of healing, but
more 'preachable' sayings such as 1: 17; 5: 36; 11:
17 which occur in the course of a narrative
important in its own right); B, sayings set in a
narrative context where the saying appears to be the
raison d'être for the narrative (this will cover the
pronouncement-stories and controversies of classical
form-criticism); and C, isolated sayings or more
extended sections of teaching which are accompanied
either by no narrative context or by a purely formal
introduction.

In category A, sayings incidental to the
narrative, I have placed 75 verses. Of these 43
have no appreciable teaching content, but consist of
questions (5: 9,30; 6: 38; 8: 5,23,27,29; 9: 16,21,
33; 10: 36,51; 12: 16) or other incidental
utterances whose relevance is limited to the
narrative context (2: 14; 4: 35; 5: 39; 6: 37; 7:
27; 8: 2f,26; 10: 49; 11: 2f; 12: 15; 14: 13-15), or
words of healing or command in the context of a
miracle or exorcism story (1: 25,41; 2: 5,11; 3: 3,
5; 4: 39; 5: 8,34,41; 7: 29,34; 9: 25; 10: 52; 11:
14). The remaining 32 occur in settings where the
narrative is apparently the author's primary
concern, or at least is of equal weight with the
sayings (i.e. narratives which are not told simply
to introduce the sayings), but nonetheless contain
material suitable for preaching or teaching
purposes; they include sayings about faith (4: 40;
5: 36; 6: 50; 9: 23,29) and discipleship (1: 17; 5:
19; 6: 10f,31; 10: 19; 12: 34), and sayings bearing
on the mission and person of Jesus (1: 38,44; 9: 19;
10: 18; 11: 17; 14: 62; 15: 2), particularly the

passion (14: 27f,30,32,34,36-38,41f,48f; 15: 34).
These last 32 verses, while formally incidental to
the narrative, contain in fact some quite crucial
christological and other teaching, which must not be
left out of account in our general assessment.

In category B, sayings set in a narrative
context where the saying appears to be the raison
d'être for the narrative, we include those sayings
which occur in controversial dialogues (2: 8-10,17,
19f,25f; 3: 4,23-27; 7: 6-13; 8: 12; 10: 3,5-9,11f;
11: 29f,33; 12: 17,24-27) and in pronouncement-
stories (3: 33-35; 6: 4; 8: 33; 9: 35,37,39-40; 10:
14f,21,23-25,27,38-40; 11: 22f; 12: 29-31,43f; 13:
2; 14: 6-9,18,20f,22,24f). These two formal groups
are of course often easily inter-changeable, but
this would not affect the resultant total of 76
verses in our second category. This is a minimum
figure, as I have not included sayings which are
joined onto the end of these pericopae but which
appear to be originally independent of them, such as
2: 21f,27f; 3: 28f; 7: 14ff; these have been
included in the third category.
In the third category, C, sayings with little
or no narrative context, we may distinguish from the
formal point of view particularly the six parables
of Mark (4: 3-8 with 13-20; 4: 26-29,30-32; 12: 1-
11; 13: 28f,34-37). The other major block of
teaching is of course the apocalyptic discourse of
chapter 13 (13: 5-37, of which verses 28f and 34-37
have already been included in the list of parables).
Other relatively extended passages of teaching are
7: 14f and 18-23; 8: 15 and 17-21; 8: 34-38; 9: 43-
49; 10: 42-45; 12: 35-37,38-40. All this adds up to
99 verses of clearly didactic material introduced
not primarily as part of the narrative but in
significant blocks of teaching as such. To these
may be added a further 29 verses which consist of
brief sayings, sometimes occurring with no
appreciable context, sometimes attached to a
pronouncement-story, controversial dialogue or other
narrative; many of them are introduced with the
Marcan redactional formula καὶ ἔλεγεν αὐτοῖς or a
similar clause (2: 27f; 4: 9,11f,21f,24f; 9: 1,12f,
31) /41/, or by a more elaborate introduction

(1: 15; 10: 29f,33f), but others follow on without
introduction from the material to which they are
attached (2: 21f; 3: 28f; 4: 23; 9: 41,42,50; 10:
31; 11: 24f). These brief sayings may also be
regarded therefore as units of teaching inserted
into the gospel as such and not because the narrative
in any way required them.

The foregoing somewhat untraditional
classification of sayings-material in 'Mark /42/ has
been made with a view to determining how it fits
into the plan of the gospel as a whole. It is thus
an entirely formal classification, without regard to
content (as is the case with much so-called form-
criticism). It is debatable in several points of
detail, particularly in distinguishing as isolated
units a few sayings which may have a less tenuous
connection with their context than I have suggested,
but I believe that as a whole it provides a clear
enough indication of the role of the sayings-
material in Mark's composition.

It indicates first that 128 verses of Mark
(virtually 20% of the whole gospel) contain teaching
material introduced into the work <u>as teaching
material</u>, neither required by nor, in most cases,
integrally related to the narrative sequence, but
fitted in throughout the work either in larger
blocks of sayings-material or as isolated
insertions with only a tenuous link with the
surrounding material (our category C). This group
of material alone is sufficient to disprove a
simplistic view of Mark as portraying Jesus as
mighty in deed and word but uninterested in the
content of what he taught.

We find a further 76 verses (11.5% of the
gospel) which contain the sayings of Jesus within
narrative situations which apparently exist only to
lead up to those sayings (our category B).
Statistically, therefore, not only these sayings but
their accompanying narrative (which is there only to
introduce them, not for its own sake) ought to be
included in our reckoning; this adds a further 84
verses, and results in a figure of 24% of the gospel

for the controversy and pronouncement-story material
whose presence in the gospel not only presents Jesus
as a controversialist and authoritative teacher but
spells out the content of his pronouncements on a
wide variety of issues.

Even in those utterances which are closely
integrated into the narrative without being
themselves the reason for its existence (our
category A) we found that 32 verses (5% of the whole
gospel) contain material suitable for didactic or
preaching purposes, including some of the most
profound teaching on the mission and passion of
Jesus. It occurs within the narrative of the events
in which that mission is carried out, and by its
presence there indicates the significance which
Jesus himself saw, and taught his disciples to see,
in those events.

These results surely refute the suggestion that
Mark was uninterested in telling his readers what
Jesus taught. Nor do they support the idea that the
teaching material only found its way into his gospel
almost by accident, by association with the
narratives which were supposedly his primary
interest. Without wishing in the least to deny that
Mark wanted his readers to see Jesus as the Messiah
mighty in deed and word, I would deny that this
entails that he would not want to set out the
content of his teaching. He has in fact done so,
not only by showing Jesus the teacher in action in
debate and authoritative pronouncement, but also by
incorporating considerable sections of his teaching
as such, scattered widely within the overall
narrative structure of his gospel.

Certainly there is no Marcan equivalent to the
formal collection of Jesus' teaching in the Sermon
on the Mount. The nearest approaches to this in
Mark are the collection of parables in chapter 4 and
the eschatological teaching in chapter 13. These
are quite deliberate 'teaching collections', the
latter being particularly impressive in this regard.
Elsewhere the plan of the gospel involves a heavier
concentration of teaching material in some areas

than in others, as was pointed out by C.F. Evans in
his demarcation of five main teaching sections
(excluding chapter 13), in 2: 1 - 3: 6 (debates); 4:
1-34 (parables); 7: 1-23 (defilement controversy);
9: 33 - 10: 31 (discipleship); and 11: 27 - 12: 44
(Jerusalem debates) /43/. But even within these
'teaching sections' narrative is constantly
interspersed with the teaching, and they exclude a
significant amount of teaching scattered elsewhere
/44/.

So Mark does not set out the teaching of Jesus
as formally as Matthew or Luke, nor in as
concentrated a form as the Gospel of Thomas or the
hypothetical Q. But the fact remains that virtually
50% of his gospel is devoted to presenting Jesus'
teaching, and I believe that if we did not have
these other documents for comparison (and we may
assume that Mark himself did not!) /45/ we would not
have been conscious of any disparity between Mark's
emphasis on Jesus as a teacher and the not
inconsiderable amount of actual teaching he
includes. Judged on his own terms, Mark has
achieved an entirely appropriate balance between
narrative and teaching.

The dilemma from which we started is therefore
a false one: Mark not only emphasises Jesus'
teaching activity, but he also deliberately includes
a significant selection of the teaching of Jesus.

### 3. The Subject-Matter of the teaching material.
Why is all this material included? What does
the character of the teaching tell us about Mark's
purpose in writing, or about the readership he had
in mind?

In the previous section I attempted a
classification of the Marcan sayings-material in
terms of its formal place in the structure of the
gospel. A similar rough and ready classification in
terms of the subject-matter follows (omitting of
course those sayings in category A which were
regarded as having no teaching content). There are
necessarily areas of overlap between the classes,

as many sayings relate to more than one subject, but
such a classification should serve to indicate the
main areas of Mark's interest in Jesus' teaching.

   (i) Legal matters.
   These are the point of several of the
controversial dialogues, resulting in rulings on the
specific issues of the sabbath (2: 25f,27f; 3: 4),
fasting (2: 19f), defilement (7: 14f,18-23) and
divorce (10: 3-12), a more general pronouncement on
the role of tradition in legal matters (7: 6-13),
and a declaration of the greatest commandments of
the law (12: 29-31). There is also a potential
legal precedent in the command to the cleansed leper
(1: 44). All this is material of practical
relevance to a Christian community in working out
its position on legal issues vis-a-vis scribal
tradition.

   (ii) Ethical issues.
   The legal matters just listed are, of course,
mostly concerned with ethical issues, but there are
also sayings, not specifically concerned with the
interpretation of the law, but relevant to the
ethical conduct of the Christian community, such
as the teaching on wealth and giving (10: 23-27;
12: 43f), civil obedience (12: 17) and forgiveness
(11: 25). The controversy in the temple implicitly
commends a right attitude to worship (11: 17), and
blasphemy is dealt with in 3: 28f. The ethical role
of the decalogue is reaffirmed in 10: 19 (and cf.
12: 29-31). All these were suitable to serve both
as guidance for the ethics of the individual and for
the discipline of the community, and the same is
true of a lot of the teaching on discipleship which
we consider next.

   (iii) Discipleship.
   Several sayings focus on the nature and
definition of discipleship (1: 17; 3: 33-35; 9: 39f;
10: 14f; 12: 34). It is a position of privileged
revelation (4: 11f), consisting of a special
relationship to Jesus (9: 37,41) and bringing great
rewards (10: 29f). But emphasis is laid on the
costly commitment involved (8: 34-38; 9: 43-49;

10: 21 and 23-27; 10: 38-40; 13: 9-13), a cost which
derives in part from the disciple's responsibility
to engage in a mission to other men with the message
of Jesus (1: 17; 4: 21f; 5: 19; 6: 7-11).  It is a
life of service, demanding constant alertness (13:
34-37; cf. 4: 9,23,24f; this is also at least one
application of the parable of the sower and its
interpretation) and a readiness to break with old
patterns (2: 21f).  It requires a radical reversal
of the world's standards in the relationships within
the disciple community (9: 35,37,42,50; 10: 31,42-
45; 11: 25), but its essence lies in the
relationship of the disciple with Jesus himself (6:
31; cf. 3: 14), a relationship exemplified in the
frequent calls to faith in connection with the
healing and miracle narratives (4: 40; 5: 36; 6: 50;
9: 23,29; 11: 22-24; perhaps the enigmatic passage
8: 15,17-21 should also be included here).  We
therefore find some 35% of the teaching material in
Mark devoted fairly directly to the theory and
practice of discipleship, and of course much of the
other teaching also has implications for this
subject.  This makes discipleship, statistically at
least, a very prominent theme in Mark's
presentation of the teaching of Jesus.

   (iv) Christology.
     While Mark's christology can be discerned in
his account of Jesus' deeds, and in his editorial
material, he has also provided a firm basis for
christology in his selection of Jesus' sayings.
Thus Jesus' preaching is introduced as focused on
the arrival of the kingdom of God (1: 15), and this
theme is explored in 4: 26-29,30-32; 9: 1; 14: 25.
(Further aspects of the kingdom, more concerned with
participation in it than with its arrival, are found
in 4: 11f; 10: 14f,23-25; 9: 47; 12: 34.)  Jesus'
mission is to preach the kingdom's arrival (1: 15,
38) and so to call men to repentance (2: 17) and to
offer them forgiveness (2: 8-10); and this preaching
is to be continued in a worldwide preaching of the
gospel (13: 10; 14: 9).  This ministry constitutes
an assault on the power of Satan (3: 23-27), and is
opposed and misunderstood (6: 4; 8: 2,33; 9: 19),
but it is carried out with the authority of God

himself (11: 29-33; 12: 1-11). Jesus' status as
Messiah is dealt with obliquely in 12: 35-37 and 15:
2, but explicitly in 14: 61f. But it is of course
in the term Son of Man that the christological
content of the sayings of Jesus is focused,
presenting both his earthly authority (2: 10,28) and
his future vindication and glory (8: 38; 13: 26; 14:
62). As Son of Man his mission is one of suffering,
death and resurrection, a message made explicit not
only in the suffering Son of Man sayings (8: 31; 9:
9,12f,31; 10: 33f,45; 14: 21,41) but also in a
variety of other sayings looking forward in
different ways to the passion (2: 19f; 10: 38-40;
12: 1-11; 14: 8, and all the subsequent sayings in
the course of the passion narrative). In all some
32% of the sayings in Mark are concerned with
elucidating the mission and passion of Jesus.

(v) <u>The Future</u>.
Mark 13 is, of course, entirely devoted to
Jesus' teaching about the future - not in the sense
of a detached forecast, but of the continuation of
the inbreaking of the kingdom of God which he had
set in motion. It is perhaps artificial to separate
this from the teaching on the mission of Jesus just
considered, for it is only a division between two
stages of the same divine act. The future aspect of
the coming of the kingdom is barely indicated
elsewhere (8: 38; 9: 1; 14: 62), but the prominent
position of chapter 13 ensures the recognition of
this as an important concern of the author.

This rough classification of the sayings was
not set out according to a predetermined scheme of
systematic or practical theology, but on the basis
of the content of the sayings themselves. It
suggests that Mark and those for whom he wrote were
interested in the teaching of Jesus for guidance on
ethical questions, and particularly for determining
the Christian stance in relation to Jewish legal
requirements; this was to be expected in a community
emerging into self-conscious communal existence.
But more prominent was their concern with the inner
dynamics of Christian discipleship, its nature,
demands and privileges, which must define the

Christian's position in relation to his fellow-
Christians and his Lord. And fundamental to this
concern was the desire to understand the nature and
significance of Jesus' mission, particularly its
culmination in suffering and death, and the sequel
both in the church's present experience and in the
expected culmination.

In all this there are no surprises, nor
anything which has not been frequently observed
already. But it suggests two observations relevant
to our present theme of Mark's attitude to the
teaching of Jesus.

(a) The teaching recorded is not only extensive
(sections 1 and 2 above), but wide-ranging in its
content. The view that Mark was interested in the
christological theme of Jesus as teacher but not in
what he taught would lead us to expect that such
teaching as he did record would focus on
christological themes. But in fact christological
themes, even including the future aspect, account
only for some 43% of the teaching recorded. The
remainder deals with more practical issues of
Christian life, serving not to increase
understanding of the mission and person of Jesus,
but to guide his followers in the existential
concerns of discipleship. It is recorded therefore
not to strengthen the image of Jesus as the Messiah
in deed and word, but for its own value as
authoritative guidance for the church. The content
of Jesus' teaching was very much the concern of the
author of this gospel. The church needed it.

(b) The content of practically all the
recorded teaching is self-evidently relevant to the
concerns of a Christian community in the post-Easter
period, either for its theological understanding of
the mission of Jesus or for the practical direction
of the life of the church. This is true of all the
subject categories listed above, and virtually all
the sayings-material fits suitably into one of those
categories. The only pericopae which have failed to
find a natural place within them are 12: 18-27, the
debate about resurrection, which is the nearest
thing in Mark to discussion of a theological point
for its own sake (though this too might well be

useful as material for Christian apologetics), and
12: 38-40, a detached denunciation of the scribes,
which would have an obvious polemical value in the
sort of situation which required recourse to the
accounts of Jesus' legal controversies. The record
of Jesus' teaching was not made therefore from mere
antiquarian interest, but because of its relevance
to the Christian community at the time of the
writing of the gospel.

This last point is again a very obvious one,
and it is exactly what would be expected: few have
been able to regard Mark as a disinterested compiler
of records of Jesus out of mere academic interest.
It must be modified by the observation, which we
shall consider in the next section, that Mark
nonetheless displays a tendency to preserve the
sayings in forms different from those which would
have been natural in his community /46/. But these
two observations are not in conflict. The reason
for the selection of the tradition recorded is its
relevance for the teaching, preaching and practice
of the Marcan community, but it is the tradition
which is recorded, even where its details may prove
irrelevant or even embarrassing to the Christian of
Mark's day.

Our study of the teaching material recorded by
Mark therefore leads to the conclusion that Mark not
only wished to portray Jesus as a teacher for
christological reasons, but that he deliberately
worked into his gospel a significant amount of the
content of Jesus' teaching, not merely to illustrate
his teaching activity but for the sake of the
teaching in its own right. Just because Jesus was
for Mark the teacher who taught with a unique
authority, he presented in considerable detail the
content of what he taught, selected with a view to
its teaching value in Mark's own situation.

IV   Mark's Handling of the Tradition

I have talked of Mark's 'selection' of teaching
material. It has in fact been suggested that the
selective process had already occurred in the church

before Mark's time, leaving him only a very limited
amount of traditional sayings available /47/. It is
certainly hard to explain why, if Mark had access to
the Q material, he did not include so many sayings
which would admirably fill out the particular themes
emphasised in his own sayings-material. In the
light of our conclusion that Mark was concerned with
preserving the content of Jesus' teaching, we can
hardly claim that he omitted so much suitable
teaching because it fell outside his purpose in
writing /48/. If the above account is correct, we
must assume that a great deal of the sayings-
material available to Matthew and Luke was not
available to Mark /49/.

But this does not entail that he had no
material available besides what he included in his
gospel. Some features in the gospel in fact
indicate that he was aware of other teaching of
Jesus: the Marcan phrase ἐν τῇ διδαχῇ αὐτοῦ (4: 2;
12: 38) suggests that the sayings so introduced are
consciously excerpted from a larger corpus, and the
reference to Jesus' teaching 'many things' in
parables (4: 2) and using 'many such parables' (4:
33f) would come strangely from an author who knew
only the six parables /50/ recorded in Mark. Of
course, if the author of the gospel was in fact John
Mark, and an associate of Peter, he would have
access to a large amount of Jesus' teaching not only
from Peter and from the wider church circles in
which he had moved (with Barnabas and Paul) but also
perhaps from his own early memories of Jesus
teaching in Jerusalem. But even apart from this
identification, it would be surprising if Mark's
community, with the attitude to Jesus' teaching as a
medium of instruction in the church which we have
noted in this gospel, had succeeded in preserving no
more of his sayings than we in fact find in Mark.

We may therefore fairly assume that Mark has
made a deliberate selection among the available
teaching of Jesus /51/. We have seen an indication
in the last section of the principles on which he
made his selection. It was intended to be relevant
to the needs of his church for instruction in both

the theory and the practice of Christian
discipleship.  There is little sign that Mark was
interested in preserving teaching of Jesus on
subjects remote from contemporary Christian concerns
(though it is admittedly not easy to imagine many
subjects on which Jesus might have taught which
would not also interest his followers).

From this observation it is a small step to the
suggestion that what mattered to Mark was the
relevance of the teaching rather than its origin;
that is, that relevant sayings could as easily be
created as preserved.  A small step, but an
illegitimate one.  For a study of the sayings in
Mark reveals that while each pericope can be
accounted for in terms of its contemporary
relevance, as the last section showed, the form in
which the teaching is presented and the details
included within the pericope are often contrary to
what one would expect in teaching which <u>originated</u>
in the Marcan situation.

An extreme example of this phenomenon would be
the famous 'foundation-pillars' listed by P.
Schmiedel /52/, passages so embarrassing or
distasteful to early Christianity that no-one would
have introduced them into the sayings-tradition.
They include three sayings of Jesus found in Mark
which give rise to christological problems unlikely
to be created gratuitously:  Mark 10: 18 ('Why do
you call me good?'); 13: 32 ('No-one knows, not even
the Son'); 15: 34 ('Why hast thou forsaken me?').
Nor are Mark and his community likely to have found
very acceptable the apparently anti-Gentile thrust
of 7: 27; and C.F.D. Moule has suggested that the
uncompromising displacement of other OT law in
favour of the Great Commandment (12: 28-31) was 'an
almost unendurably radical pronouncement.' /53/

Other details are not so much embarrassing as
irrelevant to the concerns of the mid-century church.
E. Best has pointed out how a number of pericopae
preserved in Mark contain individual sayings which
in themselves are irrelevant to the context in which
he has placed them, but which were apparently

retained as part of an existing catena (9: 49f; 11:
22-25; 4: 24) /54/.  The Corban question would not
have been the natural illustration to choose in a
church for which it had, as far as we know, no
existential application (7: 11f), and even the
sabbath question, on which Jesus' conflict with
scribal legalism is centred, does not seem to have
been a live issue in early Christianity /55/.  Other
features of the teaching of Jesus as presented in
Mark are widely agreed not to have been typical of
post-Easter formulation, such as the use of 'Son of
Man', the focus of the proclamation on the kingdom
rather than on the person of Jesus, the use of the
parable form, of ἀμὴν λέγω ὑμῖν, etc.  Best has
further pointed out that the formulation of the
passion predictions in 8: 31; 9: 31; 10: 33f is not
in terms of the 'cross' and the 'third day', as one
would expect ex eventu, but of 'being killed' and
rising 'after three days' /56/.  No doubt the list
could be extended, but the point is that there is
considerable evidence of earlier tradition 'forcing
its way through a generation which had itself
forgotten its relevance and perspective'/57/.

On the basis of such evidence it seems
justifiable to assert that, while Mark selected and
presented the teaching of Jesus with a view to its
relevance to the church, in his actual handling of
the tradition he shows a respect for the form of the
teaching of Jesus as such which leads him to
perserve that form even where it is apparently
irrelevant or embarrassing /58/.

It is in this sense that R. Pesch characterises
Mark as follows:  'Der Redaktor Markus ist kein
Inventor, sondern Bearbeiter von Tradition, er
verhält sich kaum literarisch produktiv, sondern
"unliterarisch" konservativ.' /59/  Best likewise
concludes that 'faced with a piece of tradition Mark
altered it internally as little as possible.'  His
creativity is seen not in inventing or even in
significantly altering the material he has received,
but 'in the way in which he has placed the tradition
in his total context supplying audience, place, time
and sequence and in the summaries he has

written. . . . Perhaps we should think not of an
author but of an artist creating a collage.' /60/

    This concern to preserve the tradition /61/ is
consistent with the christological interest of Mark
in Jesus as the authoritative teacher. His interest
is not just in 'teaching', but in the teaching of
Jesus. It is, of course, for its relevance to his
own community, not just from antiquarian interest,
that he preserves it; there is no reason to imagine
that he put in all the teaching of Jesus that he
knew, irrespective of its usefulness to his intended
readers. But in what he did record he seems to have
been careful to set down the tradition substantially
as he received it, even where its frame of reference
or its incidental details related to a situation
which no longer obtained.

    At the beginning of this paper I protested
against the assumption that any one distinguishable
purpose in the writing of the gospel need exclude
other purposes, even if they do not fit neatly
together. This study has filled out that protest
by indicating that Mark was at one and the same time
concerned both to portray Jesus as the authoritative
teacher, the Messiah in word as well as deed, and to
record a substantial selection of his actual
teaching for the guidance of his readers in the
contemporary church situation; and further that he
was interested both in the contemporary relevance
and in the authentic form of what he set down as the
teaching of Jesus. Nor are these concerns so
incompatible as they are sometimes supposed to be.
Indeed one might wonder what was the cash value of a
respect for Jesus as a teacher if it did not entail
a desire both to preserve his teaching and to see it
applied to the church situation.

                    V  Conclusion

    This paper does not claim to have isolated 'the
purpose of Mark'. I hope rather that it has
indicated the inappropriateness of looking for one
controlling theme or purpose in a book which
reflects the varied interests of its author, writing

in and for a Christian community which itself had
many different needs and concerns.

So I do not claim that Mark's gospel is only,
or even chiefly, a presentation of Jesus as the
Teacher. But neither should we allow that any other
prominent theme of the gospel, such as the portrayal
of Jesus as the protagonist in a cosmic struggle, or
as the secret and suffering Messiah, or as the
founder of the eschatological community, can be used
to exclude this aspect from the author's intention.
All of these facets of Jesus' ministry, and more,
are reflected in the gospel, and all were no doubt
important to its author. The same book could be
used to combat theios aner christology, proto-
gnosticism, ultra-Paulinism, or some other
deviation. But Mark was concerned positively to
tell about Jesus, and the very complexity of the
historical mission of Jesus as well as the
variegated character of the subsequent church
situation for which he was writing would necessarily
result in a book of many nuances. Among these,
Jesus the Teacher was a not unimportant theme.

Mark stressed Jesus' teaching activity not only
as a bare fact about how he spent his time and the
image he had among his contemporaries, but as a part
of his messianic role, alongside and closely
connected with his mighty works of healing and
miracle. But he was not only interested in teaching
as an activity. His gospel is not only a record of
what Jesus did (including teaching with messianic
authority) but also of what he taught, and this
teaching is included not only to illustrate Jesus'
teaching role, but for its own sake as guidance for
the Christian community. If Mark's gospel is judged
in its own right, instead of being weighed against
Matthew and Luke, the balance between the
presentation of Jesus' activity and of the content
of his teaching is seen to be well maintained, with
nearly half the gospel devoted to presenting the
teaching.

The teaching included is selected with a view
to its applicability to the needs and interests of

the Christian community in Mark's day.  It is
teaching 'with authority', and it is part of Mark's
intention to see that authority exercised in
guiding his contemporaries in their theology and
practice as Christian disciples.  But because it is
with authority, Mark has taken care to present it in
the form in which it has come to him.  He presents
it as the teaching of Jesus, with a demonstrable
respect which excludes the possibility that he was
himself responsible for its creation /62/.  As far
as the author of the second gospel is concerned, we
may be confident that the tradition of the sayings
of Jesus has been preserved with care.  It is only
what we would expect from an author who laid such
stress on the character of Jesus as the
authoritative Teacher.

## Notes

1. Cf. the sane remarks of E. Best, NTS 23 (1976/7)
   378 on the alleged polemical purpose of Mark.
2. The History of the Synoptic Tradition 347,
   following Dibelius, From Tradition to Gospel,
   e.g. 260.
3. Sanh. 43a and A.Z. 17a refer to his 'disciples'
   as to those of a rabbi.  He is described as a
   teacher in Jos. Ant. 18.63, if we may assume
   this description to be part of the presumed
   original core of the Testimonium Flavianum.  See
   further C.H. Dodd, 'Jesus as Teacher and
   Prophet' in G.K.A. Bell and A. Deissmann (ed.),
   Mysterium Christi (London: Longmans, Green &
   Co., 1930) 53-66; T.W. Manson, BJRL 27 (1942/3)
   326-330; W.D. Davies, The Setting of the Sermon
   on the Mount (Cambridge: University Press, 1963)
   418f.
4. For a full account of Mark's interest in Jesus
   as a teacher see R.P. Meye, Jesus and the Twelve
   (Grand Rapids: Eerdmans, 1968), esp. 30-87.
5. In addition to this word-group, cf. the Marcan
   phrase ἐλάλει ( αὐτοῖς) τὸν λόγον (2: 2; 4: 33;
   8: 32).  See E. Best, The Temptation and the
   Passion: the Markan Soteriology (SNTS Monograph
   2. Cambridge: University Press, 1965) 70f, and
   on the importance of the words of Jesus in Mark

see R.P. Meye, 'Messianic Secret and Messianic
Didache in Mark's Gospel' in F. Christ (ed.),
Oikonomia. Heilsgeschichte als Thema der
Theologie (für O. Cullmann) (Hamburg: Herbert
Reich, 1967) 66f. For other 'teaching'
terminology in Mark see 4: 11; 7: 14; 8: 34; 10:
32; 12: 1; 13: 5; see further R.P. Meye, Jesus
and the Twelve (note 4) 48-51.

6.  1: 21f; 2: 13; 4: 1f; 6: 2,34; 10: 1; 11: 18;
    12: 35,38. See further E. Best, Temptation
    (note 5) 71f.

7.  ὡς εἰώθει, 10: 1; cf. ἐδίδασκεν πολλά, 4: 2;
    περιῆγεν διδάσκων, 6: 6.

8.  Of Mark's 15 uses of διδάσκειν of the teaching
    of Jesus, 6 are in the imperfect, 4 in the
    present participle (3 of them with an imperfect
    verb to form a periphrastic imperfect), 4 in the
    form ἤρξατο διδάσκειν, and one (in direct
    speech) in the present indicative.

9.  For the titular character of ὁ διδάσκαλος  in
    Mark see below p. 109.

10. See below pp. 106-109.

11. E. Schweizer, 'Anmerkungen zur Theologie des
    Markus' in Neotestamentica et Patristica.
    Freundesgabe Oscar Cullmann (Supplements to
    Novum Testamentum 6. Leiden: E.J. Brill, 1962)
    37.

12. So e.g. E. Best, Temptation (note 5) 72,
    referring to the parallel between 6: 12 and 6:
    30, in which, however, the preaching is that of
    the disciples, not of Jesus.

13. Matthew links κηρύσσειν with διδάσκειν in his
    summaries of Jesus' activity in 4: 23, 9: 35;
    11: 1.

14. E. Trocmé, The Formation of the Gospel according
    to Mark (1963. ET London: SPCK, 1975) 191f,
    distinguishes between the initial 'trumpet
    blast' of the missionary preaching and the
    διδαχή which then follows. Cf. H. Riesenfeld,
    The Gospel Tradition (Oxford: Blackwell, 1970)
    60-64, though it is questionable whether there
    is such a deliberate temporal separation between
    the two activities in Mark as his treatment
    suggests. Trocmé also goes too far in
    suggesting that the occurrence of διδαχή

terminology in 1: 21f,27, before the last
reference to Jesus' preaching activity,
indicates a premature, and therefore
unsatisfactory, attempt to teach without the
initial preaching to 'destroy the old
framework'.

15. On the relation of κηρύσσειν to διδάσκειν in
Mark see further R.P. Meye, Jesus and the Twelve
(note 4) 52-60.

16. See e.g. R.P. Meye (the works noted in notes 4
and 5); S. Freyne, The Twelve: Disciples and
Apostles. A Study in the Theology of the First
Three Gospels (London: Sheed and Ward, 1968)
esp. 106-150; K.-G. Reploh, Markus - Lehrer der
Gemeinde. Eine redaktionsgeschichtliche Studie
zu den Jüngerperikopen des Markus-Evangeliums
(Stuttgart: Katholisches Bibelwerk, 1969); K.
Kertelge, 'Die Funktion der "Zwölf" im Markus-
evangelium', Trierer Theologische Zeitschrift
78 (1969) 193-206; E. Best, 'Discipleship in
Mark: Mark 8.22 - 10.52', SJT 23 (1970) 323-337;
idem, 'The Role of the Disciples in Mark', NTS
23 (1976/7) 377-401; idem, 'Mark's Use of the
Twelve', ZNW 69 (1978) 11-35; G. Schmahl, Die
Zwölf im Markusevangelium: Eine redaktions-
geschichtliche Untersuchung (Trierer
Theologische Studien 30. Trier: Paulinus-Verlag,
1974); K. Stock, Boten aus dem Mit-Ihm-Sein. Das
Verhältnis zwischen Jesus und den Zwölf nach
Markus (Analecta Biblica 70. Rome: Biblical
Institute Press, 1975); E. Trocmé, Formation
(note 14) esp. 159-162.

17. This aspect of discipleship is clearly brought
out by E. Best in SJT 23 (1970) 323-337. Cf.
also the remarks of K.H. Rengstorf in TDNT IV
406f on the paucity of uses of μανθάνειν in the
gospels, which leads him to conclude 'that
ἀκολουθεῖν rather than μανθάνειν is the true
mark of the μαθητής.'

18. We cannot here go into the vexed question of the
relation of the Twelve to the μαθηταί.
According to R.P. Meye (esp. 'Messianic Secret'
(note 5) 63-65) and S. Freyne, The Twelve (note
16) 107-119 they are identical, while for E.
Best (esp. NTS 23, 380f) and K. Stock, Boten

(note 16) 199-203 they are clearly
distinguished. In view of this diversity of
opinion it is improbable that Mark maintained
either a clear distinction or a consistent
identification; rather he presented the Twelve
as an inner circle among the disciples, so that
the terms are to some extent interchangeable,
and his description of the Twelve may fairly be
taken as a part of his total presentation of
discipleship.

19. See R.P. Meye, 'Messianic Secret' (note 5) 62-68
    for a suggestive presentation of this theme (and
    more fully his Jesus and the Twelve).
20. See E. Best, Temptation (note 5) 72f for the
    observation that in several places in Mark the
    failure of the disciples to understand 'is
    balanced by a corresponding attempt by Jesus to
    enlighten the disciples.' Cf. ibid 80f.
21. See the valuable discussion of this pericope and
    its place in Mark's redactional scheme by R.H.
    Stein, 'The "Redaktionsgeschichtlich"
    Investigation of a Markan Seam (Mc 1 21f.)', ZNW
    61 (1970) 70-94.
22. Temptation (note 5) 72.
23. The comparative material in this section is
    expressed in terms of Marcan priority, but the
    overall impression of Mark's special interests
    would not be significantly different on another
    synoptic theory.
24. The following Marcan uses are not reproduced in
    either Matthew or Luke:   2: 13; 4: 1,2; 6: 34;
    8: 31; 9: 31; 10: 1; 11: 17; 12: 35.
25. It should be noted, however, that Matthew allows
    Jesus himself to talk about the relationship of
    his disciples with their διδάσκαλος or ῥαββί
    (10: 24f; 23: 8).
26. See further on ὁ διδάσκαλος as a title of Jesus
    K.H. Rengstorf, TDNT II 155-157.
27. These last two uses are retained by Luke, not by
    Matthew.
28. So R.H. Stein, ZNW 61, 90 f; cf. E. Schweizer,
    'Anmerkungen' (note 11) 38f.
29. E. Best, Temptation (note 5) 110; R.P. Meye,
    Jesus and the Twelve (note 4) 214.  Cf. above on
    1: 27.

30. The Problem of History in Mark (Studies in
    Biblical Theology 21. London: SCM, 1957) 43-46.
31. C.F. Evans, The Beginning of the Gospel. . . .
    Four Lectures on St. Mark's Gospel (London:
    SPCK, 1968) 55.
32. So R.H. Stein, ZNW 61, 91, with references in
    n. 71. The long discussion by W.D. Davies,
    Setting (note 3) 109ff, of the place of Torah in
    Jewish messianic expectation concludes with a
    less certain verdict, but indicates that
    expectation of a New Torah was present in some
    Jewish circles, and is likely to have been more
    widely current than the extant literature
    indicates (ibid 184-187).
33. For the connection see E. Best, Temptation (note
    5) 77f.
34. TDNT II 140f; cf. E. Schweizer, 'Anmerkungen'
    (note 11) 38.   E. Best, Temptation (note 5) 80f
    suggests that in these absolute uses there is
    generally in the context an indication of the
    puzzling or obscure nature of Jesus' teaching
    for 'those outside'.
35. H. Riesenfeld, Tradition (note 14) 51-74, esp.
    62.
36. So E. Schweizer, NTS 10 (1963/4) 422f; cf. idem
    'Anmerkungen' (note 11) 44f.
37. See above note 2.
38. For references see below p. 114.
39. 3: 12,14f; 5: 43; 6: 7-9; 7: 36; 8: 30,31; 9: 9;
    14: 35,39.
40. The judgment as to which utterances have
    'teaching' content is, of course, subjective.
    I have attempted to exclude those which do not
    seem to offer material for purpose of preaching
    or catechesis.  But the exact classification is
    not essential to the validity of the overall
    statistic.
41. On this introductory clause see further H.C.
    Kee, Community of the New Age. Studies in Mark's
    Gospel (London: SCM Press, 1977) 51f.  It is
    used also to introduce some of the sayings
    treated in earlier sections (3: 23; 4: 2; 6: 4,
    10; 7: 14; 11: 17), or occasionally within a
    pericope (7: 9; 8: 21).
42. A classification in some ways similar was set

out by Morton Smith in J. Reumann, ed.,
<u>Understanding the Sacred Text, Essays in honor
of Morton S. Enslin</u> (Valley Forge: Judson
Press, 1972) 155-164, but with interestingly
different observations and conclusions.

43. C.F. Evans, <u>Beginning</u> (note 31), followed by
R.P. Martin, <u>Mark, Evangelist and Theologian</u>
(Exeter: Paternoster, 1972) 113.

44. 26 verses in our category C, 28 in category B
(plus their accompanying narrative), and 29
with teaching content in category A.

45. Again Marcan priority is assumed. See below n.
48 for further comments.

46. See below pp. 125-126.

47. So E. Best, <u>Temptation</u> (note 5) 103, though he
does not press this suggestion to the point of
denying any selection by Mark.

48. Some such explanation seems required by the
Griesbach and similar hypotheses, whereby Mark
had the whole of Q, M and perhaps L material in
front of him, and deliberately chose to omit it.
See e.g. W.R. Farmer, <u>NTS</u> 23 (1976/7) 283-286.
If the findings of this paper are correct, that
the recording of Jesus' teaching <u>was</u> a real
interest of Mark, his omission of so much
suitable material from sources supposedly in
his hands becomes a serious problem for the
Griesbach hypothesis.

49. For some other views on Mark's relation to Q
see R.H. Stein, <u>ZNW</u> 61, 93.

50. Including the two eschatological 'parables' in
13: 28f, 34ff which are not presented in the
same formal way as the other parables in Mark.

51. Cf. Dibelius, <u>From Tradition to Gospel</u> 236f,
even though Dibelius' further conclusion that
'Mark did not to any large extent include the
words of Jesus' does not follow from his
evidence that Mark's record is selective. Cf.
also E. Trocmé, <u>Formation</u> (note 14) 38f, 44f.

52. <u>Encyclopaedia Biblica</u> (London: 1899-1903) vol 2,
s.v. 'Gospels', §§ 139-140.

53. C.F.D. Moule, <u>The Phenomenon of the New
Testament. An Inquiry into the implications of
certain features of the New Testament</u> (Studies
in Biblical Theology, second series 1. London:

SCM Press, 1967) 62f.

54. 'Mark's Preservation of the Tradition' in
L'Evangile selon Marc. Tradition et Rédaction
(Bibliotheca Ephemeridarum Theologicarum
Lovaniensium 34. Gembloux: Duculot, 1974) 30-32.

55. See F.F. Bruce, Tradition Old and New (Exeter:
Paternoster, 1970) 48f.

56. E. Best, 'Preservation' (note 54) 26f.

57. C.F.D. Moule, Phenomenon (note 53) 67. H.
Riesenfeld, Tradition (note 14) 69-74 argues for
a similar phenomenon with regard to the
narrative framework of the gospel, some aspects
of which he believes to be incompatible with
Mark's intended scheme, but preserved out of
respect for the tradition.

58. This subject is usefully explored in C.F.D.
Moule, Phenomenon (note 53) 56-76 and in E.
Best, 'Preservation' (note 54) 21-34. Cf. also
E.F. Harrison in C.F.H. Henry (ed.), Jesus of
Nazareth: Savior and Lord (Grand Rapids:
Eerdmans, 1966) 165-173; F.F. Bruce, Tradition
(note 55) 48-54.

59. R. Pesch, Das Markusevangelium (Herders
Theologischer Kommentar zum Neuen Testament 2.
Freiburg: Herder, 1976) I, 22.

60. E. Best, 'Preservation' (note 54), 33.

61. See W.D. Davies, Setting (note 3) 415-418 for
the general probability of such a concern in the
post-Easter church. It can claim greater
historical verisimilitude than the attempt by
E. Schweizer, NTS 10, 422f, to present Mark as
engaged in an existentialist-style polemic
against the 'historical Jesus' and the 'mere
repetition of his sayings', or that of E.
Trocmé, Formation (note 14) esp. p. 85 to
suggest that Mark was 'seeking to shake' the
'supreme authority' of the tradition, to 'break
the hold of "the sayings of Jesus"'.

62. This paper has dealt only with the handling of
the tradition by Mark himself, and its argument
does not per se establish the same preservative
concern for the earlier stages of the tradition
(or, of course, for the other gospels). It is
not therefore a demonstration of the dominical
origin of the sayings recorded by Mark, but only

of the way he himself treated what had come to
him, by whatever means, as 'the teaching of
Jesus'. (Cf. the concluding remarks of E.
Best's article 'Mark's Preservation of the
Tradition' (note 54) 34.) Whether a similar
attitude can be postulated for the earlier
stages of the tradition must be considered on
other grounds, and it will necessarily be a
more difficult subject to control, in the
absence of direct evidence. Perhaps we may at
least dare to suggest, on the principle of
elucidating the unknown from the known, that a
preservative concern similar to that of Mark
may fairly be assumed where there is no
evidence to the contrary.

# The Authenticity of the Ransom Logion (Mark 10:45b)

Sydney H. T. Page,
North American Baptist College,
11525 23 Avenue,
Edmonton, AB., Canada   T6J 4T3.

In his magisterial commentary on the Gospel of Mark, Vincent Taylor described the saying, 'For the Son of man also came not to be served but to serve, and to give his life as a ransom for many' (Mark 10:45), as 'one of the most important in the Gospels'/1/. The saying is so important because it is an especially clear example of a statement, purporting to come from Jesus, which attributes a soteriological significance to His death. As such it must be taken into account in any attempt to reconstruct the self-understanding of Jesus, or to trace the development of the Christological thought of the early church.

Whether this saying faithfully represents the thinking of the historical Jesus is a question of great consequence for the student of Christian origins, but by no means has it received a unanimous answer. Indeed, more than three decades ago William Manson wrote: 'The authenticity of few words in the Synoptic tradition has been more hotly contested than that of this word about Jesus giving his life as a 'ransom''/2/. Nor has the debate subsided since those words were penned /3/. The issue remains a live one, and certainly is deserving of a fresh appraisal.

Prior to discussing the genuineness of any specific saying in the Gospel tradition, one must face the broader question of the fidelity with which the teaching of Jesus was transmitted in the period before the Gospels were written. Is the nature of the tradition such that, before accepting a saying as genuinely dominical, 'we must be able to show that the saying comes neither from the Church nor from ancient Judaism'/4/? Or are we justified in presuming, unless there is compelling evidence to the contrary, that the substance of what is found on the lips of Jesus in the Gospels was actually spoken by Him /5/? In other words, is the burden of proof upon the claim to authenticity or inauthenticity? Though this issue is

obviously a critical one, it would be impossible to do it
justice in a paper such as this. We can do little more than
state the position which is adopted here, and make brief
reference in the notes to some of the literature in which these
matters are handled at greater length.

In contemporary Biblical study it is often taken for
granted that a sceptical approach to the sayings material in
the Gospels is required. The need for such scepticism has been
called into question by a number of writers however /6/. To be
sure, it is clear that the logia tradition underwent modification during the oral period of its transmission; but, evidence
has not yet been produced to demonstrate that there was a
wholesale creation of 'sayings of Jesus' at that time. In fact
the very reverse is the case. There is good reason to believe
that the early Christians preserved the teachings of Jesus with
great care /7/. This being the case it is methodologically
sound to assume that the content of Jesus' teaching is
faithfully reproduced by the evangelists unless there is
definite reason to think otherwise. Applying this to the
problem at hand, we may conclude that the onus is upon those
who doubt the authenticity of Mark 10:45b to prove that it could
not have come from Jesus. Our task is to evaluate the arguments
that are put forward by those who regard the text as inauthentic
to see whether they are conclusive, and, in the course of doing
so, to give some attention to the question of whether the saying
is the sort of thing Jesus might have been expected to say. Our
working assumption is that if it can be shown that the data can
be interpreted satisfactorily without recourse to the hypothesis
of inauthenticity, the saying should be accepted as expressing
the mind of Jesus.

C. E. B. Cranfield summarizes the major considerations that
have been advanced in support of the inauthenticity of the
ransom logion as follows:
    It is alleged that (i) it is out of harmony with its
    context which is concerned with service; (ii) the use of
    ἦλθεν implies a date after the completion of Jesus' life
    and work; (iii) λύτρον and the ideas associated with it
    are found nowhere else in his teaching; (iv) the original
    form of the saying is preserved in Lk. xxii.27, and Mk. x.
    45 is a 'dogmatic recast' of it made under the influence of
    Pauline theology /8/.
Some combination of these four major arguments is generally
appealed to by those who deny the genuineness of the saying,

and therefore it is to a careful examination of them that we must now turn.

I

The first line of argument which is brought against the authenticity of Mark 10:45b is that there is a measure of tension between it and the first half of the verse. According to Mark 10:45a, it is said, Jesus taught that the purpose of His existence was to serve others, and that the disciples were to follow the pattern which He set in this regard. Mark 10:45b, however, introduces a new thought which destroys the correspondence between the behaviour of the Son of man and that expected of the twelve. It is alleged that service and giving one's life as a ransom are very different ideas, and that, because the exemplary character of the former does not extend to the latter, a transition between them would be very awkward. This is seen by several scholars to be evidence of the secondary nature of the ransom saying /9/.

Undoubtedly there is a significant difference between the concepts of service and redemption, but they are hardly mutually exclusive. To argue that Jesus could not have made the transition from one to the other is pedantic, and in effect assumes that He was incapable of using synthetic parallelism. As a matter of fact such a transition is neither unusual nor inappropriate. 'If Jesus was going to refer to his own serving as the ground of the rule which he had just stated', says Cranfield, 'it was only natural that he should refer to the self-giving in which his serving was to culminate' /10/. Jesus' service is presented as an example in Mark 10:45a, whereas His self-sacrifice, mentioned in the second half of the verse, is clearly unique, but Mark did not regard that as a problem. Since Mark saw no difficulty in the transition from one thought to the other, it is difficult to see how the argument that such a transition would have been impossible for Jesus can be sustained. Indeed Mark 10:45 is not the only place where these two ideas are found in juxtaposition. Chapters 12 and 13 of the Gospel of John also contain examples of this in the teaching of Jesus. In John 12:23-27 Jesus presents the theme of life which comes through death, both in connection with the service He expects from His followers, and in connection with His own approaching passion. Similarly, in the following chapter, the feet-washing incident has a double significance - portraying what is about to happen on the cross, as well as providing an example of humble service for the disciples. In both of these

passages the ideas of service and atonement are combined in a
manner reminiscent of Mark 10:45. An especially significant
instance of this combination of concepts is found in I Pet 2:21-
24. V 21 explicitly states that Christ has provided us with an
example in His suffering, but v 24 equally clearly refers to the
sin-bearing character of His passion, and its benefits for
others. The transition between these two thoughts is made
easily because Peter interprets Christ's suffering in the light
of Isaiah 53. Since the idea of substitutionary suffering is so
prominent in the description of the Servant of the Lord, it is
only natural that Peter should attribute it to Jesus. This is
of importance for the interpretation of Mark 10:45 because it
has traditionally been believed that it also alludes to Isaiah
53. If this be accepted, and if it be granted that Jesus saw
Himself in the role of the Isaianic Servant, the flow of thought
in Mark 10:45 is not only unexceptionable, but exactly what
might have been expected /11/. Unfortunately reservations have
been expressed about the influence of the Suffering Servant
conception on Mark 10:45 specifically and upon the thought of
Jesus generally.

C. K. Barrett's painstaking examination of the possible
links between the ransom saying and Isaiah 53 has led him to
conclude that the latter does not constitute the background of
Mark 10:45 /12/. His presentation is impressive, and his major
thesis has been endorsed by M. D. Hooker /13/ and E. Best /14/.
Nevertheless serious weaknesses in his arguments have been
detected by a number of scholars, including A. J. B. Higgins
/15/, F. Hahn /16/, R. T. France /17/, and W. J. Moulder /18/.
They have charged, with justification, that he has failed to
produce adequate grounds for denying that the ransom saying is
indebted to the fourth Servant Song. In spite of Barrett's
attempt to prove otherwise, it remains highly probable that
Isaiah 53 is alluded to in Mark 10:45.

The following points of contact between the ransom saying
and Isaiah 53 constitute sufficient warrant for thinking that
the former was based on the latter. The phrase, δοῦναι τὴν
ψυχήν, seems to recall the ʾim tāśîm ʾāšām napšô in Isa 53:10
(a connection Barrett does not mention), and the λύτρον of Mark
10:45 corresponds very adequately to the ʾāšām of Isa 53:10,
even though it is not used to translate it elsewhere /19/. The
link between πολλῶν and the catch word, rabbîm, which appears in
Isa. 52:14,15 and 53:11,12, has often been pointed out, but it
has not always been appreciated that what makes it significant
is the occurrence in both Mark 10:45 and Isaiah 53 of the notion

of one dying in the place of the 'many'. These similarities of
detail, along with the fact that the general ideas of service
and vicarious death are held in common, lead us to the
conclusion that the ransom saying was formed in conscious
dependence upon the Isaianic picture of the Suffering Servant.

If it be granted that it is probable that Isaiah 53 has
influenced the ransom saying in Mark, there is still the
question of whether Jesus interpreted His mission in the light
of that passage. This issue will be dealt with below /20/, and
at this point it need only be pointed out that if Jesus did see
Himself as the Servant of the Lord described in Isaiah, the
first objection to the genuineness of the saying becomes vacuous.
If Mark 10:45b does allude to Isaiah 53, and if this chapter had
a significant influence upon the self-understanding of Jesus,
the train of thought in Mark 10:45 is perfectly natural, and is
closely paralleled in I Pet 2:21-24. Even if the Suffering
Servant associations were rejected, it would be unjustifiable to
argue against the genuineness of Mark 10:45 on the basis of the
combination of ideas found there, since similar combinations are
found in John 12 and 13.

II

A second reason why doubt has been expressed about the
authenticity of the ransom saying is based on the fact that the
main verb (ἦλθεν) is in the aorist tense. This is taken as an
indication that the saying views Jesus' life from the perspective
of the later Christian community /21/. Rudolf Bultmann has even
gone so far as to make the generalization that all of the sayings
which speak of the 'coming' of Jesus fall 'under suspicion of
being Church products because this terminology seems to be the
means of looking back to the historical appearance of Jesus as a
whole' /22/. Whether the use of the aorist tense in Mark 10:45b
exposes it as a creation of the Church is the question to which
we must now turn.

It should be observed right at the outset that it is
illegitimate to assume a late origin for the ransom saying
because of the tense of the leading verb. As is well known the
Greek tenses primarily express the kind of action rather than
the time of the action /23/, and it is hard to imagine how Jesus
could have made a statement about His mission without using the
aorist tense. Certainly the tense does not necessarily imply
that Jesus' entire life is viewed as being in the past. In fact
there is reason to think it should not be understood in this way.

Apparently Mark did not think that the aorist tense suggested
that Jesus' life was over, for, if he had, he could have altered
it in the interests of verisimilitude. By placing the saying
on the lips of Jesus in its present form, Mark indicates that he
saw no difficulty with Jesus making such a statement.

The ransom saying is only one of a substantial number of
sayings attributed to Jesus in the Synoptics which speak of His
coming. The others are found in Mark 1:38; 2:17 (Matt 9:13;
Luke 5:32); Matt 5:17; 10:34-36 (Luke 12:51); 11:19 (Luke 7:34);
Luke 12:49; 19:10. There are also a number of sayings in which
Jesus speaks of having been sent, and they should be considered
along with the 'coming' sayings since both reflect His
consciousness of having a divine mission /24/. In Mark 9:37
(Luke 9:48); Matt 10:40 (Luke 10:16); 15:24; and Luke 4:43 we
find sayings of Jesus in which he describes Himself as one who
was sent. Similar sayings about Jesus' coming are also to be
found in John 8:14; 9:39; 10:10; and 12:46,47, and the fourth
Gospel contains a host of sayings which speak of His having been
sent. In addition to the sayings found on the lips of Jesus,
there are remarks made by others about Him which imply that He
came from God. Representative of these would be the cry of the
demoniac in the synagogue at Capernaum: 'Have you come to
destroy us?' (Mark 1:24; Luke 4:34) /25/.

Considering the evidence of these sayings as a whole it is
clear that the notion that Jesus was conscious of having a
divine mission, which He expressed in terms of 'having come' or
'having been sent', is deeply imbedded in the Gospel tradition.
Not only is it found in all of the Gospels, but it is also found
in each of the sources postulated by the four document
hypothesis. This in itself lends a high degree of probability
to the view that Jesus spoke of His coming as a past event.
This conclusion receives corroboration from the fact that some
of the sayings which speak of Jesus' coming or being sent
presuppose that His ministry had not yet been completed. These
bear eloquent witness to Jesus' sense of mission and it is
unlikely that they originated in the early Church. An
outstanding example of this is a saying recorded in Luke 12:49,
'I came (ἦλθον) to cast fire upon the earth; and would that it
were already kindled' /26/. The origin of such a statement can
more easily be traced to the historical Jesus than to the
Christian community.

In view of the wealth of evidence that Jesus believed
Himself to have been sent from God, and that He spoke of His

having come, the argument that the ἦλθεν marks the ransom saying
as a church creation must be judged inconclusive.  Indeed, as
C. H. Dodd has noted, 'The form of pronouncement, ἦλθεν with the
infinitive of purpose or an equivalent ἵνα-clause, is one of the
most widely established forms in which the sayings of Jesus are
transmitted' /27/.  It appears that it was common for Jesus to
refer to His mission in such terms, consequently, insofar as its
form is concerned, the ransom saying is credible as a dominical
logion /28/.

III

The genuineness of Mark 10:45b has also been contested on
the basis that it attributes to Jesus words and thoughts which
are not found elsewhere in His teaching.  Professor Nineham
says:  'Though Jesus may have included his death in his work of
service and love for men, there is little or no evidence
elsewhere in the Gospels that he thought of it in terms of
sacrifice or ransom' /29/.  The supposed uniqueness of the
saying in the Gospel tradition is seen as rendering it suspect,
and all the more so because of the prominence of the idea of
redemption in the early church, and most notably in the writings
of Paul.  In fact some critics have explained the origin of the
saying in terms of Pauline influence /30/.

It is not difficult to see why it might be supposed that
there is some connection between Mark 10:45b and Pauline
theology, since Paul alludes to the redemptive significance of
Jesus' death in several places /31/.  On the other hand,
although there is an undeniable similarity of thought, there is
little verbal similarity between these passages and the ransom
saying in Mark.  The designation of Jesus as 'the Son of man'
finds no parallel in Paul at all, and when Paul speaks of the
self-giving of Christ, he uses the reflexive pronoun ἑαυτοῦ
rather than using the noun ψυχή /32/.  The noun λύτρον is also
absent from the Pauline corpus, though ἀντίλυτρον is used in
I Tim 2:6 and λυτρόω, in Titus 2:14.  In addition, there is no
exact parallel to ἀντὶ πολλῶν in Paul's writings.  Paul never
uses ἀντί when speaking of Christ's death, preferring ὑπέρ
instead, and he uses πολλοί of the beneficiaries of Christ's
death only in Rom 5:15,19.

Paul's writings do not contain an exact counterpart to
Mark 10:45b, but there is a conceptual link between them.  This
must be seen, however, in the light of the widespread belief in
the early Church that Christ's death had redeeming value.  The

imagery of redemption was not confined to Pauline circles, but
comes to expression in such passages as Heb 9:12,15; I Pet 1:18;
and II Pet 2:1.  I Pet 1:18 is especially significant because
the opening phrase, εἰδότες ὅτι, indicates the presence of
commonly accepted beliefs.  Furthermore, the question must be
asked whether it is more likely that Mark is indebted to Paul,
or that an authentic saying of Jesus underlies the soteriological teaching of Paul and other Christian writers.  In his
commentary on Matthew, A. H. McNeile suggested that 'the
universal acceptance of Christian writers of the 'redeeming'
value of His (Christ's) death must owe its origin to some words
from him' /33/.  While it may be presumptuous to say that the
soteriological teaching of the epistles could only be explained
as a development of teaching originally given by Jesus, the
possibility that He was the first to regard His death as a
redemptive act must certainly be considered.  This possibility
is particularly attractive because the redemption theology of
Mark 10:45 is expressed in a comparatively simple form, and
betrays a semitic background.  To assess it accurately, however,
we must consider how probable it is that Jesus would have spoken
of His death in this way.

The evidence that Jesus foresaw His death is so overwhelming
that its historicity may be considered to be assured.  To begin
with it is solidly rooted in the Gospel tradition.  Not only is
it expressed in the three major passion predictions of the
Synoptics (Mark 8:31; 9:31; and 10:33,34, with their parallels),
but, more importantly, in numerous intimations and allusions
which cannot easily be dismissed as church creations.  These
occur in a variety of forms.  The saying about the removal of
the bridegroom (Mark 2:20; Matt 9:15; Luke 5:35), for instance,
is found in a pronouncement story; the killing of the son of
the owner of the vineyard (Mark 12:7,8; Matt 21:38,39; Luke 20:
14,15) is mentioned in a parable; and Jesus' reference to the
anticipatory anointing of His body (Mark 14:8; Matt 26:12)
appears in a narrative section /34/.  The extensiveness of the
sayings which refer to Christ's death, their allusive character,
and the variety of forms utilized demonstrate convincingly that
Jesus was aware that He would meet with a violent end.

The direct testimony of the Gospels with regard to Jesus'
expectation of an early death is strikingly confirmed by other
considerations.  The history of the persecution of prophets, and
especially the martyrdom of John the Baptist would have forced
Jesus to reckon with the possibility of His own death.  The
opposition which He encountered throughout His ministry,

particularly from the religious hierarchy of Judaism, would also
have prepared Him for it. Finally, He could hardly have failed
to appreciate that both His teaching and His actions, because of
their radical and provocative nature, would lead to attempts to
silence Him. Taken altogether the evidence that Jesus expected
His life to end prematurely is overwhelming.

In several places where Jesus' death is spoken of, it is
presented as a divine necessity /35/. Jesus' consciousness of
the fate awaiting Him is not presented merely as an inference
drawn from His observation of the antagonism that accompanied
His ministry. As Geerhardus Vos rightly notes: 'His death
appeared to Him not so much *inevitable* as *indispensable*' /36/.
According to Matt 26:54 Jesus related the necessity of His death
to the fulfilment of Scripture, and this is supported by a
number of instances where the passion is described as having
been prophesied. In Mark 9:12, e.g., Jesus asks: 'how is it
written of the Son of man, that he should suffer many things and
be treated with contempt?' /37/. The Gospels clearly indicate
that Jesus' conviction regarding the necessity of His death was
grounded in its having been 'written', and there is no reason
to reject their testimony.

In only one of the passages where Jesus speaks of the
passion as having been predicted, does he actually cite the OT
source from which He drew the idea, and that is in Luke 22:37,
which includes a quotation from Isa 53:12. No doubt Jesus
believed that His end had been foretold elsewhere in the OT as
well, but the fact remains that, insofar as our records are
concerned, Isaiah 53 is the sole passage cited by Him in this
connection. Until relatively recently it was generally accepted
that Isaiah 53 was a major source for Jesus' view of His mission.
Now, particularly as the result of the work of Professor Hooker
in this area, many scholars appear to have misgivings about the
possible influence of the Servant of the Lord concept on Jesus'
thinking /38/. In fact R. H. Fuller has boldly declared: 'we
must surely now agree that between them Tödt and Miss Hooker
have demolished the thesis that Jesus understood himself as the
Servant of the Lord' /39/. Although some of the recent studies
in this area have raised serious questions about the origin and
development of the Servant Christology, Fuller's dogmatism is
unwarranted. The conclusions of these studies have not gone
unchallenged, and by no means have all scholars abandoned the
position that Jesus interpreted His ministry in the light of
the Servant passages of Isaiah /40/. As a matter of fact an
examination of these studies reveals several major weaknesses.

It is especially noteworthy that those who deny that the
Servant Christology can be traced back to Jesus emphasize that
there is only one direct quotation from Isaiah 53 on the lips
of Jesus in the Gospels.  They are inclined to overlook or
underestimate the significance of the fact that this is the only
OT passage cited by Jesus with reference to His death.  They
also tend to disregard or minimize the import of allusions to
the chapter in His teaching.  Both the ransom saying in Mark
10:45 (Matt 20:28) and the cup-word in Mark 14:24 (Matt 26:28;
Luke 22:20) ought to be accepted as sayings which are based on
the description of the Suffering Servant.  In addition, the
passion predictions as a group exhibit a general similarity to
it, and should not be ignored.  These indirect references to
Isaiah 53 attest even more strongly than the single direct
quotation from it to Jesus' application of the passage to
Himself /41/.

A second weakness in the arguments of those who doubt that
the Servant Christology goes back to Jesus is that references to
Servant passages which do not specifically mention suffering are
often dismissed from consideration without adequate reason.
While it would be anachronistic to read back into the first
century a modern analysis of the Servant Songs as a distinct
grouping, it would be equally mistaken to suppose that Isaiah 53
was viewed in total isolation from the other Servant passages.
Allusions to other Servant passages ought to be taken into
account, and the possibility that Jesus may have linked them
with Isaiah 53 should be investigated.  It is well known that
the words of the voice from heaven at Jesus' baptism, and later
at His Transfiguration, seem to echo Isa 42:1.  The baptism
incident is particularly interesting in that it suggests that
Jesus may have identified Himself with the Isaianic Servant from
the very inception of His public ministry /42/.  The fact that
the catch phrase, 'Behold my servant', is found in Isa 42:1 and
52:13 could easily account for the two passages so introduced
being associated with one another.  Jesus' understanding of His
mission is also reflected in the incident in the  synagogue at
Nazareth which is recorded in Luke 4:16-21.  There, after
reading from Isa 61:1,2, He proclaimed:  'Today this scripture
has been fulfilled in your hearing'.  In all probability Jesus
related the anointing of the Spirit mentioned in Isa 61:1 with
His baptism.  This would coincide with the allusion of the
heavenly voice to Isa 42:1 in that an anointing with the Spirit
is also spoken of there /43/.  If Jesus interpreted Isa 42:1 and
61:1,2 of Himself, it is not difficult to see how He could have
come to the conclusion that Isaiah 53 also pertained to Him.

Those who oppose the traditional view that Jesus saw Himself as the Servant of the Lord face the problem of offering a more satisfactory explanation of the source of His convictions about His death, and their failure to do so constitutes a third weakness in their position. All of the Biblical data are intelligible on the assumption that Jesus believed that He was fulfilling the role of the Isaianic Servant /44/, but this is not the case with rival hypotheses. The main alternatives are that Jesus' conceptions were formed on the basis of either the martyr theology of late Judaism, or the Son of man prophecy in Daniel 7 /45/. The former fails to carry conviction because it does not do justice to the texts which speak of Jesus' death as a Scriptural necessity, and the latter, because Daniel 7 does not specifically associate suffering with the one 'like a son of man', and there is no solid evidence that either Jesus or the early church interpreted the passage as doing so /46/. Neither Jewish martyr theology nor Daniel 7 are nearly as plausible as Isaiah 53, which speaks so clearly of representative suffering, as possible sources for Jesus' view of His passion.

We have seen that there are solid grounds for believing that Jesus expected that He would meet with a violent end, that He believed this was predicted in the Old Testament, and that Isaiah 53 was one of the major sources from which he derived this conviction. In the light of these considerations it is difficult to see how it can be maintained that the ideas expressed in the ransom saying are foreign to the teaching of Jesus elsewhere. It is in complete harmony with the rest of the Gospel tradition relating to Jesus' view of the end of His life, and has an especially close parallel in the cup word at the Last Supper, where the influence of Isaiah 53 may also be detected. There is no inconsistency between this saying and Jesus' general teaching concerning His passion. On the contrary, along with the cup word, it represents the culmination to which the other sayings lead, and, without which, they would be incomplete. These are the only two sayings preserved in the Synoptic tradition which clearly indicate the significance Jesus attached to the passion which He knew to be predetermined. What is said in Mark 10:45b is what we might have expected from Jesus on the basis of the rest of His teaching, and also provides a satisfactory explanation for the origin of the Church's belief in the redemptive power of His death /47/.

IV

The final and most formidable of the arguments commonly
urged against the authenticity of Mark 10:45b is based on the
similarities between Mark 10:42-45 and Luke 22:24-27.  These two
passages parallel each other so closely that it is generally
believed that they reproduce the same discourse.  Both conclude
with statements about Jesus' serving, but only Mark follows that
with a reference to redemption.  This has prompted the
suggestion that the Marcan version contains a theological
expansion of an authentic saying about service, preserved more
accurately in Luke.  So Bultmann asserts:  'Lk. 22:27 is
doubtless original over against Mk. 10:45, which has formed its
conception of Jesus from the redemption theories of Hellenistic
Christianity' /48/.

A comparison of the Marcan and Lucan pericopae reveals
substantial resemblances between them, particularly in their
overall structure.  In both, the issue which gives rise to
Jesus' teaching is the disciples' concern with greatness, and,
in both, His teaching includes three elements - (a)  He
contrasts the way greatness is expressed among Gentiles with
that which ought to appertain among His followers,  (b)  He
advocates a reversal of the pattern normally encountered in the
world, and  (c)  He appeals to His own example of service to
illustrate His teaching.  Such a correspondence between two
passages, with the main ideas appearing in the same sequence, is
noteworthy, and warrants an investigation of the relationship
between them; however, regarding the Marcan version as a
modification of the Lucan in the interests of later doctrinal
views is not the only way of construing the relationship.

The fact that Mark has a theological emphasis which is
lacking in Luke does not in itself prove that Mark is secondary,
and, indeed, a linguistic analysis suggests that the Marcan
version is the more ancient of the two.  Mark 10:45 exhibits a
number of striking semitisms /49/.  Features such as the title
'Son of man', the avoidance of the divine name, the epexegetic
καί, the parallelism, the use of ψυχή rather than the reflexive
pronoun, and the expression πολλῶν are unmistakeably semitic,
and thus favour a Palestinian origin.  By way of contrast,
hellenistic characteristics are to be found in the Lucan account,
and some of the terms used appear to have been borrowed from the
vocabulary of the Church /50/.  For instance, in Mark 10:43 we
find the positive form of the adjective μέγας, which, in

accordance with semitic usage, can stand for the comparative or the superlative, but Luke 22:26 has the comparative μείζων. There are also a number of significant terms in Luke 22:24-27 which are not found in Mark. The use of εὐεργέτης in Luke 22:25 is important because of its extensive use as a title in the Graeco-Roman world, and νεώτερος and ἡγούμενος in the following verse are of interest because they are used elsewhere to designate specific groups of people within the Church /51/. Careful study of Mark 10:42-45 and Luke 22:24-27 leads irresistibly to the conclusion that, linguistically at least, the Lucan account gives evidence of Gentile Christian influence from which Mark is free. Naturally this does not prove that Mark has preserved the *ipsissima verba Jesu*, but it does support the relative antiquity of Mark's account, and suggests that it probably originated in Palestine.

Insofar as the language of Mark 10:42-45 and Luke 22:24-27 is concerned, Mark has the appearance of being more primitive; but it is doubtful that we ought to think of a direct development from one to the other /52/. There is very good reason to believe that they represent independent traditions. Mention has been made of the similarities between the two accounts, but it should also be observed that there are striking dissimilarities as well. In Mark the dispute among the disciples is concerned with positions of honour in the future, but that future orientation is lacking in Luke. With regard to the wording of the two accounts, Vincent Taylor has pointed out that only 21 of the 67 words in the Lucan version are found in Mark, and that most of the verbal agreement is in Luke 22:25,26a /53/. Even these statistics give an exaggerated impression of the extent of the verbal agreement, since only 16 words appear in the same form in both, and that includes 4 definite articles, 4 conjunctions, 3 third person plural pronouns, and the phrases οὐχ οὕτως and ἐν ὑμῖν. No verbs appear in exactly the same form in both passages, and the only noun they have in common is ἐθνῶν. The verbal agreements are so slight that direct dependence of one upon the other seems very unlikely.

Besides the variations in terminology and content, there is the obvious difference in setting. Mark places his version of Jesus' teaching in the later Perean ministry of Jesus (cf. Mark 10:1), whereas Luke puts his in the upper room. This divergence is highly important since Luke generally follows the Marcan order of events quite closely, and it would be a departure from his normal practice, if he derived Luke 22:24-27 from Mark 10:42-45, to insert it into the narrative at a later point than

Mark. In Luke 18:15-43 he has taken over the material found in Mark 10:13-52 with the sole exception of Mark 10:35-45, which he omitted. Why does he depart from Mark here? The answer may be found in Luke's editorial technique. One of the observable principles of Luke's method of composition is that he omits sections of Mark where he has parallel material in another source, apparently to avoid duplication /54/. This may account, at least in part, for his deletion of Mark 10:35-45, assuming that he had similar material in another source which he intended to use later. His respect for James and John, and his natural reluctance to call attention to their shortcomings, may also have contributed to his decision not to use Mark 10:35-45 /55/. Consideration of Luke's editorial methods and the different settings of Mark 10:35-45 and Luke 22:24-27 reinforce the conclusion drawn from a study of the verbal agreements between them that Luke 22:24-27 is non-Marcan /56/. It is most probable that it was drawn from his special source, and if so, one must beware of pressing too much significance from the fact that it does not contain the disputed ransom saying. The absence of the saying from Luke may simply be due to his decision to use material from another source that was similar to Mark 10:35-45, and need not imply anything about Luke's estimation of its authenticity. Nor does the absence of the saying from Luke's special source necessarily tell against its genuineness. Perhaps, for instance, the saying was originally independent of its context in Mark. If so, its presence or absence from Luke's source would have little bearing on its claim to be authentic.

It is possible that Mark and Luke not only reflect independent traditions, but actually refer to separate incidents, and that Mark 10:45 and Luke 22:27 contain distinct logia. It is commonly acknowledged that Jesus may have said substantially the same thing on different occasions /57/, but that possibility is generally dismissed as being excessively harmonistic when similar accounts are compared. In this case it is deserving of serious consideration /58/. To form a proper estimate of it we must evaluate the historical credibility of the setting in which the similar material is placed in each of the Gospels.

As Mark relates the story Jesus' thoughts were centred upon His impending death as He and the twelve made their way towards Jerusalem, and James and John brought forward their request for positions of prominence /59/. Jesus had already told His disciples of the suffering that lay before Him on three occasions /60/, but the disciples failed to grasp the significance of what He had said, and were obsessed with notions

of future glory.   When the sons of Zebedee made their selfish
request, Jesus attempted to bridge the gulf between His thinking
and theirs by speaking of the cup He was to drink, and the
baptism with which He was to be baptized /61/.   This veiled
reference to His suffering was then followed by His teaching
about the way to attain true greatness, which concludes with the
ransom saying.   The overall sequence of thought is natural and
thoroughly believable, and the teaching of the   self-giving
of the Son of man is very appropriate in this context.   It is
anticipated in a general way by the preceding passion
predictions, and it makes explicit what is implicit in the
imagery of the cup and baptism used by Jesus in His initial
reply to James and John.   Indeed, it might well be said that,
in Mark's presentation, the ransom saying constitutes the climax
of Jesus' teaching about His death /62/.   The logion itself, and
the pericope in which it is found, both fit smoothly into their
respective contexts, and this suggests either that Mark has
edited the material with great skill or that the contexts are
historical.   Careful Marcan redaction is certainly a possibility,
but it is more likely that Mark is simply recording the actual
sequence of events.   If Jesus did make a final trip to Jerusalem
with the awareness that He would die there, it would have been
natural for Him to instruct His followers concerning what lay
before Him and the meaning He attached to it /63/.

When we turn our attention to Luke 22:24-27 we find that it
is not as solidly wedded to its context as its Marcan parallel,
but its setting is credible nonetheless.   The Lucan pericope
appears in the narrative of the Last Supper, where it follows
the account of the institution of the eucharist and the
announcement concerning the betrayal of the Son of man.   It has
been argued above that Luke derived this section from a source
other than Mark, and it is most probable that it was connected
with the Supper in this source, since it is difficult to imagine
why Luke would have made this connection unless he believed it
to be historical /64/.   That Luke's source was correct in
placing a dispute about greatness which prompted teaching on
service in the context of the Last Supper finds support in the
Johannine tradition /65/.   The account of the feet-washing in
John 13 (vv 13-16 especially) confirms that this matter arose at
that time.   The appropriateness of Jesus' teaching in Luke 24:27
to the situation described in the Fourth Gospel is particularly
impressive.   The contrast which is drawn between sitting at
table and serving, and Jesus' statement, 'But I am among you as
one who serves', accord much better with the circumstances
described in John 13 than with those of Mark 10.   Since Luke and

John were both familiar with traditions that Jesus taught about
greatness and service at the Last Supper, there is good reason
to believe that such teaching was given on that occasion /66/.

We have seen that the teaching found in Mark 10:42-45 and
Luke 22:24-27 fits the contexts provided by the evangelists very
well, which would suggest that Mark and Luke record teaching
given on two distinct occasions. The chief difficulty with this
is the similarity between the passages, and especially the
similar sequence of ideas in Mark 10:42,43 and Luke 22:25,26.
How is this to be explained if these are not different versions
of the same teaching? One possibility is that Luke borrowed
some material from Mark 10, and used it in relating an incident
spoken of in another source. He could have filled out what
Jesus said at the Last Supper with the teaching he found in
Mark. This is unlikely, however, since the verbal agreement is
not at all close, and Luke tends to avoid conflating his sources.
More attractive is the simple suggestion that Jesus gave similar
teaching on the two occasions. It is even possible that at the
Last Supper He deliberately repeated the main features of the
teaching He gave on the way to Jerusalem, to call the earlier
dispute to the minds of the disciples. At any rate the fact
that similar teaching is found, not only in Mark 10:42-45 (Matt
20:25-28) and Luke 22:24-27 (John 13:14-16), but also in Mark
9:33-37 (Matt 18:1-5; Luke 9:46-48) and Matt 23:11 suggests that
Jesus broached the subject on more than one occasion. Since
such parallel material has been preserved in various contexts,
and there is a natural presumption that Jesus often repeated the
same teaching in different forms, it is quite possible that Mark
10 and Luke 22 relate distinct conversations between Jesus and
His disciples. When the unity of the Marcan context and the
correspondence between Luke 22 and John 13 are also taken into
consideration, one is inclined to look upon this possibility
favourably, though the fact that Mark 10:42,43 and Luke 22:25,26
have such similar structures forbids dogmatism about their being
entirely independent accounts /67/.

If Luke believed, as is probable, that he was describing a
different conversation than that recorded in Mark 10, there is
no reason to think that he deliberately suppressed the
soteriological teaching of the ransom saying by omitting it.
It is likely that his special source did not have the saying in
the account of the Last Supper, and that his preference for that
source and his tendency to avoid doublets constitute the reasons
why he does not have it. It would be hazardous to draw far-
reaching conclusions about Luke's theology from such an omission.

Luke apparently did not have as great an interest in the
redemptive effects of the death of Christ as many other NT
writers, but the view that he did not connect salvation with the
passion is to be rejected /68/. The longer text of the account
of the institution of the Lord's Supper unambiguously makes this
connection, and it is deserving of acceptance as Lucan /69/.
Even if the shorter text be followed, the concept of atoning
death is implicit in Jesus' identification of the bread with
His body /70/. That Luke interpreted Christ's death in
redemptive categories is also evident from his account of Paul's
sermon to the Ephesian elders, where he speaks of 'the church of
the Lord, which he obtained with his own blood' (Acts 20:28)
/71/.

Assessing the relationship between Mark 10:42-45 and Luke
22:24-27 is not an easy matter, and any proposals in this
connection must inevitably be tentative. Nonetheless we have
seen that the hypothesis that the Marcan version is secondary,
and has been expanded to include a dogmatic emphasis not
originally present in the teaching of Jesus, is not the only
way of understanding that relationship. In fact, it is not the
most satisfactory explanation since it is quite possible that
Mark and Luke relate two distinct conversations. Even if they
do have a common origin it is probable that the Lucan account is
based on a separate tradition from the Marcan, and,
linguistically-speaking, the Marcan version appears to be the
more primitive of the two.

Our scrutiny of the arguments which have been levelled
against the authenticity of Mark 10:45b has shown them to be
inconclusive. The evidence which is believed by many to point
in the direction of inauthenticity, can be interpreted
differently, and, indeed, should be so interpreted. There is no
need to abandon the authenticity of the saying, if one accepts
that the Synoptics contain a substantially reliable account of
Jesus' teaching.

One question remains to be answered, and that is whether
any positive evidence can be adduced to 'prove' that the ransom
saying goes back to the historical Jesus. Absolute proof in
this area is unattainable, but it should be observed that
several features of the saying are consistent with its being
authentic. The semitic character of the saying has been noted,
and that is in keeping with its being dominical, though it
could, of course, be accounted for in other ways. In this
connection the use of the title 'Son of man' is of special

interest, since it appears as a characteristic self-designation
of Jesus in the Gospels. Secondly, the content of the saying
accords well with the rest of the teaching of Jesus regarding
His passion. Particularly significant is the way this saying
corresponds with the cup-word at the Last Supper. Finally, a
number of writers have been struck by the restraint of the
saying, and have correctly observed that this would be expected
in a saying of Jesus, but not in something formulated by the
Church /72/. As Vincent Taylor puts it: 'the saying leaves
many points open, and in no way characterizes the need or
condition of the 'many'. As a 'community-product', the saying
is much too discreet; as an utterance of Jesus, it has just that
air of mystery, and the note of provocativeness, constantly
found in His words' /73/. The ransom logion shows little sign
of reflecting the developed theology of the atonement found
elsewhere in the NT, but may well be seen as the fountainhead
of later developments. None of these considerations is
decisive, and it is doubtful that they will carry much weight
with those who adopt a sceptical approach to the logia
tradition in the Synoptics. They are, however, consonant with
the genuineness of the saying, and consequently provide
confirmation of that position for those who are otherwise
predisposed towards it.

NOTES

/1/  V. Taylor, *The Gospel According to St. Mark* (London:
Macmillan, 1952) 444.  Cf. H. E. Tödt's comments on the
importance of the saying in *The Son of Man in the Synoptic
Tradition* (London:  SCM, 1965) 136.

/2/  W. Manson, *Jesus the Messiah* (London:  Hodder and
Stoughton, 1943) 131.

/3/  Among the studies in which objections have been raised to
the genuineness of the saying should be mentioned H. Rashdall,
*The Idea of Atonement in Christian Theology* (London:  Macmillan,
1919) 29-37, 49-56; and, more recently, Tödt, *Son of Man* 135-137,
202-211; and E. Arens, *The HΛΘΟΝ - Sayings in the Synoptic
Tradition* (Freiburg:  Universitätsverlag, 1976) 135-156.  On the
other hand, the authenticity of the saying is vigorously
defended in J. Jeremias, 'Das Lösegeld für Viele (Mk. 10,45)',
*Judaica* 3 (1947) 249-264 (cf. J. Jeremias, 'παῖς θεοῦ' *TDNT* 5
[1967] 712-717); and A. Feuillet, 'Le Logion sur la Rançon', *Rev
Sci Phil Theol* 51 (1967) 365-402.

/4/  N. Perrin, *Rediscovering the Teaching of Jesus* (New York: Harper & Row, 1967) 39. Cf. R. H. Fuller, *The Foundations of New Testament Christology* (London:  Collins, 1965) 18.

/5/  Cf. J. Jeremias, *New Testament Theology* (London:  SCM, 1971) 1. 37; and J. A. T. Robinson, *Can We Trust the New Testament?* (London:  Mowbrays, 1977) 132.

/6/  Cf. M. D. Hooker, 'Christology and Methodology', *NTS* 17 (1970-71) 480-487; Hooker, 'On Using the Wrong Tool', *Theology* 75 (1972) 570-581; R. S. Barbour, *Traditio-Historical Criticism of the Gospels* (London:  SPCK, 1972) 1-27; D. Hill, 'On the Evidence for the Creative Role of Christian Prophets', *NTS* 20 (1973-74) 262-274; and especially R. T. France, 'The Authenticity of the Sayings of Jesus', *History, Criticism & Faith* (ed. C. Brown; Leicester:  Inter-Varsity, 1976) 101-143.

/7/  Among the factors which favour the reliability of the Gospel tradition, two are worthy of special mention.  They are the presence in the early church of those who had been personal disciples of Jesus and who would have prevented misrepresentation of what He had taught, and the existence in the culture of first century Palestine of methods of transmitting traditions with considerable accuracy.  On the former see V. Taylor, *The Formation of the Gospel Tradition* (London:  Macmillan, 1933; 2d ed., 1935) 41-43; and T. W. Manson, 'The Foundation of the Synoptic Tradition:  the Gospel of Mark', *Studies in the Gospels and Epistles* (ed. M. Black; Philadelphia:  Westminster, 1962) 28-45.  On the latter see H. Riesenfeld, 'The Gospel Tradition and Its Beginnings', *The Gospel Tradition* (Philadelphia:  Fortress, 1970) 1-29; and B. Gerhardsson, *Memory and Manuscript* (Lund:  Gleerup, 1961) *passim*.
     Another noteworthy study in which the essential reliability of the logia material in the Gospel tradition is maintained is J. A. Baird's, *Audience Criticism and the Historical Jesus* (Philadelphia:  Westminster, 1969).

/8/  C. E. B. Cranfield, *The Gospel According to Saint Mark* (*CGTC*; Cambridge:  Cambridge University, 1959) 343. Cranfield's own evaluation of these arguments leads him to say:  'The balance of probability is surely on the side of the authenticity of the saying' (p. 344).

/9/  Cf. W. E. Bundy, *Jesus and the First Three Gospels* (Cambridge, Mass.:  Harvard University, 1955) 409; Tödt, *Son of Man* 206,207; and E. Trocmé, *The Foundation of the Gospel According to Mark* (London:  SPCK, 1975) 157.  Rather surprisingly Rashdall suggested that this might be the strongest objection to the authenticity of the saying (*Atonement* 51).

/10/ Cranfield, *Mark* 343.

/11/ D. E. Nineham appears to appreciate the significance of this consideration, for, in his discussion of the authenticity of the ransom logion (*The Gospel of St. Mark* [Pel Gosp Comm; London: Penguin, 1963] 281), he says, 'a good deal clearly turns on the possible influence upon Jesus of the suffering servant conception'.

/12/ C. K. Barrett, 'The Background of Mark 10:45', *New Testament Essays* (ed. A. J. B. Higgins; Manchester: Manchester University, 1959) 1-18.

/13/ M. D. Hooker, *Jesus and the Servant* (London: SPCK, 1959) 74-79.

/14/ E. Best, *The Temptation and the Passion* (Cambridge: Cambridge University, 1965) 142,143.

/15/ A. J. B. Higgins, *Jesus and the Son of Man* (London: Lutterworth, 1964) 41-47.

/16/ F. Hahn, *The Titles of Jesus in Christology* (London: Lutterworth, 1969) 56,57.

/17/ R. T. France, *Jesus and the Old Testament* (London: Tyndale, 1971) 117-121.

/18/ W. J. Moulder, 'The Old Testament and the Interpretation of Mark x.45', *NTS* 24 (1977) 121-123.

/19/ Cf. Cranfield, *Mark* 342; and Arens, ΗΛΘΟΝ-*Sayings* 137-139.

/20/ See the discussion of argument 3 below.

/21/ Cf., e.g., Bundy, *Jesus* 409.

/22/ R. Bultmann, *The History of the Synoptic Tradition* (Oxford: Basil Blackwell, 1963) 155.

/23/ Cf. *BDF* 166.

/24/ That it is legitimate to correlate the 'coming' and 'sending' sayings is confirmed by the observation that the 'coming' saying in Mark 1:38 is paralleled by a 'sending' saying in Luke 4:43.

/25/ Cf. Matt 8:29; 11:3 (Luke 7:20).

/26/ Cf. similar sayings in Mark 1:38; 2:17 (Matt 9:13; Luke 5:32); Matt 5:17; and Luke 4:43.

/27/   C. H. Dodd, *Historical Tradition in the Fourth Gospel*
(Cambridge:   Cambridge University, 1963) 355.

/28/   Jeremias (*Theology* 1.83) criticizes the argument from a
linguistic perspective, arguing that 'the underlying Aramaic
'*atayit* ... can simply mean 'I am there', 'I will', 'it is my
task''.   Cf. 'Lösegeld' 259.   W. Manson (*Jesus* 132), on the
other hand, points out that even if the form of the saying
reflects later influence, the content of the saying need not
be late.

/29/   Nineham, *Mark* 281.   Tödt (*Son of Man* 206) sees the fact
that it is the only Son of man saying which expresses the idea
of dying for man's salvation to be especially telling in this
regard.

/30/   Cf. C. G. Montefiore, *The Synoptic Gospels* (London:
Macmillan, 1909) 1.260; B. H. Branscomb, *The Gospel of Mark*
(*MNTC*; London:   Hodder and Stoughton, 1937) 191; and Bundy,
*Jesus* 409.   Although Cranfield (*Mark* 343) mentions the
possibility of Pauline influence in connection with the fourth
argument, it is more naturally dealt with in connection with
the third.

/31/   Cf. Rom 3:24; I Cor 6:20; 7:23; Gal 3:13; and Col 1:14.

/32/   Gal 1:4; I Tim 2:6; and Titus 2:14.

/33/   A. H. McNeile, *The Gospel According to St. Matthew*
(London:   Macmillan, 1915) 291.   Cf. C. H. Dodd, *According to
the Scriptures* (London:   Nisbet, 1952) 109,110; and I. H.
Marshall, 'The Development of the Concept of Redemption in the
New Testament', *Reconciliation and Hope* (ed. R. Banks; Exeter:
Paternoster, 1974) 153-169, especially p. 169.

/34/   Other pertinent references are Mark 9:12 (Matt 17:12);
10:38 (Matt 20:22); 14:21 (Matt 26:24; Luke 22:22); 14:22-25
(Matt 26:26-29; Luke 22:17-20); 14:49 (Matt 26:55,56; Luke
22:53); Matt 12:40; 26:2; Luke 12:50; 13:32,33; 17:25; and
John 2:19-21; 3:14; 6:51; 7:33; 8:28; 10:11,15,17,18; 12:23,24,
32,33; 13:1,36; 14:28; 16:5,7,10,16,17,28.

/35/   Cf. Mark 8:31 (Matt 16:21; Luke 9:22); Matt 26:54; Luke
13:33; 17:25; 22:22,37; 24:7,26,44,46; and John 3:14; 12:34.
The use of δεῖ in all of these verses, except Luke 22:22, is
worthy of special note.

/36/   G. Vos, *The Self-Disclosure of Jesus* (Grand Rapids:
Eerdmans, 1954) 280 (italics his).

/37/  Cf. Mark 14:21 (Matt 26:24); 14:49 (Matt 26:56); Luke
18:31; 22:37; 24:25-27,44-46.

/38/  Cf. Hooker, *Jesus passim*.  See also John Knox, *The Death
of Christ* (New York:  Abingdon, 1958) 77-107; Barrett,
'Background' 1-18; Hahn, *Titles of Jesus* 54-67; and Tödt, *Son
of Man* 141-221.

/39/  Fuller, *Foundations* 118,119.

/40/  Cf. B. Lindars, *New Testament Apologetic* (London:  SCM,
1961)  77-88; R. T. France, 'The Servant of the Lord in the
Teaching of Jesus', *Tyn Bull* 19 (1968) 26-52; R. N. Longenecker,
*The Christology of Early Jewish Christianity* (London:  SCM,
1970) 106,107; and France, *Jesus* 110-135.

/41/  Cf. V. Taylor, *Jesus and His Sacrifice* (London: Macmillan,
1959) 48.  Other possible allusions to Isaiah 53 in the teaching
of Jesus include Mark 9:12; Matt 3:15; Luke 11:22.  John the
Baptist's description of Jesus as 'the Lamb of God, who takes
away the sin of the world' in John 1:29,36 may be an allusion
to Isa 53:7 as well.

/42/  On the value of the story of Jesus' baptism as a guide to
His self-understanding, see Taylor, *Mark* 158-162, 617-619.

/43/  The Q material found in Matt 11:2-6; Luke 7:18-23 clearly
echoes Isaiah 61 and thus confirms that Jesus interpreted that
passage of Himself.

/44/  It is somewhat surprising that Luke 22:37 contains the
only example of a direct quotation from Isaiah 53 on the lips
of Jesus, but that may be explained, at least in part, by the
fact that Jesus directed His teaching about His passion
primarily to His disciples.  Cf. Jeremias, 'παῖς θεοῦ' 716,717.

/45/  Cf. Barrett, 'Background' 11-15; C. K. Barrett, 'Mark
10.45:  A Ransom for Many', *New Testament Essays* (London:  SPCK,
1972) 20-26; and M. D. Hooker, *The Son of Man in Mark* (Montreal:
McGill University, 1967) 189-198.

/46/  Cf. the insightful comments of France in *Jesus* 128-130.

/47/  Cf. Marshall's conclusion ('Concept of Redemption' 169)
that 'the concept of redemption is to be traced back to the
teaching of Jesus and has undergone a rich development,
leading to its use with various shades of meaning and in
different associations of thought'.

/48/  Bultmann, *History* 144.  Cf. W. Bousset, *Kyrios Christos*
(Nashville/New York:  Abingdon, 1970) 39; and Montefiore,

*Synoptic Gospels* 1. 258,259.

/49/   Cf. Jeremias, 'Lösegeld' 260-262; and Feuillet, 'Logion' 373-375.   Even Fuller admits that the ransom saying is 'certainly Palestinian' (*Foundations* 118), and Tödt says it 'has its linguistic roots definitely in the Palestinian sphere' (*Son of Man* 203).

/50/   Cf. Feuillet, 'Logion' 375,376.

/51/   On εὐεργέτης see the entry in J. H. Moulton and G. Milligan, *The Vocabulary of the Greek Testament* (Grand Rapids: Eerdmans, 1930;   reprinted 1976) 261; on νεώτερος see Acts 5:6; I Tim 5:1,2,11,14; Titus 2:6; and I Pet 5:5 (cf. νέος in Titus 2:4); and on ἡγούμενος see Acts 15:22 and Heb. 13:7,17,24.

/52/   Contra J. A. Bailey, *The Traditions Common to the Gospels of Luke and John* (Leiden:   Brill, 1963) 34-37.

/53/   V. Taylor, *The Passion Narrative of St. Luke* (ed. O. E. Evans; Cambridge:   Cambridge University, 1972) 61-64.

/54/   Cf. A. Wikenhauser, *New Testament Introduction* (Dublin: Herder and Herder, 1958) 225,226, 240,241; and J. M. Creed, *The Gospel according to St. Luke* (London:   Macmillan, 1965) lviii, lix, lxiii.

/55/   Luke's tendency to refrain from picturing the disciples in a poor light is obvious elsewhere.   E.g., in his account of Peter's confession at Caesarea Philippi he omits the account of Peter's rebuke found in Matthew and Mark, and in his account of the arrest of Jesus he does not mention, as the other evangelists do, that the disciples forsook Him and fled.

/56/   Cf. Taylor, *Passion Narrative* 61-64.

/57/   E.g., J. M. Rist writes:   'If we ask the question; 'Did Jesus ever say the same thing twice, or even three times in more or less the same words?', we can only answer, 'What preacher doesn't?' So we should be surprised if we did *not* find in the Gospels very similar passages, regardless of whether or not we subscribe to a theory of literary dependence' (*On the Independence of Matthew and Luke* [Cambridge:   Cambridge University, 1978] 92).

/58/   Cf. Leon Morris, *The Apostolic Preaching of the Cross* (Grand Rapids:   Eerdmans, 1956) 27; and I. H. Marshall, *The Gospel of Luke* (*NIGTC*; Exeter:   Paternoster, 1978) 811-814.

/59/   The reliability of the Marcan framework has come under considerable criticism, most notable from D. E. Nineham in 'The

Order of Events in St. Mark's Gospel - an examination of Dr.
Dodd's Hypothesis' (*Studies in the Gospels* [ed. D. E. Nineham;
Oxford: Basil Blackwell, 1967] 223-239). Nevertheless C. H.
Dodd's contention in 'The Framework of the Gospel Narrative'
(*ET* 43 [1931-32] 396-400; reprinted in his *New Testament
Studies* [Manchester: Manchester University, 1953]) that the
early Church preserved an outline of the life of Christ still
has merit.

/60/   Mark 8:31; 9:31; 10:33,34.

/61/   Cf. Mark 14:36 (Matt 26:39; Luke 22:42) and John 18:11
regarding the significance of Jesus' reference to the cup, and
Luke 12:50 regarding the reference to baptism.

/62/   Discussing the relationship of the ransom saying to its
context, James Denney says:  'The words are perfectly in place.
They are in line with everything that precedes.  They are
words in the only key, and of the only fulness, which answer to
our Lord's absorption at the time in the thought of his death'
(*The Death of Christ* [ed. R. V. G. Tasker; London:  Tyndale,
1951] 31).

/63/   V. Taylor advocates the originality of the Marcan context
in *Mark* 443.

/64/   A. Plummer correctly observes:  'If Lk. merely knew what
Jesus said on that occasion, but did not know the occasion, he
would hardly have selected the Last Supper as a suitable place
for the incident.  He probably had good reason for believing
that a dispute of this kind took place at the supper' (*A
Critical and Exegetical Commentary on the Gospel according to
S. Luke* [*ICC;* Edinburgh:  T. & T. Clark, 1896; 4th ed., 1901]
500).

/65/   This connection has often been noted.  Cf., e.g., N.
Geldenhuys, *Commentary on the Gospel of Luke* (*NICNT*; Grand
Rapids:  Eerdmans, 1951) 561,562.

/66/   The originality of the Lucan setting is favoured by
Marshall (*Luke* 811).

/67/   Naturally it is possible to maintain the authenticity of
the ransom saying and accept that Mark 10:42-45 and Luke 22:24-
27 are different versions of the same conversation.  E.g.,
A. J. B. Higgins (*Jesus and the Son of Man* [Philadelphia:
Fortress, 1964] 36-50) makes the ingenious, but unconvincing,
suggestion that the ransom saying finds its most suitable
setting in the Last Supper, and concludes that Mark has

preserved a basically authentic saying, and Luke, its authentic
setting. The possibility that Mark and Luke are referring to
different incidents must not be ignored, however, and, in the
opinion of this writer, it provides the most reasonable
explanation for the data.

/68/  Cf. H. Conzelmann, *The Theology of St. Luke* (New York:
Harper, 1960) 201.

/69/  The shorter text has been supported by G. D. Kilpatrick
('Luke XXII.19b - 20', *JTS* 47 [1946] 49-56) and A. Vööbus ('A
New Approach to the Problem of the Shorter and Longer Text in
Luke', *NTS* 15 [1968-69] 457-463).  The case for the longer text
is still much more persuasive however.  Among the notable
studies favouring it are N. B. Stonehouse, *The Witness of Luke
to Christ* (Grand Rapids:  Eerdmans, 1951) 130-141; and J.
Jeremias, *The Eucharistic Words of Jesus* (London:  SCM, 1966)
139-159.  An excellent, concise statement of the issues
involved is found in B. M. Metzger, *A Textual Commentary on
the Greek New Testament* (London:  United Bible Societies,
1971) 173-177.

/70/  Cf. Stonehouse, *Witness of Luke* 138-140.

/71/  A useful discussion of the Lucan teaching on the
redemptive death of Christ is found in Leon Morris, *The Cross
in the New Testament* (Grand Rapids:  Eerdmans, 1965) 63-143.

/72/  Cf. Taylor, *Jesus* 105; Feuillet, 'Logion' 398,399;
France, *Jesus* 117; and C. Colpe, 'ὁ υἱὸς τοῦ ἀνθρώπου', *TDNT* 8
(1972) 455.

/73/  Taylor, *Jesus* 105.

# The Authenticity of the Parable of the Sower and its Interpretation

Philip Barton Payne
Kyoto Christian Studies Center
34 Sandan Nagamachi, Matsugasaki
Sakyo-Ku, Kyoto, Japan 606

## Introduction

The parable of the Sower is, perhaps, the pivotal test case for studying the authenticity of Jesus' parables; for it alone not only occurs in each of the synoptic gospels, but also has a detailed interpretation.

## The Parable: Mark 4:3-9

There seems to be no serious challenge to the authenticity of the parable of the Sower./1/ It occurs with slight variations in Mark, Matthew, Luke, and the Gospel of Thomas. Its structure, content, Semitisms, and message follow patterns characteristic of Jesus.

The overall structure of the Sower parallels that of many of the other parables of Jesus: A. a familiar setting, B. a pattern of response to that setting leading to C. a climax. The familiar setting is the sowing of seed, which is easily visualized (ἰδού Mark 4:3; Matt 13:3). A fourfold pattern of response is described:

4:4    ὃ μὲν ἔπεσεν παρὰ τὴν ὁδόν, καί ... κατέφαγεν (aor.)

4:5-6 καὶ ἄλλο ἔπεσεν ἐπὶ τὸ πετρῶδες, καί ... ἐκαυματίσθη (aor.)

4:7   καὶ ἄλλο ἔπεσεν εἰς τὰς ἀκάνθας, καί ... συνέπνιξαν (aor.)

4:8   καὶ ἄλλα ἔπεσεν εἰς τὴν γῆν τὴν καλήν, καί ... ἔφερεν (imp.)

The climax falls on the fourth response. In contrast to the prior three graphic examples of destruction, the seeds falling on good soil are bountifully

fruitful. The three multiples of fruitfulness
(30-fold and 60-fold and 100-fold) balance the former
three cases of devastation. As the final example,
the good soil receives end stress. It is highlighted
further by the shift from singular to plural ( ἄλλα ),
from aorist to imperfect tenses ( ἐδίδου . . . ἔφερεν ),
and in the use of ἀναβαίνω , now of wheat rather
than thorns (4:7).

Each of the ten parables listed in Table I
follows this same threefold structure (A. a familiar
setting, B. a pattern of responses to that setting
leading to C. a climax) and describes the patterned
responses in parallel as does the parable of the
Sower. Thus, the Sower follows a structural pattern
that is characteristic of Jesus' parables.

Table I   Parables with a Climax which Reflects
          Parallel Patterns of Response to a Familiar
          Setting

| parable | pattern | number of parallel examples | climax |
|---------|---------|------------------------------|--------|
| The Sower<br>Mark 4:3-8<br>Matt 13:3-8<br>Luke 8:5-8 | reception of seed | 4 groups | fruitfulness dependent on reception |
| The Wicked Husbandmen<br>Mark 12:1-11<br>Matt 21:33-44<br>Luke 20:9-18 | rejection of the master's servants | Mark many & son, Matt 2 groups &son Luke 3 &son | destruction of the husbandmen; vineyard given to others |
| The Good Employer<br>Matt 20:1-16 | hiring vineyard laborers at various times | 5 hirings | equal payment |
| The Marriage Feast<br>Matt 22:1-10 | rejected invitations | many | destruction |
| The Great Supper<br>Luke 14:16-24 | rejected invitations | 3 in Luke 4 in the G. of Thomas | they shall not taste the banquet |

Table I  (Continued)

| parable | pattern | number of parallel examples | climax |
|---------|---------|----------------------------|--------|
| The Talents Matt 25:14-30 | investment proportionate to what was entrusted | 3 responses | only those investing wisely are entrusted with more |
| The Pounds Luke 19:12-27 | varied investment of what was entrusted | 3 responses | rewards in proportion to wise investment |
| The Good Samaritan Luke 10:25-37 | response to the assaulted man | 3 responses | generous care |
| The Barren Fig Tree Luke 13:6-9 | examination for fruitfulness | 4 examinations | be fruitful or be destroyed |
| The Shrewd Steward Luke 16:1-8 | action in crisis | 2 acts | commendation |

   The content of the Sower is also characteristic
of Jesus' parabolic teaching.  It develops
contrasting responses of the different kinds of soil
to the seed, which may be paralleled to the
contrasting responses in the Two Houses, the
Unmerciful Servant, the Two Sons, the Two Debtors,
the Servant Entrusted with Supervision, the Talents,
the Pounds, the Marriage Feast, the Great Supper, the
Ten Virgins, the Closed Door, the Children in the
Marketplace, and the Prodigal Son.

   Likewise, the focus on elements from nature
(birds, rocky soil, soil, sun, root, thorns, fruit)
is frequent in the parables of Jesus:  the Seed
Growing Secretly, the Mustard Seed, the Wicked
Husbandmen, the Budding Fig Tree, the Tares among the
Wheat, the Leaven, the Pearl, the Dragnet, the Lost
Sheep, the Good Employer, the Barren Fig Tree, the
Good Shepherd, the Hireling, the Grain of Wheat, and
Childbirth.  This contrasts with the relative paucity

of elements from nature in the writings of Paul./2/

The extent of Semitic expressions in the Sower
is sufficient for M. Black and V. Taylor to affirm:
'Here in Mark we may speak with confidence of a
literal translation Greek version of a parable of
Jesus.'/3/  These include: (v 4) καὶ ἐγένετο . . .
ἔπεσεν ;  (v 4) ἐν τῷ σπείρειν ;/4/  (v 7) καρπόν. . .
ἔδωκεν ;  (v 8) ἐδίδου καρπόν ;/5/  (v 7) ἀνέβησαν ;
(v 8) ἀναβαίνοντα ;/6/  (v 8) ἐν . . . ἐν . . . ἐν ;/7/
and (vv 3,4,5,7,8) unexpected uses of the definite
article./8/  In addition, παρὰ τὴν ὁδόν  reflects the
ambiguity of    עַל אְרַח ,/9/ and there is not one
instance of a hypotactic aorist participle./10/  The
translation into Aramaic given by Black indicates the
key sounds to be laryngals and the sonant ר./11/

The occurrence of the Sower in each of the
synoptic gospels and the Gospel of Thomas, its
structure and content following patterns
characteristic of Jesus, and its language in Mark
giving strong evidence that it is a literal
translation from Aramaic all give support to the
authenticity of this parable.  But what stage of
Jesus' ministry does it reflect?

### The Place of the Parable of the Sower
### in Jesus' Ministry

The parable of the Sower seems to reflect a
period in Jesus' ministry when Jesus anticipated or
He and His disciples faced discouragement.  According
to the gospels, these discouragements were a result
of poor response to Jesus' message about the Kingdom
of God.  There were times when some of Jesus'
followers left Him.  John pictures a dwindling of
Jesus' popularity when 'many of His disciples drew
back and no longer went about with Him'(John 6:66)
and when 'even His brothers did not believe in Him'
(John 7:5)./12/  A similar reaction seems to be
described preceeding the Sower.  Mark 3:21 tells that
His friends "went out to seize Him, for they said,
'He is beside himself.'", and 3:31 includes even His
mother and brothers.  All the synoptic gospels tell
of rejection of Jesus in His own country, Nazareth./13/
The reliability of these accounts is high since

events derogatory to the disciples and family would not be expected in later additions to the gospel tradition. As well as describing those who turned away from following Jesus, all the gospels describe immediate rejection and growing opposition from certain groups, notably religious leaders such as the Sanhedrin, Pharisees, priests and scribes.

The unfruitfulness of seeds on the path, in rocky areas, and among thorns gives an apt picture of various ways people were responding inadequately to Jesus' message. But by highlighting the abundant fruitfulness of the good soil, the realistic parable is hopeful and encouraging in tone. It reflects the confidence Jesus had in the blessing of God on His ministry. Discouragements did not destroy His trust.

'Devoured', 'scorched' and 'choked' may depict the tragic destiny of those who rejected Jesus' message, contrasting sharply with the hopeful prospect of fruitfulness. The Sower seems to be able either to warn or to encourage, like the double-edged Hebrew prophecies of judgment and blessing, judgment to those who reject and blessing to those who receive the prophetic word. Such a combination of judgment and blessing was typical of Jesus' contrast parables, eschatological blessing for those who are prepared and receive God's invitation aright, judgment for those who do not. This occurs in the parables of the Men Awaiting their Master's Homecoming, the Two Houses, the Tares among the Wheat, the Dragnet, the Unmerciful Servant, the Marriage Feast, the Great Supper, the Servant Entrusted with Supervision, the Ten Virgins, the Pounds, the Talents, the Closed Door, the Rich Man and Lazarus, and the Pharisee and the Publican. Whether in fact these parables became to any particular hearer a threat or a promise depended on how he responded to it. They are all challenges to respond properly to Jesus' message.

To those who were rejecting Jesus' message outright, like many of the scribes (Mark 2:16; 3:21,22,30), Pharisees (Mark 2:16,18,24; 3:2,5,6), Herodians (Mark 3:2,5,6), and Sadducees (Mark 12:18), the Sower warned implicitly that they were losing something of great potential. As the path did not

receive seed at all, but birds devoured it, these men
are depicted as being totally unresponsive and even
hostile to Jesus' proclamation.

The crowds welcomed Jesus' teaching,/14/ but
often flocked to Him out of curiosity (Mark 3:8), for
healing (Mark 3:10), or for free food (Mark 6:37-44 &
parallels;  8:1-9 & parallels;  John 6:26);  and many
had no depth of commitment to Jesus or to the Kingdom
(as οἱ ἔξω in Mark 4:11, cf. v 34).  To them the
Sower could have been a warning not to lose interest
and find their eagerness withered.  They were like
thin soil in which seeds sprouted but were scorched
by the sun and withered away.

Those who had begun to follow Jesus, even His
friends (Mark 3:21), family (Mark 3:31), and
disciples (Mark 14:10-13), could have found this
parable an appropriate warning not to be distracted
from the life of the Kingdom by concerns which could
choke out their fruitfulness.  They could easily
become like the thorny soil.

Finally, there were those whose response was
faithful, like the twelve whom Jesus appointed and is
recorded to have sent out to preach and have authority
to cast out demons./15/  These did the will of God
(Mark 3:35).  They, as the good earth, were proving
fruitful.  To all who would respond in this way the
Sower offered the hope of rich fruitfulness.

### The Interpretation:  Mark 4:13-20

Although the authenticity of the interpretation
of the parable of the Sower is usually denied by
critical scholars,/16/ its congruity with the parable
is generally acknowledged./17/  Paralleling the major
focus of the parable, which is a contrast between the
unfruitful reception of seed on various types of poor
soil and the fruitful reception of good soil, it
gives examples of how people were receiving Jesus'
message, contrasting the loss of the unfruitful with
the bountiful fruitfulness of the truly receptive.

The major objections to the authenticity of the
interpretation are:

1. Explanation is inappropriate to parables.
2. Jesus did not use allegory.
3. Most of Jesus' parables have no interpretation; therefore this one probably did not.
4. It is inconsistent with itself.
5. Its vocabulary reflects a later period.
6. Its style is not Hebraic.
7. It presupposes a situation in the early church's experience.
8. Its concentration on losses destroys the balance of the parable.
9. It misses the original eschatological focus on the amazing harvest.

Each of these objections, however, seems to warrant re-examination.

### 1. Is explanation inappropriate to parables?

The alleged instant clarity of parables was not a requirement of מְשָׁלִים./18/  Examples of detailed allegorical interpretation are listed in Str-B I,664-65.  Explanation can be helpful, particularly when the reality referred to is largely unknown to the hearers, as was the Kingdom as Jesus proclaimed it. Explanation could be especially helpful for this parable since it deals with the importance of proper reception of Jesus' message,/19/  in effect setting the foundation for understanding any of Jesus' parables.

### 2. Is it true that Jesus did not use allegory?

Jeremias was incorrect to say that Mark 4:14-20 "interpreted each detail allegorically.'/20/  The interpretation does not explain the sower, the path, the rocky ground, or the 30- and 60- and 100-fold; and the root and fruit are repeated without being identified.  Similar degrees of allegorical interpretation are found in Rabbinic parables and the OT, so this objection is not a solid basis for rejecting authenticity./21/  The omission of the interpretation from the Gospel of Thomas seems insignificant because of its theological bias favoring omission of explanations and because of the indications that its version is secondary.  Since some scholars point to this omission as the main textual evidence against the authenticity of Mark 4:13-20, the parable of the Sower in the Gospel of

Thomas is considered in detail in the appendix to
this article.

The most questioned part of the semi-
allegorical interpretation in Mark is that birds are
used to depict Satan. D. Via asked, 'Could any
hearer have surmised from the story itself that the
birds who ate the seed (4:4) really represent Satan
(4:15)?'/22/ An examination of the range of meaning
of 'birds' in the OT and Judaism, however, reveals
that its connotations were predominantly negative.
The same word as in Mark 4:4, κατέσθειν , 'to
devour', is used in the LXX of birds plundering
people's corpses (3 Kgs 14:11 A; 12:24 B; 16:4;
20:24 A), baked food (Gen 40:17), and fruit from
vines and fig trees (Hos 2:14). Rabbinic literature
commonly pictures birds as robbers./23/

Birds are the instruments of Satan or Mastema in
what seems to be the closest Jewish parallel to birds
devouring seed in the process of sowing, Jub. 11:
5-24./24/ In the Apocalypse of Abraham XIII the
fallen archangel Azazel (or Satan, cf. XIV, XXIII,
XXXI) descends in the form of an unclean bird./25/
Satan is identified with a bird by R. Joḥanan in
Sanhedrin 107a: 'Now Bath Sheba was cleansing her
hair behind a screen, when Satan came to him [David],
appearing in the shape of a bird. He shot an arrow
at him, which broke the screen, thus she stood
revealed, and he saw her.'/26/ A similar suggestion
can be seen in Rev 18:2, 'Fallen, fallen is Babylon
the great. It has become a dwelling place of demons,
a haunt of every foul and hateful bird.' Here, the
use of 'demons', 'foul spirit', and 'foul and hateful
bird' in parallel shows that they were associated in
thought together. As the Holy Spirit could be
pictured as a dove, so it was natural to depict the
action of evil spirits with birds' evil actions.

In the parable of the Sower just such an evil
action is pictured. Thus, in first century Palestine
the interpretation of birds as Satan could be natural
and not artificial as one might think today when
birds have a more positive connotative range.
Furthermore, a reference to Satan as hindering Jesus'
message is consistent with Mark's presentation of

Jesus.  Prior to the Sower in Mark, Jesus' ministry
is depicted in conflict with Satan (1:13;  3:22-27)
and unclean spirits (1:23-27,32-34,39;  3:11-12).

### 3.  Is it true that most of Jesus' parables have no interpretation?

Although this is commonly assumed, the fact is
that as well as the parables with a detailed point
by point interpretation:
  The Sower (Mark 4:3-9,13-20;  Matt 13:3-9,18-23;
            Luke 8:5-8,11-15)
  The Tares among the Wheat  (Matt 13:24-30,37-43)
  The Dragnet  (Matt 13:47-48,49-50)
  The Good Shepherd  (John 10:1-5,6-16,26-28),
many have an interpretation corresponding closely to
the parable narrative:
  The Divided House  (Mark 3:23-26;  Matt 12:25-28;
            Luke 11:17-20)
  The Budding Fig Tree  (Mark 13:28-29;  Matt 24:32-
            33;  Luke 21:29-31)
  The Children in the Marketplace  (Matt 11:16-19)
  The Two Sons  (Matt 21:28-32)
  The Burglar  (Matt 24:43-44;  Luke 12:39-40)
  The Unjust Judge  (Luke 18:1-8)
  Childbirth  (John 16:21-22).
Furthermore, a summary interpretation is given for
each of the following parables:
  The Doorkeeper  (Mark 13:33-37)
  The Lost Sheep  (Matt 18:12-14;  Luke 15:4-7)
  The Unforgiving Servant (Matt 18:23-35)
  The Friend Asked for Help at Night (Luke 11:5-8)
  The Rich Fool  (Luke 12:16-21)
  The Men Awaiting their Master's Homecoming  (Luke
            12:35-38,40)
  The Closed Door  (Luke 13:24-30)
  The Choice of Places at Table  (Luke 14:7-11)
  The Tower Builder  (Luke 14:28-30,33)
  The King Contemplating a Campaign  (Luke 14:31-33)
  The Lost Coin  (Luke 15:8-10)
  The Shrewd Steward  (Luke 16:1-13)
  The Servant's Reward  (Luke 17:7-10)
  The Pharisee and the Tax Collector  (Luke 18:9-14)
  The Grain of Wheat  (John 12:24-26).
Most of the rest of Jesus' recorded parables have
some sort of interpretive comment such as, 'The

Kingdom of God is like unto . . .' or 'So shall it
be with this generation.' We see that the parables
of Jesus as recorded in the gospels contain a whole
range of interpretations from brief to detailed. To
say that Jesus did not give interpretations to His
parables or did so only rarely flies flat in the face
of the testimony of each of the gospels as well as
explicit statements about Jesus interpreting His
parables (e.g. Mark 4:10-13,34; Matt 13:10-18,36,51;
15:15-20; Luke 8:9-11; John 10:6-7).

### 4. Is Mark 4:13-20 really inconsistent with itself?

The authenticity of Mark 4:13-20 as dominical is
frequently doubted on the ground that it is
inconsistent, identifying both the word and groups of
people with the seed which is sown./27/ A simple
explanation of this seeming inconsistency is that the
οἱ σπειρόμενοι phrases may not identify hearers with
seed, but rather serve as a general formula to tie
that section of the interpretation to the revelant
section of the parable./28/ Usually when Mark's
seeming inconsistency is excused it is on the valid
grounds that both Semitic and Rabbinic parables are
characterized by a lack of concern for logical
consistency. In fact, a similar shift in usage
occurs in Col. 1:6 and 10, where the metaphor of
'bearing fruit and growing' is applied first to the
gospel and then to believers. The similarity of this
passage and Mark 4:14-20 in terminology, shift in
metaphorical usage, and focus on proper reception of
the word (Col 1:5-12) may indicate that Paul before
the writing of the gospels was familiar with the
parable of the Sower and its interpretation. 4 Ezra
also pictures as seed both men sown by God (8:41) and
God's word (9:31).

It is possible that this seeming shift in usage
in the interpretation of the Sower is not
necessitated by the Greek of Mark, influenced as it
is at many points by Aramaic style, but arises from a
failure on our part to understand the way in which
that Greek was intended. Maldonatus explained the
passage in such a way as to avoid its apparent
inconsistency, 'The expression, "is sown", may refer
either to seed which is sown or to soil which is

sown. Here it more naturally applies to the soil in
which seeds are sown. Therefore, the one who hears
the word of the kingdom and does not understand it,
is described not as seed sown but as soil.'/29/  This
evaluation of Mark's intention is conveyed in the
translation of Mark 4:16,18, and 20 in the JB and NEB,
'who receive seed', and the NASB, 'on whom seed was
sown', which takes σπειρόμενοι as an elliptical
expression for 'sown [with seed]'.

The reason why these versions translated
σπειρόμενοι 'received seed' is that this usage of σπείρω
is particularly appropriate to the context, a parable
and interpretation about reception of the word.  The
groups of people who are said to 'be sown' are
associated throughout the interpretation with the
soils:  'These are the ones along the path where the
word is sown . . . the word which is sown in them'
(4:15).  They are said to hear (4:15,16,18,20),
receive (4:16), and accept (4:20) the word.  It is
the word which is equated with seed (4:14,15,16,18,
19,20).  In each of the three instances where the
Greek would seem to favor understanding 'those who
were sown' as identifying the people with the seed
which was sown (4:16,18,20), the text immediately
speaks of their hearing and receiving the word, an
abrupt and awkward incongruity.

Yet the prepositions ἐπί and εἰς in Mark 4:16,
18,20 usually, though not necessarily,/30/ suggest
motion and so are more appropriate to seed than to
soil.  Hence, when σπειρόμενοι is linked with these
prepositional phrases, the groups of people are
naturally associated with seed, contrary to the
analogy which the interpretation develops.  It would
be natural for readers of Mark to associate σπειρόμενοι
with seeds for a further reason as well.  The use of
σπείρω with soil as object seems to have been
infrequent in first century Greek.  References in
classical Greek to sowing a field are listed by LSJ
from the seventh to the early third century B.C., and
Moulton-Milligan gives examples from papyri of the
second and third centuries A.D.  But the scarcity of
σπείρω with soil as object in the first century A.D.
is indicated in its non-occurrence elsewhere in the

NT and BAG. Of the eighty-three occurrences of σπείρω
in Philo listed by Leisegang, only one clearly
specifies land being sown./31/

Words equivalent to σπείρω with soil as object
are common, however, in Aramaic and Hebrew/32/
literature as in English. ‏זְרַע‎ is used in the
passive to describe soil being sown in Deut 21:4 Tg.
Ps.-J. and Tg. Onq. (unless ‏ב‎ is transferred
elliptically); Deut 29:22(23 MT) Tg. Onq. (unless ‏ב‎
is transferred elliptically); Jer 2:2 Tg. Ps.-J.;
and Ezek 36:9 Tg. Ps.-J.. ‏זְרַע‎ is used as an active
verb to depict the sowing of soil, which is
introduced with the sign of the direct object, ‏יָת‎ in
Gen 47:23 Tg. Onq., Tg. Ps.-J., and Tg. Neof.
(marginal variant); Exod 23:10 Tg. Neof., Tg. Onq.,
and Tg. Ps.-J.; and Isa 30:23 Tg. Ps.-J. Other
active uses of ‏זְרַע‎ with soil are found in Lev 19:19
Tg. Neof., Tg. Onq., and Tg. Ps.-J.; Lev 25:3,4
Tg. Onq. and Tg. Ps.-J.; Judg 9:45 Tg. Ps.-J. (with
double accusative, 'sowed it [the city] with salt');
and Ps 107:37 (Lagardiana Recension of the Targum).

In each of the Targum references to soil being
sown, "with seed" is not stated but is implied. If
Mark 4:16,18 and 20 follow this Aramaic pattern,
'the ones sown' would imply 'with seed', and the
awkward shift would be eliminated of people being
compared first with soils and later with seed.

This is one of several clues that, as with the
parable of the Sower so with its interpretation,
there may have been an underlying Aramaic tradition.
Such an underlying tradition might account for the
problematic use of 'those who were sown' in Mark 4:
16,18 and 20. In light of the major parallels a
possible Aramaic source behind Mark 4:16 may be
hypothetically reconstructed, transliterating the Old
Syriac and Peshitta into square characters:/33/
Mark 4:16 καὶ οὗτοί εἰσιν ὁμοίως/34/οἱ ἐπὶ τὰ πετρώδη σπειρόμενοι, οἳ ὅταν...
Old Syriac:      ‏דעל שוע הינון אנון דמר‎   ‏הינון‎
'Those on the rock, those are they who when..[no 'sown]
Peshitta  :     ‏הינון דעל שוע אדרעו: ומא‎
'Those who on the rock were sown, these are they who..!
Aramaic(?):     /35/‏וכד‎ ‏:הינון אנון דעל שוע דאזדרעו‎
'Those are they on/36/the rock who were sown, and when!

The grammatical difference between the Peshitta (and
the Greek) and the proposed Aramaic may be diagrammed
as follows:

Peshitta:     Those | are \ they
(and Greek)                \who | were sown
                                 \on patches of rock

Aramaic:     Those | are \ they
                         on patches of rock
                         who | were sown

The difference between these two diagrams is that in
the proposed Aramaic 'on patches of rock' (suggesting
motion when modifying 'were sown') no longer modifies
'were sown'. Thus, 'were sown' can appropriately
refer to soil.

The syntax of the proposed Aramaic original
supports a focus on soil receiving seed, since if it
were intended with focus on seed as being cast onto
soil it would be more natural to use only one
relative pronoun as in the Peshitta, ܙܪܥܝܢ ܐܝܠܝܢ
The sense of Mark 4:16 in Aramaic would be: 'Those
are they on the rock who are sown (i.e. receive seed),
and when they hear the word, immediately receive it
with joy.'

The present Greek text: οἱ ἐπὶ τὰ πετρώδη σπειρόμενοι,
οἱ ὅταν . . . ('those-sown-on-the-rocky-ground, who,
when . . .') could have resulted through a single
natural scribal shift from an original Markan text,
still reflected in the Codex Vaticanus, which
followed the proposed Aramaic more closely: οἱ ἐπὶ τὰ
πετρώδη, οἱ /37/ σπειρόμενοι, /38/ ὅταν /39/ ἀκούσωσιν . . .
('those-on-the-rocky-ground, who being sown, when
they hear . . .'). The relative pronoun οἱ preceding
σπειρόμενοι removes any necessity of linking σπειρόμενοι
with a preposition of motion (ἐπί or εἰς) and allows
'those who were sown' to be analogous with the soil
rather than seed.

The present thesis, that the seeming
inconsistency of the Greek of Mark 4:16,18 and 20 may
simply be due to our misunderstanding of Mark's
translation from Aramaic, does not depend on the
textual reconstruction just given. The Greek text of
Mark exactly as it stands may have been Mark's (or

his tradition's) rendering of an oral or written
Aramaic original similar to that proposed.  Although
superficially σπειρόμενοι in Mark 4:16 seems to be a
fairly literal translation of the proposed Aramaic,
it muddles the original analogy because, once in
Greek, it becomes unidiomatic and would no longer
suggest that soil is being sown.  Such clumsiness
seems to be typical of Mark's style, translating
Aramaic idiom fairly literally without sensitivity to
the shifted nuance it may carry in Greek./40/

The textual variations indicate three things
that certain of the coypists recognized which support
the original association of σπειρόμενοι with  soils,
an association clouded in Mark 4:16,18,20.  First is
a focus on personal reception of the word as seen in
the variant οἷς in Mark 4:15 and the variants of εἰς
αὐτούς in Mark 4:15./41/  Second is a recognition of
four parallel situations depicted by the four soils
(analogous to four types of reception of the word).
There is strong manuscript evidence for the inclusion
of ὁμοίως in 4:16, and the introduction of οὗτοι in
4:18 and 20 reinforced the parallelism./42/  Third is
awareness of the incongruity in the Greek text caused
by σπειρόμενοι which identifies people with seed and
breaks the patterned symbolism of seed as word and
soil as people.  This is seen in the omission of
σπειρόμενοι in the Old Syriac and Luke, who with his
more fluent Greek, was more likely than Mark to
recognize this incongruity./43/

Lest it be thought that a shift from seed to
soil as the object of σπείρω in such close proximity
is unlikely, exactly the same shift is made in the MT
and LXX of Leviticus, where we find the shift from
25:3,4 (soil) to 25:11,20 (seed) to 25:22
(unspecified) to 26:16 (seed), and in the MT and LXX
of Exodus, where we have 23:10 (soil) and 23:16
(seed).

The conclusion of this study is that the seeming
inconsistency in the Greek of Mark 4:16,18 and 20 may
simply be due to our misunderstanding of Mark's
Greek, affected as it is by his Aramaic background.
Our trouble comes when we try to interpret Mark's
literal translation from Aramaic according to strict

rules of Greek grammar. $\sigma\pi\epsilon\iota\rho\acute{o}\mu\epsilon\nu o\iota$ in these verses was probably intended by Mark to suggest <u>soil</u> being sown with seed just as the context demands and as a literal Aramaic rendering would have suggested.

### 5.  Does the vocabulary of Mark 4:13-20 reflect a later period?

Jeremias affirmed, 'This interpretation must be ascribed to the primitive Church . . . on linguistic grounds alone it is unavoidable.'/44/  He bases this affirmation on nine words or word usages occurring in Mark 4:13-20 which do not occur elsewhere in the teaching of Jesus recorded in the Synoptic gospels but which he claims to be common in the rest of the NT and on a few other words which occur only once elsewhere in the Synoptics.

The conclusiveness, however, of such verbal statistics has often been questioned, since it depends so much on the subject matter at hand, the audience, the mood of the speaker, and the freedom which may have been taken by the translator. Humphrey Palmer has shown that valid statistics demand a large control group which can only be achieved with words of high frequency, unlike those cited by Jeremias./45/  In any event, the corpus of Jesus' sayings is far too limited for any scholar to determine what words would not have been appropriate to Him on linguistic grounds, particularly after parallel accounts are excluded and when the freedom of various translators is taken into account.

The unreliability of Jeremias' statistical criterion is evident in its application to the parable of the Sower, a pericope which is almost universally affirmed as authentic to Jesus.  Eight terms occur in the Sower which apart from their occurrence in the parable and its interpretation, are absent elsewhere either from the Synoptic record ($\pi\epsilon\tau\rho\tilde{\omega}\delta\epsilon\varsigma$, $\dot{\epsilon}\xi\alpha\nu\alpha\tau\acute{\epsilon}\lambda\lambda\omega$, $\kappa\alpha\nu\mu\alpha\tau\acute{\iota}\zeta\omega$, $\kappa\alpha\rho\pi\grave{o}\nu$ $\delta\acute{\iota}\delta\omega\mu\iota$, and $\check{\epsilon}\nu$ or $\dot{\epsilon}\nu$ or $\epsilon\grave{\iota}\varsigma$ used with a numeral to mean '-fold') or from the teaching of Jesus ($\sigma\nu\mu\pi\nu\acute{\iota}\gamma\omega$, $\tau\rho\iota\acute{\alpha}\kappa o\nu\tau\alpha$, $\dot{\epsilon}\xi\acute{\eta}\kappa o\nu\tau\alpha$).  Apart from these, $\beta\acute{\alpha}\theta o\varsigma$ occurs elsewhere in the Synoptics only once (Luke 5:4), $\acute{o}$ $\sigma\pi\epsilon\acute{\iota}\rho\omega\nu$ twice (Matt 13:37,39), and $\kappa\alpha\tau\epsilon\sigma\theta\acute{\iota}\omega$ in two other sayings (Mark 12:40 & parallels and Luke 15:30).  And

elsewhere in the sayings of Jesus $ρίζα$ occurs only
once (Matt 3:10 = Luke 3:9) and $ἀνατέλλω$ twice (Matt
5:45 and Luke 12:54). Statistics such as these and
Jeremias' do little more than reflect how limited the
corpus of Jesus' teaching is.

Jeremias ascribed the interpretation of the
Sower to the early church because most of the words
in it which are unique in the teaching of Jesus occur
several times elsewhere in the NT. The occurrence,
however, of so many specialized word usages both in
the interpretation and in church tradition does not
in itself establish the direction of dependence, if
there is any. Such an extensive overlap in word
usage might favor the authenticity of Mark 4:14-29
since Jesus' teaching was likely to affect church
terminology. In any event, it is natural that the
translation of Jesus' teaching into Greek in the
church community would use 'church vocabulary' where
that vocabulary faithfully expressed Jesus' teaching.
Greek vocabulary statistics cannot determine the
authenticity of Jesus' Aramaic sayings. Moreover, in
order to compare word frequencies, the size of the
two corpuses being questioned must be taken into
account. The Synoptic teaching of Jesus is not
nearly as extensive as the rest of the NT. This
factor is omitted from Jeremias' discussion.

The major linguistic stumbling block to the
authenticity of Mark 4:13-20 is its use of 'the word'.
Jeremias alleges that 'the use of $ὁ λόγος$ absolutely
is a technical term for the gospel coined and
constantly used by the primitive Church; this
absolute use of $ὁ λόγος$ by Jesus only occurs in the
interpretation of the parable of the Sower.'/46/
Although Jeremias shows that the absolute use of
$ὁ λόγος$ for the gospel is frequent outside the
sayings of Jesus, his assertion that it was 'coined'
by the early church is undemonstrated. And by
stating 'the use . . . constantly used' he gives the
impression that the absolute use of $ὁ λόγος$ always
refers to the gospel, when in fact it does not.
Excluding Mark 4:13-20, Mark uses $ὁ λόγος$ absolutely
four times referring to a specific message and only
twice referring to Jesus' message in general./47/
Even when $ὁ λόγος$ does refer to the gospel, 'the

gospel' may be understood in a variety of senses.
The meaning which became common in the church, i.e.
ὁ λόγος as the content of church preaching, does not
occur at all in Mark./48/  Each of Mark's uses of
ὁ λόγος absolutely referring to the gospel has the
meaning of Jesus' proclamation of the Kingdom.

Jeremias continues by alleging:
the fact that in this short passage a number of
sayings about 'the Word' occur, which are not
found elsewhere in the teaching of Jesus, but on
the other hand are common in the apostolic age:
the preacher preaches the word;  the word is
received, and that with joy;  persecution arises
on account of the word, the word is a cause of
stumbling, the word 'grows', the word brings
forth fruit./49/
But the sayings 'the preacher preaches the word' and
'the word grows' do not occur in Mark 4:13-20.  Of
the other sayings Jeremias mentions, most of his
examples either have no reference to λόγος or λόγος
is not in the absolute./50/  The sum total of all the
occurrences of these sayings throughout the rest of
the NT is only three:  Acts 17:11;  1 Thes 1:6;  and
1 Pet 2:8.  This is hardly 'common'.

Jesus may have interpreted the Sower with an
initial reference to seed as 'the word of the
Kingdom' as in Matt 13:19./51/  It would be natural
for Him to use an abbreviated form such as 'the word'
in its following occurrences (5 in Matthew, 7 in
Mark and 3 in Luke).  When in the course of tradition
the meaning of ὁ λόγος became established, it could
easily be substituted for the initial 'the word of
the Kingdom' to make all the occurrences uniform, as
is the case in Mark and Luke.

Of the eight remaining words which Jeremias says
'do not occur elsewhere in the Synoptists, but . . .
are common in the rest of the New Testament
literature, especially in Paul,'/52/ four develop the
imagery of the parable: σπείρειν , ῥίζα , ἄκαρπος ,
καρποφορεῖν ;  and two others reflect an event in the
parable: παραδέχεσθαι , πρόσκαιρος ./53/  Jeremias
claims that πρόσκαιρος is 'a Hellenism, for which
there is no corresponding adjective in Aramaic.'/54/

But Cranfield noted that 'there is a Syriac adjective
zabnaya="temporary", "transient"';/55/   C. F. D. Moule
added that 'the Peshitta . . . represents πρόσκαιρος
by dzbn', "temporary";'/56/  and J. Bowker added that
the Aramaic qzr 'catches the nuance of being before
one's time, of being short-lived or transitory.'/57/
All of the words challenged by Jeremias occur in the
LXX, and πλοῦτος is the only word common in the rest
of the NT./58/

A close examination of the vocabulary used in
Mark 4:13-20 does not seem to demand ascribing it to
the primitive church.  But as any discourse is
influenced by the vocabulary current in the language
in which it is written, the choice of particular
words may have followed usage current at the time the
interpretation was first written in Greek.  The
translation into Greek in the church community of
parables which Jesus originally said in Aramaic
allows quite naturally for 'church terminology' in an
authentic parable.

### 6.  Is the style of Mark 4:13-20 unhebraic?
It is false to say that the style of the
interpretation is not Hebraic in light of its
fourfold parallelism, the frequency of redundant
definite articles (4:15,16,18,20), the use of birds
symbolizing Satan, the awkward use of 'these are
those who were sown' (whether Semitic lack of concern
for consistency or as suggested above, the result of
translation from Aramaic), the uninterpreted
threefold ἐν, and the striking parataxis./59/

### 7.  Does Mark 4:13-20 presuppose a situation in the early church's experience?
It is hardly an objection that this interpreta-
tion could be applied profitably to the experiences
of the early church;  this can be said of almost all
of Jesus' teaching.  The content of Mark 4:13-20 is
appropriate to Jesus' situation.  He seems to have
expected some of His followers to fall away (cf.
Matt 7:21-22;  John 6:66) and to have envisaged
opposition to His ministry from Satan (cf. Mark 3:23-
27=Matt 12:26-29=Luke 11:17-22;  Luke 10:18-19;
13:16), persecution (cf. Mark 8:34-38;  Matt 5:10-12,
22;  10:17-25), the cares of this age (cf. Matt 6:

24-34; Luke 12:22-32), and the enticement of wealth
(cf. Mark 10:23-30; Luke 12:13-21,33-34; 16:19-31).

### 8. Does Mark 4:13-20 concentrate on losses, destroying the balance of the parable?

The charge that the concentration on losses
destroys the parable's balance may rise from not
observing the balance of the parable itself, a
fourfold depiction culminating in the fruitfulness of
the good earth. The same fourfold depiction and
culmination is found in the interpretation.

### 9. Does Mark 4:13-20 miss the (supposed) original focus on the amazing harvest?

Finally, the objection that the interpretation
misses the original eschatological focus on the
amazing harvest presupposes that the parable does
focus on an amazing harvest. But no mention of a
harvest ($\theta\epsilon\rho\iota\sigma\mu\acute{o}s$) or of a harvester occurs in the
parable, unlike the parables of the Seed Growing
Secretly (Mark 4:26-29) and the Tares among the Wheat
(Matt 13:24-30).

Jeremias, who viewed the parable as a contrast
parable contrasting small beginnings and big endings,
took v 8 to refer to the yield of the whole field.
However, in contrast to the three portions of seed
described in Mark 4:3-7, 4:8 highlights the growth
and fruitfulness of individual seeds. This is
evident in the plural $\mathring{\alpha}\lambda\lambda\alpha$ and the present plural
participles, $\mathring{\alpha}\nu\alpha\beta\alpha\acute{\iota}\nu o\nu\tau\alpha$ and $\alpha\mathring{\upsilon}\xi\alpha\nu\acute{o}\mu\epsilon\nu\alpha$. The focus
in 4:8 on the reception and growth of individual
seeds is maintained through the conclusion in which
some seeds are said to be in the process of bearing
($\mathring{\epsilon}\phi\epsilon\rho\epsilon\nu$) fruit, one seed thirtyfold, and ($\kappa\alpha\acute{\iota}$) one
sixtyfold, and ($\kappa\alpha\acute{\iota}$) one a hundredfold./60/ Such
fruitfulness per grain is realistic, unlike Jewish
descriptions of the eschatological harvest.

A lack of understanding, however, of the realism
of '30-fold, 60-fold, and 100-fold' yields per grain
has led many recent interpreters astray. A detailed
investigation is therefore warranted. Such
fruitfulness is good, but by no means impossible. It
would suggest the blessing of God as in Gen 26:12:
'Isaac sowed in that land, and reaped in the same

year a hundredfold.'  This is referred to in Ms.
Neofiti I as the blessing of the Lord.  Philo
commented:
> What is the meaning of the words, 'He sowed in
> that year and found hundredfold barley?' . . .
> there is prosperity both in agriculture and in
> other things pertaining to the life of the
> world, and that which comes afterwards is many
> times greater than that which was in the
> beginning, and is fulness./61/

Dalman supports the realism of yields up to one
hundredfold, 'Jesus bleibt im Gleichnis innerhalb des
als möglich Denkbaren'/62/ and '[100-fold] nicht
übertrieben scheint'./63/  His evaluation is that
this realistic bounty would have excited a strong
sense of 'den guten Ertrag des göttlichen Samens der
Botschaft von der Gottesherrschaft' in the unhindered
hearts of men./64/

Jeremias, however, says that the fruitfulness of
which the Sower speaks 'surpasses all prayer and
understanding . . . symbolizes the eschatological
overflowing of the divine fullness, surpassing all
human measure.'/65/  He equates this fruitfulness
with 'the abnormal yield of the soil in the Messianic
Age . . . depicted . . . in the OT and in the
Rabbinic and pseudepigraphical literature.'/66/  In
defence of this he claims, incorrectly, that Gen 26:
12 is eschatological./67/  Since his interpretation
is so widely accepted, the extravagance of this yield
demands close scrutiny.

Jeremias' position fails to recognize that
although the Sower reflects the OT hope that God
would bless the fruitfulness of the land in the
Messianic Age, it is not at all like the hyperbolic
expressions of fruitfulness in apocalyptic literature.
The fruitfulness of the land in God's rule at the end
of the days is a regular feature of the OT prophetic
exaggerated yields./68/  In contrast, the
pseudepigrapha and rabbinic writings describe the
Messianic Age as fantastically fertile.  For
instance, b. Ketub.   111b says, 'There will be no
grape that will not contain thirty kegs of wine', and
112a speaks of one se'ah producing 50,000 kor of

grain, 1,500,000-fold./69/  This kind of exaggeration
is followed by Papias as recorded in Iren. haer. v.
33.3-4:  'The days shall come wherein . . . a grain
of wheat shall bring forth ten thousand ears, and
every ear shall have ten thousand grains, and every
grain shall yield five double pounds of white clean
flour.'/70/  In contrast to such fantastic
eschatological imagery is the realistic possibility
of thirtyfold and sixtyfold and a hundredfold
mentioned in the Sower.

Jeremias' insistence that the focus lies on the
eschatological harvest of superabundance is further
weakened since a seed producing one hundredfold was
not only possible but was frequently recorded.  When
Dalman spoke of $7\frac{1}{2}$-fold yield common in Palestine
today, he was not referring to the most fruitful
parts of Palestine,/71/ as is evident from Table II.

Table II  Recent Yields of Wheat in Palestine/72/

| place | yield: | bad | normal | good | very good | maximum |
|-------|--------|-----|--------|------|-----------|---------|
| Hauran | | | 40-50X | 70-100X | | |
| Jordan Valley | | 10X | | | | 100X |
| Ramallah Hills | | | 10-30X | | 50X | |
| Hebron | | | 10X | | | |
| Ḥezma | | 2X | | 6-10X | 20X | |
| Plain of Jezreel | | | 6-8X | | | |
| West Country | | 2X | 7X | 12X | | 40X |

Thus, it was improper of Jeremias to refer to Dalman's
$7\frac{1}{2}$-fold figure as demonstrating the eschatological
nature of the yield in the Sower./73/  A. Jaussen
reported that although the soil is now poor, with
care it can give large returns and even with meager
labor produces 40- or 50-fold yields./74/  Likewise,
J. Sonnen reported that 'die Bestockung ist im
allgemeinen sehr stark.  Gewöhnlich sprossen aus
einem Korn 4-5 Halme;  da jede gut entwickelte Aehre
60-70 Körner enthält, so bringt also ein Korn 240-350
Körner.'/75/

It is difficult to be sure what was the normal
yield of wheat in Jesus' day.  Dalman and Jeremias
consider it to be $7\frac{1}{2}$-fold,/76/ but Dalman (earlier),
Sprenger, and Linnemann put it as 35-fold./77/  The
crucial passage for Dalman is b. B. Meṣ. 105b:

Said R. Judah:  What is a standard stack?  But
[the standard is] if there is enough for
resowing.  And how much is needed for resowing?
R. Ammi said in R. Joḥanan's name:  'Four
se'ahs per kor' [i.e. in an area where a kor
ought to grow, only four se'ahs grew, which is
the quantity needed for sowing such an area.]
R. Ammi, giving his own opinion, said:  'Eight
se'ahs per kor.  An old man said to R. Hama, son
of Rabbah b. Abbuha:  'I will explain it to you.
During R. Joḥanan's lifetime the land was
fertile [hence the lesser quantity sufficed];
during that of R. Ammi it was poor . . . The
poor must be given the measure for resowing. . .
4 kabs per kor./78/
There are 30 se'ahs to one kor and 6 kabs to one
se'ah./79/  Thus, in this one passage three rates
seem to be given, 7½-fold, 3¾-fold, and 45-fold.  The
discrepancy is probably due to the fertility of the
soil under consideration, as suggested in the
passage.  Fertility would vary with the location and
growing conditions, such as rainfall, in the area
under consideration.  In the OT bad yields of grain
are often described./80/

Beyond these reports of normal yields, there are
many of great yields.  Dalman records 82-fold and
104½-fold yields for entire fields./81/  Within a
field there would be variable productivity depending
on the individual plants and their soil.  In good
ground a sample of 19 plants had 82  stalks and 3000
grains, averaging a 158-fold yield.  But in stony
ground a sample of 23 plants had 48 stalks and 1000
grains, averaging 43½-fold.  And on a rock layer or
by thick thistles, he recorded only few, mostly weak
and unfruitful plants.  Dalman found that the average
yield in Tiberias from a grain was 5 stalks each with
60-70 grains each, or a yield of 300-350-fold, and
even 1000 grains yield was possible from one
plant./82/  The key to large productivity is that
plants have enough time to send up numerous side-
shoots, many of which may yield grain, as is frequent
among plants sown in autumn.  K. D. White records
that in many places this provides a 300-fold yield
from one seed./83/  J. Sonnen attested, 'Ich habe bei

Weizen aber schon 19 Halme auf einem Stock, also aus
einem Korn gezählt . . . 10-12 Halme kommen häufig
vor.'/84/  Dalman records that H. Auhagen reported
seeing in Hauran a barley plant with 30 stalks and
2100 kernels./85/

Great yields were also recorded in antiquity.
Pliny in <u>H.N.</u> XVIII.xxi.94-95 says:
Nothing is more prolific than wheat -- Nature
having given it this attribute because it used
to be her principal means of nourishing man --
inasmuch as a peck of wheat, given suitable
soil like that of the Byzacium plain in Africa,
produces a yield of 150 pecks . . . [He even
records] 400 shoots obtained from a single grain
of seed . . . [and] 360 stalks from one grain.
At all events the plains of Lentini and other
districts in Sicily;  and the whole of
Andalusia, and particularly Egypt reproduce at
the rate of a hundredfold.  The most prolific
kinds of wheat are branched wheat and what they
call hundred-grain wheat.
Varro (born in 116 B.C.) recorded yields of a
hundredfold near Gadara on the slopes of Mt. Gilead,
near Jesus' Galilean ministry (<u>De Re Rustica</u> I.44.2).
Theophrastus, <u>Historia Plantarum</u> VIII.7.4, reported of
corn in Babylon, 'if the ground is ill cultivated, it
produces fiftyfold, if it is carefully cultivated, a
hundredfold.'  Herodotus I.193 calls Babylon 'by far
the most fertile in corn . . . its corn is so
abundant that it yields for the most part 200-fold,
and 300-fold when the harvest is best.'  Strabo's
<u>Geography</u> XV.3.11 states that 'Suis abounds so
exceedingly in grain that both barley and wheat
regularly produce 100-fold, and sometimes even 200',
and XVI.1.14 notes that Armenia-Babylon 'produces
larger crops of barley than any other country
(bearing 300-fold, they say).'  <u>B. Ketub.</u>    112a
lists the maximum yield in Zoan in Egypt as 2100-fold
and records that R. Meir claimed to see a 2100-fold
yield in beth Shean, but these Rabbinic figures may
have been intentional hyperbole as suggested by their
apocalyptic context./86/

From such abundant evidence of the productivity
both now and in ancient Palestine, it can be said

that the variable yield per grain of seeds in the
Sower of 30- and 60- and 100-fold is not at all
fanciful, but would probably have suggested the
blessing of God in Jesus' day.

## Conclusion

None of the objections raised to the
authenticity of the parable of the Sower or of its
interpretation have been found upon close scrutiny to
be at all convincing. Both the parable of the Sower
and its interpretation in Mark 4:3-9,13-20 follow the
structure most typical of Jesus' parables (A. a
familiar setting, B. a pattern of response to that
setting in which each response is described in nearly
identical terminology, leading to C. the climax).
Both show many signs of translation from Aramaic, and
the message evident in the parable and its
interpretation is typical of Jesus' ministry, i.e.
how one responds to Jesus' message will determine his
destiny.

In the light of all the arguments and counter-
arguments adduced, it seems that both the parable of
the Sower and its interpretation are authentic to
Jesus; therefore, the commonly made generalization
that Jesus did not use allegory or give interpretations to His parables does not stand up under
investigation.

Appendix:    The Parable of the Sower in the Gospel of
             Thomas

     Since the discovery of the Gospel of Thomas
there has been much discussion concerning the
possibility that it contains early traditions
independent of the Synoptic gospels./87/ This
Sahidic Coptic gospel from Nag Hammadi should
probably be dated either in the second half of the
fourth century or in the beginning of the fifth
century A.D. It is a recension of the Gospel of
Thomas known from the P. Oxy. 1,654 and 655, dating
in their present form from about the end of the
second century or first quarter of the third century.
Estimates of the earliest redaction of the Gospel of
Thomas in Greek range from A.D. 140 to 200.

     The Gospel of Thomas displays a distinctively
gnostic perspective. As in Valentinian teaching
there is an underlying physical dualism and contempt
for the world and sex (Sayings 22,80,87,111,112,114).
Anthropological dualism is evident in statements
about human pre-existence, predestination, and the
importance of esoteric knowledge (Sayings 1,19,49,50).
The Gospel of Thomas calls men to turn inward to know
themselves (Sayings 58,67,69a) and realize an inward
salvation (Sayings 3,5b,58,69a). Often Synoptic
sayings seem to have been modified in the direction
of inwardness (Sayings 69a,113), and more frequently
such sayings appear to be later creations. The
Christology of the Gospel of Thomas tends to be
docetic and spiritual (Saying 77), and Jesus'
controversial debate is presented as teaching
(Sayings 26,31). The parables are never understood
eschatologically, 'but rather as admonitions to find
the mysterious treasure in Jesus' words and in one's
own self.'/88/ In keeping with the desire that the
interpretation of Jesus' sayings be hidden from all
except those of spiritual insight, allegorical
interpretations or other hints to the meaning of a
parable are rarely given./89/

     The secondary character of most of the Gospel of
Thomas has been increasingly recognized in the light
of evidence underlying the text of knowledge of Paul's
letters (Sayings 17,53) and John (Saying 77). It

includes all seven of the parables of Matthew 13
(Sayings 9,20,57,96,109,76,8) and certain readings
which seem secondary to parallel Synoptic accounts
(Sayings 8,76,96,107)./90/  Although parallels to
Matthew and Luke  predominate, most of the Gospel of
Thomas probably evolved from the Synoptics not
through conscious redaction but as a gnostic
community's oral tradition.

     Many scholars have supported the reliability of
the Gospel of Thomas as based on or incorporating a
tradition independent of the Synoptic gospels./91/
H. Koester even goes so far as to 'presuppose that
the parables of Thomas are not taken from the
synoptic gospels, but derive from an earlier stage of
the tradition of the synoptic parables.'/92/  Some of
the evidence adduced for this may be no more than
what arises from the gnostic viewpoint of the gospel:
the unique structure of the book, lack of apocalyptic
imagery, paucity of generalizing conclusions, and
the absence of allegorical interpretations to the
parables.  But the variation in order and re-grouping
of sayings,/93/ lack of parallel with many Synoptic
introductory phrases, unique content, and the
apparently primitive character of many of the
features of the Gospel of Thomas may not be entirely
the work of Gnostics.  There is also some evidence
for underlying Aramaisms,/94/ which has led some to
look for the roots of the sayings in a Jewish
Christian group or oral tradition.  A comparison of
P. Oxy. 1.6 (Gos. Thom. 31) with Mark 6:1-6 has shown
that support can be given for a primitive tradition
underlying this pericope of the Gospel of Thomas./95/

     However, where the unique features of the Gospel
of Thomas appear to follow its editorial slant, they
are probably not authentic to Jesus.  J. B.
Sheppard's analysis judged that
          in each instance where a parable of Thomas
          contains a reading which appears to be more
          primitive than that found in its synoptic
          counterpart, the reading found in the synoptic
          account of the parable is inappropriate for the
          message that Thomas seeks to convey, and there
          is evidence elsewhere in Thomas' account of that
          parable that alterations have been made to bring

the account into harmony with his message./96/
If his analysis is correct, it is not justified to
suppose that the parables of the Gospel of Thomas
depended on a tradition independent of the Synoptics.

Although most of the Gospel of Thomas is
probably secondary development of Synoptic material,
there may be isolated elements reflecting a primitive
tradition independent of the Synoptics.  In order to
evaluate this possibility, the Sower in Gos. Thom. 9
is examined in detail below.

Gos. Thom. 9 (82:3-13)/97/ Mark 4:2b-8
(____indicates additions
    to Mark 4)

| | |
|---|---|
| 3  Jesus said:  Behold, 4  the sower went forth, he filled his hand, 5  he cast.  Some fell upon the road; 6  the birds came and gathered them.  Others 7  fell on the rock, | he said to them:3 'Listen! A sower went out to sow. 4  And as he sowed some seed fell along the path, and the birds came and devoured it.  5  Other seed fell on rocky ground, where it had not much soil, and immediately it sprang up, since it had no depth of soil; 6  and when the sun rose it was scorched, and since it had no root it withered away. |
| and sent no root down 8  to the earth, nor did they sprout any ear up to heaven.  9  And others fell on the thorns; 10  they choked the seed, and the worm ate them. 11  And others fell on the good earth 12  and brought forth good fruit unto heaven, 13  some sixtyfold and some an hundred and twentyfold. | 7  Other seed fell among thorns and the thorns grew up and choked it, and it yielded no grain. 8  And other seeds fell into good soil and brought forth grain, growing up and increasing and yielding thirtyfold and sixtyfold and a hundredfold.' |

Both of these versions of the Sower present a
fourfold reception of seed, only the fourth being
fruitful, and that abundantly fruitful.

'He filled his hand' (82:4) reflects a tendency
of the Gospel of Thomas to embellish with addition of
'hand', as in Saying 17 (embellishing 2 Cor 2:9) and
Saying 41, 'Whoever has in his hand, to him shall be
given' (embellishing Matt 13:12 & parallels)./98/  A
similar expression is found in the Pap. Egerton 2 1 1.
67-68, καὶ ἐκτείνα[ς τὴν] χεῖ[ρα αὐτο]ῦ τὴν δεξιὰν [ἐγέ]μισεν.

'He cast' (82:5) may simply be equivalent to
'and as he sowed' (Mark 4:4) as in 1 Clem. xxiv.5,
ἐξῆλθεν ὁ σπείρων καὶ ἔβαλεν εἰς τὴν γῆν ἕκαστον τῶν σπερμάτων....
But it may have been used in Gos. Thom. 82:5 since a
γεωργός casting σπέρμα on the earth is a well known
picture in non-Christian Gnosis, as in Corpus
Hermeticum xiv.10, ἴδε γεωργὸν σπέρμα καταβάλλοντα εἰς τὴν γῆν./99/
Another possibility that has been suggested is that
'The sower went forth, he filled his hand, he cast'
could reflect a semitizing asyndeton./100/

'Upon the road' (82:5) might be a translation of
an original Aramaic אָרְחָא לְ which can mean either
'upon' or 'beside' the road.  A similar reading to
'upon' is given in Justin Martyr's Dialogue with
Trypho 125 ( εἰς τὴν ὁδόν ),/101/ the Syriac
translation of the pseudo-Clementine Recognitions
III,14,7, the Arabic and Syriac versions of the
Diatessaron of Tatian, and Heliand 2388./102/  It has
been argued that all of these would not have
independently corrected the unanimous testimony of
the Synoptic gospels and the Syriac versions, but
rather may represent with the Gospel of Thomas a
tradition independent of the Synoptics./103/  Quispel
notes over 100 parallels between the Gospel of Thomas
and the Diatessaron at points where they differ from
the canonical gospels./104/  Heliand 2388 shows many
affinities with Gos. Thom. 9 where it diverges from
the Synoptics:
> A man began to sow on the earth (pure) corn
> with his hands.  Some fell down on hard stone,
> it did not have earth, that it might grow there
> and take root, germ and stick . . . Some,
> however, fell on a hard road, where the beat of
> horses' shoes and the pace of heroes have
> trodden it;  and the birds collected it./105/
Such close resemblances indicate some sort of
relationship, but whether that relationship is

through a primitive tradition independent of the
Synoptics is far from established. The reliability
of the sources adduced is in doubt./106/ The changes
are a natural development of the Synoptic tradition,
Luke being intermediate between Mark and the Gospel
of Thomas./107/ In particular, the Coptic of the
Gospel of Thomas for 'upon the road' is a perfectly
natural translation of the Synoptic's παρὰ τὴν ὁδόν./108/
In fact, a few minuscules (28,33,569) and lectionaries
(49,184,251,260) have substituted ἐπί for παρά .

The use of the plural for seed throughout Gos.
Thom. 9 is paralleled in variant mss. of Mark and Luke
and hence is explicable from the Synoptic tradition.

The variant 'the birds gathered' (82:6) instead
of 'devoured' the seed is also found in one version
of the Diatessaron, indicating that it was part of a
tradition current in Syria in the second century./109/
'Gathered' may have been substituted in oral
tradition for 'devoured' as the shift does not change
the meaning significantly.

The description of seed falling on 'rock' (82:7)
is similar to Luke 8:6, which may have been its
source.

'Sent no root down to the earth, nor did they
sprout any ear up to heaven' (82:7-8) and 'good fruit
unto heaven' (82:12) seem to be typically gnostic
expressions. Gos. Truth 28,16 says, 'he who has no
root also has no fruit.' The contrast between 'down
to earth' and 'up to heaven' may 'be a reference to
the heavenward ascent of the soul of the true
gnostic.'/110/ This is supported by the symbolical
use of 'roots' in Gnosticism for spiritual growth
(Gos. Truth 28,16 and 42,34-35) and 'raising ears to
heaven' in the Mysteries for the quest of God./111/
It is also possible that the reference to 'sprout any
ear up to heaven' may simply have been transferred
from Mark 4:28 or from Isa 37:31's 'take root
downward, and bear fruit upward.'

'And the worm ate them' (82:10) is probably an
embellishment since the worm does not fit the scheme
of the parable, which is about types of soil; a worm

could belong to any type of soil.  There is a similar
addition in Saying 76, 'where no moth comes near to
devour and no worm destroys'.  This may have
suggested the worm of Gehenna, as in Mark 9:48 &
parallels.

'Good' fruit (82:12), too, looks like a typical
embellishment as in Gos. Thom. 8 'a large good fish',
57 'good seed', 65 'good man', 96 'large loaves',
and 107 'the largest' sheep.

The increased yield, sixtyfold and a hundred
and twentyfold (82:13) also looks like an
embellishment./112/

The Sower was probably expounded in the
community of the Gospel of Thomas as a picture of the
growth of the true gnosis as described in various
sources to gnostic thought:  Gos. Truth 28,7-18;
Gos. Philip 8 (100,32-33); Das Johannesbuch der
Mandäer;/113/  Sophia Jesu Christi 104,13-105,3,
'that he might bear pure fruit . . . from Wisdom',
cf. 122,12-14;  Acts of Andrew 12;  Hipp. haer.
V,8,30, 'the meaning of this, he says is as follows,
that none becomes a hearer of these mysteries, except
only the perfect Gnostics';  Or. fg. in Matt 295
(GCS XII, 132), ὁ ἀληθῶς γνωστικὸς καὶ συνίησι καὶ
καρποφορεῖ εἰ δέ τις δοκεῖ συνιέναι μὴ καρποφορῶν, οὐ συνίησιν, καὶ εἰ
δοκεῖ καρποφορεῖν μὴ συνιείς, οὐ καρποφορᾷ The sower was probably
understood in most gnostic circles to be the Father,
as in Gos. Truth 36,35, 'He knows his seed, which he
sowed in his paradise.'/114/  The good earth
represents the Gnostic as in Hipp. haer. V,8,29-30;
Acts of Andrew 12;  and Ptolemaeus, Letter to Flora
7,10 (SC 24), 'receive the fertile seed like good
beautiful earth and give its issue, fruit.'

The overall impression is that Gos. Thom. 9 is
an edited form of the Synoptic tradition of the Sower
tending to follow the peculiar vocabulary and gnostic
ideas of the Gospel of Thomas./115/  Several of the
additions to the Synoptic version of the Sower show
signs of gnostic embellishment:  'he filled his hand,
he cast' (82:4), 'sent no root down to the earth, nor
did they sprout any ear up to heaven' (82:7-8), 'and
the worm ate them' (82:10), 'good fruit unto heaven'

(82:11), and 'an hundred and twentyfold' (82:12).
The remaining additions are explicable as a
development of the Synoptic tradition of the Sower:
'upon' (82:5), the references to seed in the plural
(82:6,9,10,11), 'rock' (82:7), and possibly
'gathered' (82:6). The variant 'gathered' does not
seem to be motivated by gnostic thought and appears
to have been in Tatian's _Diatessaron_, indicating that
this variant was probably current in Christian
tradition in Syria in the second century. This and
the other variants which have been given only
tentative explanations suggest that some part(s) of
Gos. Thom. 9 could have come from a tradition other
than those presented in the Synoptic gospels. 'The
nature of the variants, however, is not such that
they give the impression of a primitive tradition.'/116/

Notes to 'The Authenticity of the Parable of the
  Sower and its Interpretation   (Mark 4:3-9, 13-20)'

    1  A. Jülicher, Die Gleichnisreden Jesu (2 vols.;
Tübingen:  Mohr, 1910)  II,535, and E. Linnemann,
Parables of Jesus (London:  SPCK, 1966) 185, question
its authenticity simply because of its allegorical
features.

    2  C. C. Turner, The Metaphors of St. Paul
Classified and Discussed (Ph.D. Dissertation:
Aberdeen, 1956).

    3  M. Black, An Aramaic Approach to the Gospels
and Acts (3d ed.;  Oxford:  Clarendon, 1967) 63;  V.
Taylor, The Gospel According to St Mark (2d ed.;
London:  Macmillan, 1966) 250.

    4  Taylor, Mark, 250.

    5  This expression is a secondary Semitism found
in Lev 26:4,20; Ps 1:3; Ezek 34:27;  Zech 8:12;  cf.
συμβούλιον ἐδίδουν  in Mark 3:6;  Taylor, Mark, 250,
253;  C. E. B. Cranfield, The Gospel According to St.
Mark (Cambridge University, 1959) 149.

    6  Cf. the frequent use of ἀναβαίνω in the LXX to
translate עלה referring to vegetation springing up:
Gen 41:5;  Deut 29:23 (MT 22);  Isa 5:6;   32:13;
Hos 10:8.  ἀνέβησαν is probably a 'secondary
Semitism';  cf. Taylor, Mark, 253 and H. B. Swete,
The Gospel According to St Mark (London:  Macmillan,
1909) 73.  Both Xenophon (Oeconomicus 19.18) and
Theophrastus (Historia Plantarum VII.3.2) used
ἀναβαίνω to refer to vines climbing trees or stakes,
but this is not  exactly parallel to the Semitism,
contra Taylor, Mark, 253.

    7  The most probable explanation for the
divergence of manuscripts seems to be an original
threefold Aramaic ד, the sign of multiplication
meaning '-fold'.  For a discussion of this point and
bibliography cf. the present writer's Metaphor as a
Model for Interpretation of the Parables of Jesus,
With Special Reference to the Parable of the Sower
(Ph.D. Dissertation:  Cambridge, 1975) 177-81.

8  J. Jeremias, <u>The Parables of Jesus</u> (3d ed.; London:  SCM, 1972) 11.

9  Cf. Black, <u>Aramaic Approach</u>, 162;  C. C. Torrey, <u>The Four Gospels: A New Translation</u> (London: Hodder and Stoughton, n.d.) 298, and <u>Our Translated Gospels</u> (London:  Hodder and Stoughton, n.d.) 7-8; Jeremias, <u>Parables</u>, 12;  G. Quispel, 'Some Remarks on the Gospel of Thomas,' <u>NTS</u> 5 (1958-59) 277-78, and 'The Gospel of Thomas and the New Testament,' <u>VC</u> 11 (1957) 201, and 'Evangile selon Thomas et les Clémentines,' <u>VC</u> 12 (1958) 183, 193.

10  Black, <u>Aramaic Approach</u>, 63, and Taylor, <u>Mark</u>, 250, have noted that the hypotactic participle is frequent in the gospel parables, which, in this respect, on the whole are written in idiomatic Greek.

11  Black, <u>Aramaic Approach</u>, 162-63.

12  After the falling away (cf. also John 6: 41-43,52,60) John describes a continuing period of division (cf. 7:12,43;  9:16;  10:19-21), followed by renewed popularity after the raising of Lazarus (11:48;  12:18-19,42) before His crucifixion.

13  Mark 6:3-6;  Matt 13:55-58;  Luke 4:22-30 (preceding the Sower in Luke).  Other examples of rejection of Jesus are found in Mark 10:22 & parallels, the rich young ruler;  Luke 9:53, Samaritans;  Matt 12:30, 'he who is not with me'; Mark 14:10 and parallels, Judas Iscariot;  Mark 14: 66-72 and parallels, Peter's denial.

14  Mark 1:45;  2:2,4,12,13,15;  3:7-10,20,32; 4:1,36.

15  Cf. Mark 3:14-19;  6:7-13;  Matt 10:5-15; Luke 9:1-6,10;  10:1-20.

16  For an extensive list of exceptions, cf. Payne, <u>Parables</u>, 204.

17  Even by Jülicher, <u>Gleichnisreden</u> II,524,535, who said that one has no right to deny its allegorical interpretation as authentic to Jesus if one regards

17 (continued)  the story of the Sower in the
Synoptics as his.  Both Jülicher and Linnemann
questioned the authenticity of the Sower in light of
this congruity:  Jülicher, Gleichnisreden II, 537-38,
and Linnemann, Parables, 185, cf. 119.

18  Cf. Payne, Parables, 22 and Appendix II.

19  For a discussion of the various
interpretations the Sower has received cf. Payne,
Parables, 221-31.

20  Jeremias, Parables, 79.

21  Cf. R. Bultmann, The History of the Synoptic
Tradition (3d ed.;  Oxford:  Blackwell, 1972) 187;
E. Lohmeyer, Das Evangelium des Markus (Göttingen:
Vandenhoeck & Rupprecht, 1953) 84;  J. Schniewind,
Das Evangelium nach Markus (8th ed., NTD;  Göttingen:
Vandenhoeck & Ruprecht, 1958) 44;  J. Bowker,
'Mystery and Parable:  Mark iv. 1-20,' JTS 25 (1974)
310-12;  Str-B I,137,664-65,671.

22  D. Via, The Parables:  Their Literary and
Existential Dimension (Philadelphia:  Fortress Press,
1967) 8.

23  Cf. Gen.Rab. XLIV.15;  LXXX.5;  Lev.Rab.
III.1,4.

24  Cf. R. H. Charles, The Book of Jubilees or
the Little Genesis (London:  SPCK, 1917) 88.

25  G. H. Box and J. I. Landsman, ed., The
Apocalypse of Abraham (London:  SPCK, 1919) 51-53,
where further references are given.  Cf. the flying
serpent of Isa 14:29.  Ephrem de Nisibei in  (SC 121)
Commentaire de l'évangile Concordant ou Diatessaron/
§ 10,12 (p 190) mentions 'Satan who flew through the
air.'  2 Enoch 29:5 says that Satan's dominion after
his expulsion was the air, cf. Eph  2:2;  Rev 12:8-13.

26  I. Epstein, ed., The Babylonian Talmud
(London:  Soncino, 1935-61) Nezikin II,730.

27  Cf. A. Loisy, *Les Evangiles Synoptiques* (Ceffonds:  Chez L'Auteur, 1907) I,753;  Dodd, *Parables*, 14,181;  Jeremias, *Parables*, 79;  D. Nineham, *The Gospel of St. Mark* (London:  Adam & Charles Black, 1968) 139-40;  Jülicher, *Gleichnisreden* II,524, cf. 532-33;  S. Johnson, *A Commentary on the Gospel According to St. Mark* (London:  Adam and Charles Black, 1972) 92.

28  Cf. D. Wenham, 'The Interpretation of the Parable of the Sower,' *NTS* 20 (1973-4) 303.

29  Author's translation from F. Sausen, *Joannis Maldonati, Commentarii in quatuor Evangelistas* (5 vols.;  Mainz:  Kirchhein, Schott & Thielmann, 1840-44)  I,385.

30  M. Zerwick, *Biblical Greek* (Rome:  Pontifical Biblical Institute, 1963) 35, notes that εἰς may stand for ἐν without a sense of motion in Mark, Luke and Acts and on p 42 that ἐπί with the accusative can answer the question 'Where?' rather than 'Whither?'; cf. N. Turner, *Syntax, Vol. III of A Grammar of New Testament Greek by James Hope Moulton* (Edinburgh: T.& T. Clark, 1963)254,271-72.

31  L. Cohn, P. Wendland, and J. Leisegang, *Philonis Alexandrini:  Opera Quae Supersunt* (7 vols.; Berlin:  Georgius Reimerus, 1896-1915;  Walter de Gruyter, 1926) VI,110,4 = LCL IX,270-71.  Two other occurrences may indicate the sowing of land:  Cohn I,28,1 = LCL I,64-65, and Cohn IV,305,2 = LCL VII, 86-87.  Josephus, *Antiquities* XII.192, also used soil as the object of σπείρω .

32  זרע or σπείρω occurs in the MT and LXX of the OT with accusative of land in Gen 47:23;  Exod 23:10;  Lev 25:3,4;  Deut 21:4;  29:23;  Ps 107:37 (LXX 106:37);  Jer 2:2 (not in LXX);  Ezek 36:9;  and with two accusatives, for both land and seed in Lev 19:19;  Deut 22:9;  Judg 9:45;  Isa 30:23 (not in LXX) Cf. S. Schulz, 'σπέρμα , σπείρω , σπορά , σπόρος ,σπόριμος,' *TWNT* 7 (1964) 544, for Rabbinic references.

33  This proposal has been worked out in detail

33 (continued)  in consultation with Dr.
Sebastian P. Brock in Cambridge, who said that the
accounts in each of the Synoptics give a reasonable
translation of the proposed Aramaic original.

34  The inclusion of ὁμοίως follows the text of
Nestle, A B K π 1009 it 0133 pm; ὁμοίως εἰσίν is
found in ℵ C L Δ 33 892 1071 1241 Lect. bo . . .;
ὁμοίως is omitted from D W Θ f¹ f¹³ 28 565 700 1216
it sy^sp sa arm geo Origen <u>Diatessaron</u>.

35  Since 'those are they' is put in the first
clause, as in the Greek text of Mark 4:16, Syriac or
Aramaic would more naturally introduce the second
clause with the conjunction ) than the relative
pronoun ׳T to avoid a piling up of ׳T clauses. אויו
could be used instead of TD) .

36  Aramaic necessitates putting in a relative
pronoun while Greek and English tend to omit it
(ellipsis) when locative prepositional  phrases are
used adjectivally.  Therefore the first ׳T ('who')
is not included in the translation.

37  If such were the original form of the Greek
translation, it is obvious why copyists, especially
of an unaccented unpunctuated ms., would want to omit
this relative pronoun οἵ.  It would seem redundant,
particularly if it was read as the definite article
οἱ, since the οἱ could cover all of οἱ ἐπὶ τὰ πετρῶδη
σπειρόμενοι .  Even if not dropped intentionally, the
repetition of similar forms in OIϹΠEIPOMENOI         ,
rather like homoeoteleuton, could have led to
omission.

38  B* and 48^lect also omit οἵ at this point.
W has οἵτινες .

39  The dropping of ) ('and') in translating
׳TD) by ὅταν is no more than a stylistic change
which is almost standard since ) , being more
frequent in Aramaic than καί is in Greek, need not be
translated.  Haplography could also explain the
dropping of ) : ׳TD̲)̲ו̲ו̲ג̲ד̲ד̲א̲׳T.

40 Cf. J. C. Doudna, The Greek of the Gospel of Mark (JBL Monograph Series 12; Philadelphia: SBL, 1961) 128-36.

41 The variant from ὅπου σπείρεται ὁ λόγος in Mark 4:15 to οἷς σπείρεται ὁ λόγος in D 69² Latin versions ff g¹ l and the Syriac Peshitta is of special interest because the dative 'to whom the word is sown' shows that the focus is on the reception of what is sown. All of the variants from εἰς αὐτούς in Mark 4:15 focus on the place sown, and in all but one of them they focus on personal reception: ἐν αὐτοῖς ℵ C L Δ 579 892 bo sa; ἐν ταῖς καρδίαις αὐτῶν D E F G H K M S U V Θ Π Σ Φ Υ Ω 22 33 124 131 157 346 565; εἰς τὴν καρδίαν αὐτῶν syˢ P; ἀπὸ τῆς καρδίας αὐτῶν A Latin version l eth.

42 Cf. the variants of ὁμοίως mentioned above in n 34. ὁμοίως shows the continuity in imagery of people receiving the word as soils receive seed. This favors taking σπειρόμενοι as focusing on soil as receiving seed. Many mss. change the ἄλλοι of Mark 4:18 to οὗτοι to parallel the first two groups: A C² E F G H K M S U V Π Σ Φ Υ Ω (22 33) 131 157 579 pm. The same change (from ἐκεῖνοι to οὗτοι) is made in 4:20 by A D E F G H K M S U V Π Σ Φ Υ Ω f¹ f¹³ 22 33 157 543 579 700 1071 it pm (οὗτοι δέ in W Latin versions e ff sa). By increasing the parallelism they indicate that they recognized the fourfold pattern in the Sower and its interpretation.

43 Luke has no significant variations in regard to sowing. The Old Syriac omits any reference to 'were sown' in Mark 4:16, which suggests a recognition of awkwardness as does Luke. The next page of the Old Syriac, on which 4:18 and 20 would have been, is missing. There is a minor variation from the aorist to the present passive participle in Matt 13:19: most mss. τὸ ἐσπαρμένον , D W τὸ σπειρόμενον and syᵖ τὸν ἐσπαρμένον λόγον , further heightening the association of seed and word.

44 Jeremias, Parables, 77; cf. Dodd, Parables, 13-14; Nineham, Mark, 139. The validity of their arguments has been challenged by D. Wenham, The Composition of Mark 4:1-34 (Ph.D. Dissertation,

44 (continued) Manchester, 1970) 242-44;   C. F.
D. Moule, 'Mark 4:1-20 Yet Once More,' pp 95-113 in
Neotestamentica et Semitica:  Studies in Honour of
Matthew Black (ed. E. Ellis & M. Wilcox;  Edinburgh:
T. & T. Clark, 1969) 111-12;  Cranfield, Mark, 161-
63,  and 'St. Mark 4.1-34,' SJT 4 (1951) 409-11;
Bowker,'Mystery and Parable,' 316.

45 H. Palmer, The Logic of Gospel Criticism
(London:  Macmillan, 1968) 220-24;  cf. even A. Q.
Morton and James McLeman, Christianity and the
Computer, 24, 'If you want to be able to make any
useful judgement about Greek prose you must do
something with around 100 sentences.' (London:
Hodder and Stoughton, 1964).

46 Jeremias, Parables, 77.

47 A specific message:  Mark 1:45;  8:32;  9:
10;  10:22 (cf. 5:36).  Jesus' message in general:
Mark 2:2 and 4:33;  16:20 probably being secondary.
Jeremias' citation of 1:45 as meaning 'the gospel' in
Parables, 77 nn 8 and 10, is contrary to all the
major English versions and the commentaries of
Cranfield, Grundmann, Haenchen, Johannes Jeremias,
Lagrange, Lohmeyer, Moule, Nineham, Rienecker,
Schlatter, Schniewind, Schweizer, Swete, and Taylor.
That Jesus did speak of His message in general is
supported by 'my words' in Mark 8:38 - Luke 9:26;
Mark 13:31 = Matt 24:35=Luke 21:33; Luke 6:47; 24:44;
'these words of mine' Matt 7:24,26;  and possibly
'the word of God' Luke 8:21;  11:28.

48 The one possible exception is Mark 16:20,
probably secondary. In Mark $εὐαγγέλιον$ refers to the
story of Jesus Christ (1:1),  Jesus' proclamation of
the Kingdom (1:14,15), that to which one should be
devoted (8:35;  10:29), and the content of church
preaching (13:10;  14:9 ; and the added 16:15).

49 Jeremias, Parables, 77-78. Similar sayings,
however, do occur elsewhere in the teaching of Jesus,
as the reference to persecution on account of 'the
gospel' and 'my words' in Mark 8:34-38;  13:9-13;
Luke 9:23-26;  and reference to Jesus being a cause
of stumbling in Matt 11:5-6: $εὐαγγελίζονται \ldots σκανδαλισθῇ ἐν ἐμοί.$

50  No reference to λόγος :   2 Cor 11:4;   Col 1:10;  2 Tim 1:8.   λόγος  is not in the absolute in 1 Thes 2:13;  Col 1:5-6;  2 Tim 2:9;  Jas 1:21 (an appropriate parallel even though not absolute). Jeremias even added et al. in note 12, p 78, although there are no further examples in the NT.

51  Cf. D. Wenham, 'The Interpretation of the Parable of the Sower,' NTS 20 (1973-74) 308.

52  Jeremias, Parables, 78.

53  σπείρειν  seems to be used metaphorically of a proclamation in the LXX in Hos 2:23 (MT 25) and Nah 1:14;  cf. 4 Ezra 9:31.  ρίζα seems to indicate inward stability in the LXX in 4 Kgs 19:30;  Job 5:3; 15:29;  Prov 12:3;  Wis 3:15;  4:3;  Sir 23:25;  40: 15;  Isa 37:31;  40:24;  Jer 17:8;  cf. MT Job 8:17; 15:29;  Isa 27:6;  and 4 Ezra 8:41.  ἄκαρπος occurs metaphorically in the LXX in Wis 15:4 and 4 Macc 16:7. The same idea expressed by καρποφορεῖν occurs in Jesus' teaching in Matt 3:10 = Luke 3:9;  Luke 13:9.

54  Jeremias, Parables, 78.

55  Cranfield, Mark, 162;  cf. Cranfield, 'St. Mark 4.1-34,' 410 for a further example.

56  Moule, 'Mark 4:1-20 Yet Once More,' 112.

57  Bowker, 'Mystery and Parable,' 316.

58  πλοῦτος occurs 19 times in the rest of the NT and 101 times in the LXX.  πλουτέω occurs in Luke 1:53 and 12:21 and πλούσιος is found sixteen times in the Synoptics.  The frequencies of the others in the rest of the NT are:  σπείρειν = 'preach' 1, ρίζα = 'inward stability' 0, πρόσκαιρος  2, ἀπάτη 5 (but only 1 with the meaning Jeremias understands in Mark 4:19), ἄκαρπος 5,  παραδέχεσθαι 5,  καρποφορεῖν (metaphorically) 4.

59  Cf. Wenham, The Composition of Mark 4:1-34, 240-41, who concludes that 'in so far as style is any guide, the interpretation has as much right to be considered a translation as the parable.'

60  Linnemann, _Parables_, 117,181, and K. D.
White, 'The Parable of the Sower,' _JTS_ n.s. 15 (1964)
302, 307, affirm that the 30-fold, 60-fold, and
100-fold points not to the yields of the field as a
whole, but to individual seeds, _contra_ Jeremias,
_Parables_, 150. White has shown (p 301) that ancient
writers often recorded yield as return 'of seeds
reaped for seeds sown, in other words they are
concerned with the fertility of individual plants.'

61  Philo, _Questions and Answers on Genesis_
IV.189, cited from R. Marcus, _Philo Supplement I._
_Questions and Answers on Genesis_ (LCL, 1953) 268-69.

62  G. Dalman, _Arbeit und Sitte in Palästina_
(7 vols.; Hildesheim: Georg Olms, 1964) III,163,
where he also calls 100-fold 'das äusserste Denkbare'.

63  Dalman, _Arbeit_ II,244;  cf. his 'Viererlei
Acker,' _PJ_ 22 (1926) 120-32.

64  Dalman, _Arbeit_ III,163.

65  Jeremias, _Parables_, 150;  cf Jeremias'
Palästinakundliches zum Gleichnis vom Säemann, Mark
IV.3-8 par.,' _NTS_ (1966-67) 53.

66  Jeremias, _Parables_, 150.

67  Jeremias, 'Palästinakundliches,' 53.

68  Cf. Isa 4:2;  27:6,12;  32:15-16;  37:30-31;
62:8-9;  65:21-22;  Jer 31:5,12,14;  Ezek 34:26-27,29;
36:8-11,29-30;  Hos 6:11;  Joel 2:19-26;  Amos 9:13-
15.

69  Epstein, _Babylonian Talmud_, _Nashim_ II,720-25.
Cf. also _Exod. Rab._ XV.21;  Str-B IV,888-90, 948-50;
R. Patai, _Man and Temple in  Ancient Jewish Myth and_
_Ritual_ (London:  Thomas Nelson and Sons, 1947) 202-6;
N. A. Dahl, 'The Parables of Growth,' _ST_ 5 (1951) 153.

70  Quoted from the translation of Jeremias in
_Unknown Sayings of Jesus_ (2d ed.;  London:  SPCK,
1964) 33.

71   Dalman, _Arbeit_ III,164.

72   Data taken from Dalman, _Arbeit_ III,153-54.

73   Jeremias, 'Palästinakundliches,' 53.

74   A. Jaussen, _Coutumes des Arabes au Pays du Moab_ (Paris: Victor Lecoffre, 1908) 254.

75   J. Sonnen, 'Landwirtschaftliches vom See Genesareth,' _Bib_ 8 (1927) 84.

76   Dalman, _Arbeit_ III,164;   cf. II,153-54; Jeremias, _Parables_, 150 n 84.

77   Dalman, 'Viererlei Acker,' 128;   G. Sprenger, 'Jesu Säe- und Erntegleichnisse,' _PJ_ 9 (1913) 84; Linnemann, _Parables_, 117.

78   Epstein, _Babylonian Talmud_, _Neziḳin_ I,603-4.

79   Epstein, _Babylonian Talmud_, _Neziḳin_ I,681, and _Index_, 737.

80   Cf. Isa 5:10 (1/10-fold);   Jer 12:13;   Hos 8:7;   Mic 6:15;   Hag 1:6;   2:16-17.

81   Dalman, _Arbeit_ III,164.

82   Dalman, _Arbeit_ II,243-44.

83   White, 'The Parable of the Sower,' 302.

84   Sonnen, 'Landwirtschaftliches,' 85.

85   Dalman, _Arbeit_ III,163.

86   Epstein, _Babylonian Talmud_, _Nashim_ II,725.

87   Cf. David M. Scholer, _Nag Hammadi Bibliography 1948-69_ (Leiden: Brill, 1971) 136-65, a description of the debate by E. Haenchen, 'Literatur zum Thomasevangelium,' _TRu_ 27 (1961) 147-78, 306-38, and Payne, _Parables_, 147-55.

88   J. M. Robinson and H. Koester, _Trajectories_
_through Early Christianity_ (Philadelphia: Fortress,
1971) 117;   cf.   H. Montefiore, 'A Comparison of the
Parables of the Gospel According to Thomas and of the
Synoptic Gospels,' _NTS_ 7 (1960-61) 237 and the
frequent addition to the parables of 'whoever has
ears to hear, let him hear,' Gos. Thom. 8, 21, (24),
63, 65, 96.

89   The Gospel of Thomas does not give
explanations to the Dragnet (8), the Sower (9), or
the Tares among the Wheat (57);   and the Wicked
Husbandmen (65) is less allegorical.   However,
explanatory comments are given in Sayings 21a, 21b
(additions of 'his kingdom' and 'for the world'), 66
interpreting 65, and 76 (94:19-22).

90   Cf. the detailed form-critical work of W.
Schrage, _Das Verhältnis des Thomas-Evangeliums zur_
_synoptischen Tradition und zu den koptischen_
_Evangelienübersetzungen_ (Berlin:  Alfred Töpelmann,
1964);   J. B. Sheppard, _A Study of the Parables_
_Common to the Synoptic Gospels and the Coptic Gospel_
_of Thomas_ (Ph.D. Dissertation, Emory, 1965);   R. L.
Arthur, _The Gospel of Thomas and the Coptic New_
_Testament_ (Ph.D. Dissertation, Graduate Theological
Union, 1976);   and a bibliography in Payne, _Parables_,
148 n 4, 149 n 1.

91   Cf. the bibliography in Payne, _Parables_, 149
n 4.

92   Koester, _Trajectories_, 176.  This is the
'working hypothesis' of N. Perrin, _Rediscovering the_
_Teaching of Jesus_ (London:  SCM, 1967) 36.

93   The order of sayings may not be significant
as Haenchen has shown that the Gospel of Thomas tends
to link sayings by key words, _Die Botschaft des_
_Thomasevangeliums_ (Berlin:  Alfred Töpelmann, 1961)13.

94   On the difficulty of assessing Aramaisms and
a bibliography on this question cf. R. Kasser,
_L'Evangile selon Thomas_ (Neuchatel:  Delachaux &
Niestle, 1961) 17 n 3.

95   Cf. E. Wendling, Die Entstehung des Markus-
Evangeliums (Tübingen:  Mohr, 1908) 53-56;  Bultmann,
Synoptic Tradition, 31-32;  J. M. Robinson,
Trajectories, 129.

96   Sheppard, A Study of the Parables, 360.
H. L. Briscoe comes to the same conclusion in A
Comparison of the Parables in the Gospel according to
Thomas and the Synoptic Gospels (Th.D. Dissertation:
Southwestern Baptist Theological Seminary, Fort Worth,
1965) 202.

97   This translation is taken from E. Hennecke,
New Testament Apocrypha (2 vols.;  London:
Lutterworth, 1963 and 1965), I,512.

98   Schrage, Thomas-Evangeliums, 46-47, argues
that the Gospel of Thomas 82:4b-5a is a secondary
addition.

99   Cf. Corpus Hermeticum ix,3-4 and 6;  A. D.
Nock and A. J. Festugière, Corpus Hermeticum (2 vols.;
Paris:  Société d'édition 'Les Belles Lettres', 1945)
I,104 n 6; and R. Reitzenstein, Poimandres. Studien
zur griechisch-ägyptischen und frühchristlichen
Literatur (Leipzig:  B. G. Teubner, 1904) 143-44 for
further examples.

100  H. E. W. Turner and Hugh Montefiore, Thomas
and the Evangelists (London:  SCM, 1962) 48 n 2;
Sheppard, A Study of the Parables, 165;  cf. Turner,
Syntax, 9, 340-41.

101  PG VI, 765. This is not exactly parallel
to the Gospel of Thomas since the reading ⲈⲬⲚ (82:7)
is usually a translation of ἐπί , occurring over 400
times in the Sahidic NT as opposed to 46 times for
εἰς and four times for παρά ;  L. Th.-Lefort and
Michel Wilmet, ed., Condordance du Nouveau Testament
sahidique (CSCO Subsidia Vols. 1, 11, 13, 15;
Louvain:  Secrétariat du CSCO, 1950-59) II, 1610-12.
Justin should not, therefore, be claimed to parallel
Gos. Thom. 9 at this point;  cf. Sheppard, A Study of
the Parables, 164 contra Quispel, 'Some Remarks on
the Gospel of Thomas,' 277.

102   The Saxon an can mean 'near', 'by', or 'at'
as well as 'on' and so has a similarly ambiguous
range of meaning to    παρά and ל (Aramaic);   cf.
W. Krogmann, 'Heliand, Tatian und Thomasevangelium,'
ZNW 51 (1960) 261-62;   Sheppard, A Study of the
Parables, 164.

103   This view  held by Quispel, R. McL. Wilson
(Studies in the Gospel of Thomas [London:   Mowbray,
1960] 128), and  H. Montefiore ('A Comparison of the
Parables,' 225-26) is criticized and rejected by
Sheppard, A Study of the Parables, 163-65.

104   Quispel, 'Some Remarks on the Gospel of
Thomas,' 283.

105   Ibid., 285.  Note, however, the signs of
embellishment in 'the beat of horses' shoes and the
pace of heroes'.

106   Cf. R. M. Grant and D. Freedman, The Secret
Sayings of Jesus (New York:   Doubleday, 1960) 213-20,
268-70;   G. Strecker, Das Judenchristentum in den
Pseudoklementinen (TU 70, 1958) 117-36.

107   Cf. Hans-W. Bartsch, 'Das Thomas-Evangelium
und die synoptischen Evangelien,' NTS 6 (1959-60)
250-51;   Haenchen, Die Botschaft, 45.

108   'On the road is the translation given by
BAG, 616 (III,d) for παρά in Mark 4:4,15 & parallels
and Heb 11:12.  It is also proposed by them for Mark
1:16 & parallels and Mark 10:46 & parallels.  Cf.
E. Haenchen, 'Literatur zum Thomasevangelium,' 167;
Schrage, Thomas-Evangeliums, 45;  Sheppard, A Study
of the Parables, 164.

109   G. Quispel, 'L'Evangile selon Thomas et le
Diatessaron,' VC 13 (1959) 89;  Sheppard, A Study of
the Parables, 166.

110   Montefiore, 'A Comparison of the Parables,'
229;  cf. Acts of Andrew 12, 'seeds . . . sprout
and . . . grow and emerge into the light';  Ginza
134,11-12;  Hipp. haer. V,9,6;  Odes of Solomon 38,18,

110 (continued)  'It struck deep and sprang up';
and possibly Gos. Philip 116 (127,31-32).  'Fruit' is
used in description of the spiritual success of the
gnostic in Gos. Thom. 45 and 65 as well as here in 9,
but 'heaven' is not pictured as the goal of the
gnostic in its other occurrences in Gos. Thom. 3, 6,
11, 12, 44, and 111.

111  Cf. P. Rech, 'Aehre,' RAC I,139-40.

112   Cf. Iren. haer. ii.1.3, ii.3.2;  Hipp.
haer. VIII,9,1-8;  Schrage, Thomas-Evangeliums, 48;
W. Bousset, Hauptprobleme der Gnosis (Göttingen:
Vandenhoeck und Ruprecht, 1907) 397-98.

113  M. Lidzbarski, Das Johannesbuch der Mandäer
(Giessen:  Alfred Töpelmann, 1915) 204, 11.34-35.

114  Cf. Clem. str. I.37.2, 'He sows from above.'
A different interpretation is given by Paulus Orosius
(circa A.D. 414) in Commonitorium de Errore
Priscillianistarum et Origenistarum 2, quoting
Memoria Apostolorum, 'He was not a good sower or he
would not have been so careless.  In fact, he was the
God of this world, sowing souls into bodies.'  CSEL
18, 154, lines 4-18

115  Cf. J. D. Crossan, 'The Seed Parables of
Jesus,' JBL 92 (1973) 250; Jeremias, Parables, 28;
Schrage, Thomas-Evangeliums, 43-45;  Haenchen,
'Literatur zum Thomasevangelium,' 167;  contra
Quispel, 'Some Remarks on the Gospel of Thomas,'
277-78.

116  Sheppard, A Study of the Parables, 164.

# Jüdische Elementarbildung und Evangelienüberlieferung

Rainer Riesner
Universität Tübingen

## 1. Die Thesen von H. Riesenfeld und B. Gerhardsson

Auf dem Kongress von 1957 über die vier Evangelien skizzierte der schwedische Neutestamentler H. Riesenfeld in Oxford einen Gegenentwurf /1/ zu dem Bild, das sich die 'formgeschichtliche Schule' /2/ vom Prozess der Evangelien-Überlieferung gemacht hatte. Nach Riesenfeld begann die Jesus-Überlieferung nicht erst in der Urgemeinde, sondern schon im vorösterlichen Jüngerkreis:

> 'In the Gospels we are shown very clearly that Jesus was a teacher, and especially in his relation to his disciples. This means more than his mere preaching in their presence. He gave them instruction, and in this we are reminded, *mutatis mutandis*, of the method of the Jewish rabbi. An this implies that Jesus made his disciples, and above all the Twelve, learn, and furthermore that he made them learn by heart' /3/.

Riesenfelds Schüler B. Gerhardsson legte eine ausführliche Darstellung des rabbinischen Traditionsbetriebs vor /4/, wie er sich in Mischna und Talmud spiegelt. Gerhardsson versuchte weiter, am lukanischen Werk und bei Paulus zu zeigen, dass sich auch die Urkirche ähnlicher Überlieferungsmethoden bediente /5/.

Diese skandinavischen Vorschläge sind nicht völlig neu. Vergleichbare Thesen wurden schon früher besonders von katholischen Exegeten /6/, aber auch von einem Forscher wie B. S. Easton vertreten /7/. Bereits A. Schlatter hatte auf die formalen Analogien zwischen rabbinischer und evangelischer Überlieferung aufmerksam gemacht /8/, doch erste Hinweise darauf finden sich sogar schon bei J. L. Gieseler /9/. In der neueren internationalen Diskussion verschafften allerdings erst Riesenfeld und Gerhardsson derartigen Überlegungen Gehör. Sie selbst folgten vermutlich einer Anregung von A. Fridrichsen /10/ /11/.

In der lebhaften Debatte /12/, die den skandinavischen
Thesen folgte, wurden vor allem zwei Einwände geltend gemacht:
1) Kann man wirklich Parallelen zwischen dem Unterricht der
Rabbinen und dem Lehren Jesu ziehen, wenn er selbst im
Gegensatz zu Paulus kein akademisch ausgebildeter
Schriftgelehrter war? 2) Darf man die rabbinischen Quellen, die
nach den nationalen Katastrophen von 70 und 135 nChr. ihre
Gestalt fanden, ohne weiteres als Illustration für Vorgänge in
der ersten Hälfte des 1. Jahrhundert nChr. heranziehen? Diese
Frage hat sich besonders durch die Arbeiten von J. Neusner /13/
zugespitzt, der die rabbinischen Überlieferungen mit ähnlicher
Skepsis behandelt wie R. Bultmann die synoptische Tradition.

Bultmann selbst glaubte noch, 'dass Jesus zum Stande der
Schriftgelehrten gehörte, dass er eine zunftgemässe Ausbildung
erfahren und die vorgeschriebenen Prüfungen absolviert hatte'
/14/. Aber von Aussenseitern wie F. Cornelius /15/ abgesehen,
wird heute noch kaum jemand diese Ansicht vertreten. Die
Anrede 'Rabbi' war vor 70 nChr. noch nicht, wie Bultmann
voraussetzte, ein feststehender Titel für den akademisch
ausgebildeten Schriftgelehrten /16/. Allerdings weisen die
Evangelien darauf hin, dass die Bezeichnung bereits in
neutestamentlicher Zeit vor allem auch Personen beigelegt
wurde, die in irgendeiner Weise als 'Lehrer' wirkten /17/.
Johannes der Täufer war gewiss kein studierter Schriftgelehrter
im späteren rabbinischen Sinn, aber er wurde 'Rabbi' genannt
(Joh 3,26), weil er Schüler um sich sammelte und sie lehrte
(Lk 11,1).

In Joh 7,15 wird Jesus mē memathēkos genannt. Wenn damit
auch keineswegs gesagt ist, dass Jesus jede Art von Bildung
fehlte, so ist dieser polemische Vorwurf doch nur verständlich,
wenn Jesus kein Schriftgelehrter war /18/. In der Tat wissen
erst die mittelalterlichen Toledoth Jeschu davon zu berichten,
dass sich Jesus einem Rabbi als Schüler anschloss /19/. Aber
schon allein die chronologische Konfusion dieser
Tendenzschriften zeigt, dass es sich dabei um historisch völlig
wertlose Nachrichten handelt.

Nun waren aber Schülerkreise, wie sie sich etwa um Hillel
oder Schammaj sammelten, keineswegs die einzigen Institutionen,
in denen man sich zur Zeit Jesu Bildung aneignen konnte. In
einer Antwort auf seine Kritiker warf Gerhardsson die Frage
auf, ob sich nicht bereits vor 70 nChr. in sehr verschiedenen
jüdischen Gruppen und Einrichtungen eine Art 'popular

pedagogic' nachweisen liesse /20/. Man denke nur daran, dass
es in Jerusalem spätestens seit der Makkabäer-Zeit Schulen für
Jugendliche gab /21/.

Wenn man die Analogien zum Prozess der Evangelien-
Überlieferung nicht allein in den rabbinischen Schülerkreisen
sucht, sondern die Untersuchung auf die drei jüdischen
'Volksbildungsinstitutionen' Elternhaus, Synagoge und
Elementarschule ausweitet, dann verlieren die quellenkritischen
und chronologischen Probleme im Zusammenhang mit der
rabbinischen Literatur an Schärfe. Die populäre Pädagogik war
überall in der Antike durch einen beharrlichen Konservatismus
gekennzeichnet. Dafür dürfen wir uns durch die Inflation der
modernen Bildungsreformen nicht den Blick verstellen lassen.
Die Ursprünge der jüdischen Volksbildung lassen sich schon im
Alten Testament erkennen /22/ und eine in manchem erstaunlich
kontinuierliche Entwicklungslinie führt über die
intertestamentarische Periode bis hin zur frührabbinischen
Zeit /23/.

Ich bin überzeugt davon, dass schon allein die drei
zeitgenössischen Volksbildungsinstitutionen Jesus und der
Urgemeinde ein Mass von Traditionsbewusstsein und
Traditionsmethodik vermitteln konnten, das eine 'gepflegte
Überlieferung' /24/ ermöglichte. Als Beispiel für eine
elementare Traditionsmethode soll im folgenden das
Auswendiglernen behandelt werden, weil seine Wichtigkeit von
Riesenfeld besonders betont wurde (s.o.S.1).

## 2. Auswendiglernen als populäre<br>pädagogische Methode

a) *Das Elternhaus:* Die älteste und für lange Zeit auch
einflussreichste jüdische Bildungsinstitution war das
Elternhaus. Schulbildung blieb in der vorneutestamentlichen
Periode ein Privileg für wenige. Seit der Wende vom 1. zum 2.
nachchristlichen Jahrhundert begann dann die Schule das
Elternhaus nach und nach als Vermittlerin von Bildung zu
ersetzen.

Wenn man nach der Bedeutung des Auswendiglernens im
Alten Testament fragt, dann darf man sich nicht durch einen
ersten flüchtigen Blick auf den Wortbefund täuschen lassen.
Während im mischnischen Hebräisch *schanah* und im talmudischen
Aramäisch *tᵉnah/ᵓatni* zu einer Art termini technici geworden

sind /25/, kennt das Alte Testament noch keinen festgeprägten
Ausdruck für Auswendiglernen. Diese Tätigkeit wird dafür oft
durch Umschreibungen ausgedrückt. Dem stereometrischen Denken
/26/ der Hebräer entsprechend stehen oftmals mehrere dieser
Umschreibungen nebeneinander, um auf die gemeinte Sache
aufmerksam zu machen.

Wie schon in ägyptischen Schultexten /27/ und später im
Koran /28/ gilt auch im Alten Testament das Herz als Sitz des
Gedächtnisses /29/. Deshalb können Wendungen wie *jazar leb* und
*sim lebab* auch Auswendiglernen bedeuten /30/. Wie es im
ganzen Altertum üblich war /31/, so lernte man auch in
alttestamentlicher Zeit laut auswendig. Darum ist in
entsprechenden Zusamenhängen oft betont vom 'Mund' die Rede
/32/. In Skarabäen aus Ägypten fand man /33/ 'kurze Kernsätze
der Lehre, die der Träger des Ringes gleichsam als Devise für
sein Leben stets bei sich haben wollte' /34/ eingraviert.
Ähnliche israelitische Bräuche stehen hinter manchen bildhaften
Umschreibungen für das Auswendiglernen.

Wenn man diesen sprachlichen Sachverhalt im Auge behält,
dann entdeckt man leicht, dass Auswendiglernen als eine der
elementarsten Traditionsmethoden auch in alttestamentlicher
Zeit beim Unterricht der Söhne durch ihre Väter eine
entscheidende Rolle spielte /35/. Das vielleicht bekannteste
Beispiel für eine Überlieferung der vorexilischen Zeit, die ein
Israelit im Gedächtnis haben musste, ist das 'kleine
geschichtliche Credo' (Dtn 26,5-10), das bei der Darbringung
der Erstlingsfrüchte rezitiert wurde.

Auch in neutestamentlicher Zeit hatte das Auswendiglernen
in der häuslichen Erziehung nichts von seiner Bedeutung
verloren. Ein Text, der aus einem stoisch beeinflussten
Diaspora-Judentum des 1. Jahrhunderts nChr. stammt, beschreibt
den idealen Vater, der seine Söhne 'Gesetz und Profeten' lehrt
(*edidasken*), wobei er sich zum besseren Einprägen der
Kantillation bedient (4Makk 18,10-16). Auch Philo kann kaum
etwas anderes als Auswendiglernen meinen, wenn er von seinem
Volk sagt (*LegGaj* 210):
> 'Von frühester Kindheit an... trägt es der Gebote Bilder
> eingeprägt in seiner Seele (*en tais psychais*
> *agalmatophorousi tas tōn diatetagmenōn eikonas*)'.

Für Palästina zur Zeit des Neuen Testaments ergibt sich
kein anderes Bild. Josephus rühmte sich, in seiner Jugend

durch ein besonders gutes Gedächtnis aufgefallen zu sein (*Vit* 8). Für sein ganzes Volk hebt er die Schulung des Memoriervermögens als besonderes Charakteristikum hervor: 'Bei uns hingegen mag man den ersten besten über die Gesetze befragen, und er wird sämtliche Bestimmungen derselben leichter hersagen als seinen eigenen Namen. Weil wir nämlich gleich vom Erwachen des Bewusstseins an die Gesetze erlernen, sind sie in unsere Seelen sozusagen eingegraben (*autous emanthanontes echomen en tais psychais hōsper enkecharagmenous*)' /36/. Selbst zu einer Zeit als die Elementarschule schon weit verbreitet war, hören wir davon, dass die Väter mit ihren Söhnen sogar am Sabbat das wöchentliche Memorierpensum repetierten (*Ned* 37a), wie sie auch sonst die Schule durch weiteren häuslichen Unterricht unterstützten (*Kid* 30a).

b) *Die Synagoge*: Auch wenn immer noch kein Konsensus über die historischen und geografischen Ursprünge dieser wichtigsten jüdischen Volksbildungsinstitution besteht /37/, so ist doch unumstritten, dass sie zur Zeit Jesu existierte. Angaben bei Philo /38/ und in den rabbinischen Quellen /39/ bestätigen das Bild, das wir im Neuen Testament von einer weiten Verbreitung der Synagogen in der Diaspora und auch in Palästina erhalten. Selbst in verhältnismässig kleinen jüdischen Siedlungen muss es Synagogen gegeben haben /40/, sodass es nicht erstaunlich ist, wenn die Evangelien für Galiläa eine Vielzahl voraussetzen /42/. Ein archäologischer Beweis dafür sind neuere Ausgrabungen, die in Magdala /42/ und vielleicht auch in Gamla /43/ Synagogen aus der frührömischen Periode freilegten.

Während die öffentlichen Torahlesungen an den Markt- und Fasttagen Montag und Donnerstag sowie an den Festen erst nach der Tempelzerstörung eingeführt wurden, kann man in Palästina mindestens seit dem 2. Jahrhundert vChr. mit regelmässigen Torahlektionen am Sabbat rechnen /44/. Die Torahlesung blieb immer das Zentrum des synagogalen Gottesdienstes. Dagegen konnten alle anderen Bestandteile je nach Ort und Situation variieren. Auch wenn die Liturgie nach 70 nChr. noch eine wesentliche Bereicherung und Ausgestaltung erfuhr, so darf man doch in neutestamentlicher Zeit für einen durchschnittlichen Synagogengottesdienst mit folgenden Hauptteilen rechnen /45/:
Rezitation des Dekalogs
Rezitation des '*Sch<sup>e</sup>ma<sup>c</sup> Jisrael*'
Benediktionen

Torahlesung mit Targum
Profetenlesung mit Targum
Psalmengesang
Predigt

Das *Schema^c*, das ja auch eine entscheidende Rolle beim
persönlichen Gebet des Einzelnen spielte /46/, kam aus den
Zusammenkünften der priesterlichen *mischmarot* und der
Standmannschaften (*ma^camadot*) in den synagogalen Gottesdienst
/47/. Es wurde von der ganzen Gemeinde rezitiert /48/.
Ähnlich muss man sich auch die Rezitation des Dekalogs
vorstellen, der /49/ später aus Polemik gegen das
Urchristentum aus der Liturgie ausschied /50/. Im Neuen
Testament wird deutlich, dass die auswendige Kenntnis von
Dekalog /51/ und *Schema^c* /52/ sehr weit verbreitet war.

Lange Zeit scheint es für das dem *Schema^c* folgende Gebet
kein vorgeschriebenes Formular gegeben zu haben. Von dem
später an dieser Stelle verwandten Achtzehnbitten-Gebet waren
vor 70 nChr. die drei ersten und die drei letzten
Benediktionen bekannt /53/. Sie dürften zusammen mit anderen
als eine Art von 'Modell-Lobpreisungen' gedient haben /54/.
Der Vorbeter, der als vorbereiteter Stellvertreter für die
Gemeinde sprach /55/, konnte sich an ihnen orientieren /56/.
Dazu musste er natürlich eine grössere Anzahl solcher
'Standardgebete' im Kopf haben, die er nach den momentanen
Erfordernissen ergänzen und abwandeln konnte.

Die Schriftrezitationen und Gebete wurden ebenso wie die
Psalmen im synagogalen Gottesdienst 'gesungen' /57/. Wie die
rabbinische Wendung *ᵓamar schir* /58/ andeutet, handelte es
sich dabei allerdings um einen nur sehr wenig melodischen
Gesang. S. Krauss sprach mit Recht von 'Kantillation', das
heisst einem 'mehr vom Rhythmus und der Wortfolge abhängigen
Vortrag' /59/. Die Kantillation erhöhte nicht zuletzt die
Einprägsamkeit der vorgetragenen Stücke /60/.

Wenn auch zur Zeit Jesu noch kein einheitlicher Zyklus
für die Torah- und Profetenlektionen existierte, so gab es in
den einzelnen Synagogengemeinden doch schon Ansätze für eine
lectio continua /61/. Die Vorleser der beiden Schriftlektionen
wurden ebenso wie der Prediger vom Synagogenvorsteher (*rᵓosch
haknesset, archisynagōgos*) bestimmt /62/. In den seltensten
Fällen dürfte die Aufforderung völlig spontan erfolgt sein.
Es handelte sich ja um die schwierige Aufgabe, unvokalisierte
Texte in der nicht alltäglichen Sprache Hebräisch fehlerfrei

und flüssig zu lesen. Dazu war eine Vorbereitung unumgänglich.
Der Synagogenvorsteher oder der Synagogendiener (*chazan*,
*hypēretēs*) werden sich vor dem Gottesdienst mit einem dafür
geeigneten Gemeindeglied über die Auswahl der Lesung
verständigt haben /63/.

Von R. Me²ir wird berichtet, dass er sich einmal
weigerte, öffentlich aus der Torah vorzulesen. Zur Begründung
sagte er seinen Schülern:
> 'Ich habe mich geweigert vorzulesen, nur weil ich diesen
> Abschnitt nicht zwei- oder dreimal der Reihe nach
> durchgegangen war (mich darauf vorbereitet hatte); denn
> ein Mensch darf die Worte der Torah vor der Gemeinde
> nicht sagen, bevor er sie nicht zwei- oder dreimal vor
> sich selbst vorgetragen hat' /64/.

Auch andere Stellen in der rabbinischen Literatur weisen auf
eine derartige Vorbereitung der Schriftlektionen zurück /65/.
Oft wird diese Vorbereitung der Sabbatlesungen bedeutet haben,
dass der Vorleser sie auswendig lernte, um einen stockenden
Vortrag zu vermeiden /66/. Wenn später die Rabbinen heftig
dagegen ankämpften, die Schriftlesungen ebenso wie das Targum
auswendig vorzutragen /67/, dann zeigt das, wie sehr sich eine
solche Praxis eingebürgert hatte.

c) *Die Elementarschule*: Schon in alttestamentlicher
Zeit gab es in Jerusalem und wohl auch an anderen grösseren
Orten Schulen /68/. Zu intensiveren Bemühungen, für weitere
Bevölkerungsschichten eine Elementarbildung einzurichten, kam
es als Antwort auf die krisenhaften Hellenisierungsversuche
der Makkabäer-Zeit. Als die Pharisäer während der
Regierungszeit von Königin Alexandra Salome (76-67 vChr.) zu
Einfluss gelangten, versuchte ihr Führer Schim^con b. Schatach
eine Art öffentliche Schulpflicht einzuführen (*j Keth* 32c).
Wie allerdings der erneute Reformversuch des Hohenpriesters
J^ehoschua^c b.Gamla² zwischen 63-65 nChr. zeigt (*BB* 21a), war
kein bleibender Erfolg erreicht worden.

Ebenso wie sonst im hellenistischen Zeitalter blieben
auch Gründung und Einrichtung jüdischer Schulen vor der
Tempelzerstörung weithin eine Sache privater Initiative. Wie
gross die Zahl der Schulen im 2. Jahrhundert gewesen sein muss,
verraten die rabbinischen Quellen immer wieder, aber auch
schon im 1. muss es von Seiten der Pharisäer starke
Bestrebungen gegeben haben, einen Elementarunterricht
einzurichten. Da das Ziel der 'Bildung' vor allem darin

bestand, Gemeindegliedern die aktive Teilnahme am
Synagogengottesdienst zu ermöglichen, boten sich naturgemäss
die Synagogengebäude als Stützpunkte an /69/.

Auswendiglernen war in den Schulen des alten Ägypten
/70/, Mesopotamien /71/, Griechenland /72/ und Rom /73/ eine
pädagogische Standardmethode, obwohl in diesen Kulturen die
Schrift eine hervorragende Rolle spielte. Es gilt für die ganze
Erziehung des Altertums, was H. Brunner von der ägyptischen
Schule sagte:
> 'Stets stand das Gedächtnis im Vordergrund der Erziehung,
> weit vor der heute so früh geübten Fähigkeit zu
> Kombination und Urteil' /74/.

Auch in den Schulen des vorexilischen Israel stand das
Auswendiglernen an vorderster Stelle /75/. Nicht bloss kurze
Sprüche, sondern selbst so lange Lehrreden wie die in Sprüche
1-9 erhaltenen mussten memoriert werden /76/.

In den späteren jüdischen Elementarschulen wurde nicht
weniger reichlich auswendig gelernt /77/. Wenn man nach einem
Wort von Rab den Schüler 'wie einen Ochsen stopfen' solle (*BB*
21a), dann kann das als allgemein anerkannte Maxime gelten.
Wie schon im alten Ägypten /78/ war es auch in den rabbinischen
Schulen üblich, weite Passagen mechanisch auswendig zu lernen,
ehe der Lehrer auch nur den geringsten inhaltlichen
Erklärungsversuch unternahm /79/. Wie sein ägyptischer Kollege
/80/ teilte auch der jüdische Elementarlehrer den
Unterrichtsstoff in Memorierpensa ein /81/. Diese wurden dann
von den Schülern so lange repetiert, bis sie einwandfrei
auswendig beherrscht wurden (*Erub* 54b). Was eine Baraitha
Hillel zuschreibt (*Chag* 9b), hatte a fortiori in der
Elementarschule Geltung:
> 'Wer nämlich seinen Abschnitt hundertmal wiederholt
> (*schoneh*), ist nicht mit dem zu vergleichen, der seinen
> Abschnitt hunderteinmal wiederholt'.

Auch schon in den altägyptischen /82/ und den frühen
griechischen /83/ Schulen erleichterte man den Schülern das
Auswendiglernen durch mnemotechnische Kunstgriffe /84/. Die
Allitterationen in Sprüche 18,20-22 /85/ oder die
alphabetisierende Dichtung in Sprüche 31,10-31 /86/ zeigen,
dass derartige Gedächtnishilfen auch in den vorexilischen
Schulen Israels nicht unbekannt waren. Bei der Anordnung der
Sprüche Salomos, die in der Schule Verwendung fanden /87/, ist
auch öfter das Stichwortprinzip zu beobachten /88/. In den

späteren jüdischen Elementarschulen half man z.B. den Schülern
beim Einprägen des Alphabets, indem man sie in Gedichtform
lernen liess /89/. Dieselbe Praxis kannten auch die
hellenistischen Schulen der Umwelt /90/.

Alt ist auch der Brauch, mit Kantillation auswendig zu
lernen. Diese Memoriermethode ist für Ägypten ebenso bezeugt
wie für Griechenland /91/. Die jüdischen Schulen machten
hierin keine Ausnahme. Wie Psalm 1,1f zeigt, 'murmelte (*hagah*)'
man in der nachexilischen Tempelschule /92/ über der Torah, das
heisst man lernte mit Intonation auswendig. Bei den Essenern,
die für ihre Sorgfalt bei der Kindererziehung bekannt waren
/93/, wurde *hagah* /94/ zu einem terminus technicus für den
'Umgang mit einem Buch, bei dem man dessen Inhalt einübt und
dem Gedächtnis einprägt' /95/. Bücher dienten in der Antike
ja nicht zuletzt als Vorlagen zum Auswendiglernen /96/. Schon
den Gezer-Kalender aus dem frühen 9. Jahrhundert vChr. kann
man als 'kleine Übungstafel eines Schülers, der mit ungeübter
Hand seinen Memorierstoff schrieb' /97/ interpretieren /98/.

Auch die rabbinischen Quellen zeigen an vielen Stellen,
dass in den jüdischen Schulen laut gelesen und auswendig
gelernt wurde /99/. Besonders bedeutsam ist in diesem
Zusammenhang eine rabbinische Anekdote über den kynischen
Philosophen Oinomaios aus Gadara (*GenR* 65,20), der in der
ersten Hälfte des 2. Jahrhunderts nChr. lebte. Als Grund für
die erstaunliche jüdische Kraft zur Selbstbehauptung gibt
Oinomaios an:
> 'Geht und beobachtet ihre Synagogen und Lehrhäuser.
> Solange ihr dort Kinder findet, die mit ihrer Stimme
> zwitschern (*zafzaf $b^e kol$*), könnt ihr (die Heiden) ihnen
> nicht beikommen, denn ihr (himmlischer) Vater hat es
> ihnen versprochen'.

d) *Das Traditionsgedächtnis*: Schon Josephus rühmte das
auswendige Wissen seiner Landsleute von Jugend auf (*Ap* II 178)
und die rabbinische Überlieferung weiss mancherlei Erstaun-
liches über die immense Bibelkenntnis zu erzählen, die schon
Schulkinder besassen /100/. So soll R. Ze$^c$iri in der Mitte des
3. Jahrhunderts nChr. in einer babylonischen Gemeinde den
gestörten Text einer Schriftrolle nach den Angaben von
Schulkindern wieder hergestellt haben (*Men* 29b). Dabei wird
sogar ausdrücklich betont, dass es sich noch nicht einmal um
besonders begabte Schüler gehandelt habe.

Wenn hier im Einzelnen auch die Übertreibung mitspielt,
so kamen doch auch Nichtjuden nicht umhin, die hohen
Gedächtnisleistungen der Juden anzuerkennen. Hieronymus
geriet in Staunen darüber, dass jüdische Zeitgenossen die
Namenslisten der Chronikbücher vorwärts und rückwärts in der
richtigen Reihenfolge aufsagen konnten /101/, ja, einige sogar
Torah und Profeten auswendig beherrschten /102/. Ähnliches
weiss Eusebius zu berichten /103/ und vielleicht spielt 1 Tim
1,4 ebenfalls auf solche Fähigkeiten an /104/. Erstaunliche
Beispiele für die Fassungskraft des Traditionsgedächtnisses
lassen sich auch in moderner Zeit aus noch funktionierenden
Gedächtniskulturen beibringen /105/. Es stellt der jüdischen
Volksbildung in neutestamentlicher Zeit und nicht zuletzt der
Schulung im Memorieren ein hohes Zeugnis aus, wenn Seneca in
seiner Schrift *'De superstitione'* die Juden den übrigen Völkern
des römischen Weltreichs mit den Worten gegenüberstellte /106/:
       'Illi tamen causas ritus sui noverunt; maior pars populi
       facit quod cur faciat ignorat' /107/.

### 3. Jesus als messianischer Lehrer

Unsere Untersuchung hat gezeigt, dass Auswendiglernen als
pädagogische Methode nicht bloss in den rabbinischen Akademien
/108/, sondern auch in den drei jüdischen
Volksbildungsinstitutionen Elternhaus, Synagoge und
Elementarschule eine entscheidende Rolle spielte. Auch
Kantillation und Mnemotechnik wurden in grossem Ausmass auf der
elementaren pädagogischen Stufe eingesetzt. Man kann deshalb
mit Recht die gesamte jüdische Bildung der neutestamentlichen
Zeit als Teil einer 'Gedächtniskultur' /109/ bezeichnen.

Gab es schon vor Ostern eine Überlieferung der Worte Jesu
bei der Auswendiglernen eine Rolle spielte? Ich möchte diese
Frage mithilfe einiger Thesen bejahen /110/, die ich an anderer
Stelle ausführlich zu begründen versuche /111/.

1) Nazareth besass eine eigene Synagoge (Mt 13,54/Mk 6,
2/Lk 4,16), in der alttestamentliche Schriften zugänglich waren
(Lk 4,17). Der Synagogendiener (Lk 4, 20) konnte, wie wir das
aus rabbinischen Quellen wissen, als Elementarlehrer fungieren.
Interessierte Nazarethaner vermochten sich eine gründliche
Schriftkenntnis erwerben. Das aber hiess, wesentliche Teile des
Alten Testamentes auswendig zu lernen.

2) Das Mass an Elementarbildung, das jüdische Kinder erhielten, hing vom religiösen Interesse des Elternhauses ab. Jesus stammte aus einer sehr frommen Familie (Lk 2,22-27.42). Es deutet nicht auf einen 'wunderbaren' Vorgang, sondern auf eine gute Elementarbildung, wenn der zwölfjährige Jesus unter Lehrern sass, und durch Zuhören, Fragen und Antworten lernte (Lk 2,46f).

3) Jesu Anspruch kann nur mit der Kategorie des Messianischen richtig beschrieben werden. Nun gab es aber in sehr verschiedenen Gruppen des zeitgenössischen Judentums die Erwartung, dass der Messias als Lehrer von Worten höchster Weisheit auftreten werde /112/. Jesus hat seinen Hoheitsanspruch dem engsten Jüngerkreis enthüllt (Mk 8,29f Par.), aber auch Aussenstehenden konnte er nicht völlig verborgen bleiben. Dieser Anspruch aber stellte ein aussergewöhnliches Überlieferungsmotiv dar: Die Worte dessen, der der Messias ist oder der es zumindest sein könnte, darf man nicht einfach vergessen! Tatsächlich verweist Jesus immer wieder auf die eschatologische Tragweite seiner Worte /113/.

4) Ein grosser Teil der synoptischen Tradition besteht aus kurzen Worten, die durch Bildhaltigkeit, Hyperbolik, Kontraste uä. sehr eindringlich und damit auch einprägsam sind. Besonders poetische Stilmittel wie Parallelismus, Rhythmus, Reim usw. zeigen, dass Jesus diese Sprüche bewusst geformt hat. Die Kunst der Maschaldichtung konnte Jesus aus der intensiven Beschäftigung mit dem Alten Testament lernen. Das inhaltliche Gewicht und die stilistische Abrundung dieser Aussprüche zeigt, dass es sich um Lehrresumés handelte, die er bei verschiedenen Gelegenheiten wiederholte.

5) Einleitungsformeln wie das spezifisch jesuanische 'Amen, ich sage euch' oder der häufig auftauchende Aufruf zum 'Hören' wiesen auf solche besonderen Zusammenfassungen hin und forderten damit mehr oder weniger direkt zum Auswendiglernen auf. Der 'Heilandsruf', in dem Jesus von sich nach Art der lehrenden Weisheit (vgl. Sir 51,23-28) spricht, umfasst den Imperativ 'Lernt von mir!' (Mt 11,29).

6) Wenn Jesus dem engeren Kreis seiner Anhänger den Namen *talmid* 'Schüler' gab, so deutet das doch darauf hin, dass zu ihrer Aufgabe auch das Lernen seiner Lehre gehörte. Lk 11,1 -4 sagt ausdrücklich, dass Jesus seine Jünger ein längeres Traditionsstück lehrte. Wenn Jesus sie in seinem Auftrag zu

Verkündigung des Reiches Gottes aussandte (Mt 10 Par.), so
bedeutete das nach altorientalischem Botenrecht, dass sie die
authentischen Worte ihres Auftraggebers weitergeben konnten.
Die Aussendung forderte eine Unterweisung in den wichtigsten
Lehrresumés.

7) Da ein vorösterlicher Beginn der Jesus-Überlieferung
aus mehreren Gründen naheliegt, darf man mit Riesenfeld und
Gerhardsson ein grösseres Vertrauen in die Zuverlässigkeit der
synoptischen Tradition setzen, als das vom Ansatz der
'formgeschichtlichen Schule' her möglich ist.

ANMERKUNGEN

1.  The Gospel Tradition and Its Beginnings, *TU* 73 (1959) 43-65.
    Nachdruck: *The Gospel Tradition*, 1970, 1-29.
2.  Zum Ausdruck: H. Burkhardt, *Theologische Beiträge* 1 (1970)
    21-28.
3.  *The Gospel Tradition*, 22.
4.  *Memory and Manuscript*, 1961, 19-188.
5.  A.a.O. 193-335.
6.  Z.B. T. Soiron, *Die Logia Jesu*, 1916; J. Ranft, *Der Ursprung
    des katholischen Traditionsprinzips*, 1931.
7.  *The Gospel before the Gospels*, 1928; *JBL* 50 (1931) 148-155.
8.  *Jochanan Ben Zakkai*, 1899, 8; *Die Geschichte des Christus*,
    ²1923, 7.
9.  *Historisch-kritischer Versuch über die Entstehung und die
    frühesten Schicksale der schriftlichen Evangelien*, 1818,
    passim.
10. *ThLZ* 66 (1941) 83.
11. Vgl. L. Hartman, *Faculty of Theology at Uppsala University*,
    1976, 60f.
12. Bibliografie: B. Gerhardsson, *Die Anfänge der Evangelien-
    Tradition*, 1977, 66.
13. Z.B. *The Rabbinic Traditions about the Pharisees before 70
    A.D.* I-III, 1970.
14. *Jesus*, ²1929, 55.
15. *Jesus der Mensch*, 1973, 126.
16. Vgl. M. Hengel, *Nachfolge und Charisma*, 1968, 46-48.
17. Vgl. H. Shanks, *JQR* 53 (1962/3) 337-345; 59 (1968/9) 152-
    157.
18. Vgl. R. Schnackenburg, *Das Johannesevangelium II*, ²1977,
    184f.
19. Vgl. S. Krauss, *Das Leben Jesu*, 1902, 156f.
20. *Tradition and Transmission*, 1964, 16-21.

21. Vgl. 1Makk 1,14; 2Makk 4,9.12.

22. Vgl. L. Dürr, *Das Erziehungswesen im AT und im Alten Orient*, MVÄG 36,2 (1932); H. J. Hermisson, *Studien zur israelitischen Spruchweisheit*, 1968, 113-136; B. Lang, *Die weisheitliche Lehrrede*, 1972, 36-46; H. W. Wolff, *Anthropologie des AT*, [3]1977, 298-308.

23. N. Morris, *The Jewish School*, 1937; N. Drazin, *History of Jewish Education*, 1940; E. Ebner, *Elementary Education in Ancient Israel*, 1956; A. S. Roth, *Rabbinic Foundations of Jewish Education*, Diss. Evanston 1957; J. W. Carpenter, *The Jewish Educational System*, Diss. Washington 1958; M. Hengel, *Judentum und Hellenismus*, [2]1973, 143-152; S. Safrai, in: *The Jewish People* I/2, 1976, 945-970.

24. Davon kann man reden, wenn geformte Stoffe kontrolliert weitergegeben werden.

25. Vgl. W. Bacher, *Die exegetische Terminologie der jüdischen Traditionsliteratur*, I 1899, 194.

26. Vgl. G. von Rad, *Weisheit in Israel*, 1970, 42f.

27. Vgl. H. Brunner, *Altägyptische Erziehung*, 1957, 179.182.

28. Vgl. E. Nielsen, *Oral Tradition*, 1954, 59.

29. Vgl. Wolff, *Anthropologie des AT*, 80f.

30. Vgl. B. Lang, *Anweisungen gegen die Torheit*, 1973, 8.

31. Vgl. S. Krauss, *Talmudische Archäologie III*, 1912, 227-229.

32. Vgl. T. Klauser, *RAC* I, 1950, 1034.

33. Vgl. E. Drioton, *Annals of the Faculty of Arts*, 1 (Kairo 1951) 55-71.

34. Brunner, *Altägyptische Erziehung*, 54.

35. Vgl. Ex 13,8f.14-16; Dtn 6,7-9; 11,18-21; 31,21; Spr 4,10.

36. *Ap* II 178 vgl. *Ant* IV 210.

37. Forschungsüberblick: J. Gutmann, *AA* 87 (1972) 36-40.

38. *SpecLeg* II 62; *VitMos* II 216; *LegGaj* 132.

39. *jMeg* 73d; *jKeth* 35c; *Keth* 105a; *Git* 58a; *Ber* 8a; 30b. Allerdings sind die Zahlenangaben durchweg übertrieben.

40. Vgl. M. Avi-Yonah, *Encyclopedia of Archaeological Excavations* IV, 1978, 1129.

41. Mt 4,23/Mk 1,39; Mt 9,35; Lk 4,14f.

42. Vgl. V. Corbo, *Liber Annuus* 24 (1974) 19-28.

43. Vgl. *BAR* 5, 1979, 15-19.

44. Vgl. C. Perrot, *La lecture de la Bible dans la synagogue*, 1973.

45. Vgl. C. Perrot, *La Maison-Dieu* 126 (1976) 26-29.

46. Vgl. *Bill* IV/1 189-205.

47. Vgl. I. Elbogen, *Der jüdische Gottesdienst*, [3]1931, 236.238.

48. Vgl. *Bill* IV/1 205-207.

49. Vgl. P. Billerbeck, *ZNW* 55 (1964) 145.

50. Vgl. *jBer* 3c; *Ber* 12a. Dazu: E. Lerle, *NovT* 10 (1968) 34f.
51. Mt 19,18f/Mk 10,19/Lk 18,20; Röm 13,9. Dazu: M. J. Lagrange, *Saint Marc*, 1966, 266.
52. Lk 10,26f. Dazu: J. Jeremias, *Abba*, 1966, 74.
53. Vgl. *Bill* IV/1 208-249.
54. Vgl. Safrai, in: *The Jewish People*, 916f.
55. Vgl. Billerbeck, *ZNW* 55 (1964) 148.
56. Vgl. Safrai, in: *The Jewish People*, 922-926.
57. Vgl. *Bill* IV/1 206f.
58. Vgl. *Bill* IV/1 394.
59. *Talmudische Archäologie III*, 77.
60. Vgl. Elbogen, *Der jüdische Gottesdienst*, 503.
61. Vgl. Anm. 44.
62. Vgl. *Bill* IV/1 157f; Perrot, *La lecture*, 137f.
63. Vgl. Billerbeck, *ZNW* 55 (1964) 152.
64. *Tanch Jethro* 90a (*Bill* IV/1 158).
65. Vgl. *TBM* 2,21; *TSchab* 1,12; *Ber* 8b; *ExR* 40 (Ende); *SDtn* 11, 22.
66. Vgl. Gerhardsson, *Memory and Manuscript*, 68.
67. *Meg* 2,1; *jMeg* 74d; vgl. weiter *Bill* IV/1 160f.
68. Vgl. Hermisson, *Spruchweisheit*, 113-136.
69. Vgl. M. Hengel, *Judentum und Hellenismus*, [2]1973, 150.
70. Vgl. L. Dürr, MVÄG 36,2 (1932) 22; Brunner, *Altägyptische Erziehung*, 72-76. 128-133.
71. Vgl. A. Falkenstein, *WO* 1 (1948) 172-186; Nielsen, *Oral Tradition*, 19f.
72. Vgl. M. P. Nilsson, *Die hellenistische Schule*, 1955, 4.46f; H. I. Marrou, *Geschichte der Erziehung im klassischen Altertum*, 1957, 226.243f.
73. Vgl. Marrou a.a.O. 396.407f.
74. *Altägyptische Erziehung*, 76.
75. Vgl. Dürr, MVÄG 36,2 (1932) 115f; Hermisson, *Spruchweisheit*, 123.134f.
76. Vgl. Lang, *Die weisheitliche Lehrrede*, 39.62.
77. Vgl. Morris, *The Jewish School*, 112-145; Drazin, *Jewish Education*, 109-116; Ebner, *Elementary Education*, 88-95; Roth, *Rabbinic Foundations*, 106-113; Carpenter, *Educational System*, 205-221; Safrai, in: *The Jewish People*, 950-952.
78. Vgl. Brunner, *Altägyptische Erziehung*, 76.132.
79. Vgl. *Schab* 63a; *AZ* 19a. Vgl. weiter Gerhardsson, *Memory and Manuscript*, 126-130.
80. Vgl. Brunner, *Altägyptische Erziehung*, 74f.
81. Vgl. *jMeg* 75b; *Meg* 22a; 27a; Taan 27b. Dazu: L. Wiesner, *Die Jugendlehrer der talmudischen Zeit*, 1914, 27 Anm. 1.
82. Vgl. Brunner, *Altägyptische Erziehung*, 75f.

83. Vgl. Marrou, *Geschichte der Erziehung*, 87.
84. Vgl. Anm. 77.
85. Vgl. R. N. Whybray, *The Book of Proverbs*, 1972, 56.
86. Vgl. Nielsen, *Oral Tradition*, 59f.
87. Vgl. Lang, *Die weisheitliche Lehrrede*, 36-40.
88. Vgl. H. Gressmann, *ZAW* 42 (1924) 291.
89. Vgl. *jMeg* 71d; *Schab* 104a.
90. Vgl. Marrou, *Geschichte der Erziehung*, 222.
91. Vgl. Brunner, *Altägyptische Erziehung*, 67; Marrou, *Geschichte der Erziehung*, 226.
92. Vgl. H. L. Jansen, *Die spätjüdische Psalmendichtung*, 1937, 100-119.
93. Vgl. Josephus, *Ant* II 210; *TestN* 8,5.
94. Vgl. 1QH 11,21; 1QSa 1,7; CD 10,6; 13,2.
95. O. Betz, *Offenbarung und Schriftforschung in der Qumransekte*, 1960, 21.
96. Vgl. Nielsen, *Oral Tradition*, 32f.46f.49.
97. V. Burr, *Bibliothekarische Notizen zum AT*, 1969,6.
98. Vgl. W. F. Albright, *BASOR* 92 (1943) 16-26.
99. Vgl. z.B. *Meg* 32a; *Ned* 37a/b; *BB* 21a; *Sot* 30b *Bar*; *GenR* 52,4. Dazu: Krauss, *Talmudische Archäologie, III*, 227-229.
100. Vgl. *jHor* 48b; *Chag* 15a; *Taan* 19a.
101. *Comm in Jer* 25,26; *Ad Tit* 3,9.
102. *Comm in Is* 58,2.
103. Vgl. *PraepEv* XI 5,513.
104. Vgl. Krauss, *Talmudische Archäologie III*, 354 Anm. 243.
105. Vgl. R. Riesner, *ThB* 8 (1977) 59.
106. Vgl. T. Reinach, *Textes d'auteurs Grecs et Romains relatifs aux Judaisme*, 1895, 263 Anm. 2.
107. Nach Augustinus, *CivD* VI 10.
108. Dazu: Gerhardsson, *Memory and Manuscript*, 122-170.
109. P. Gaechter, *Das Matthäus-Evangelium*, o.J. (1963) 18.
110. Vgl. auch J. J. Vincent, Did Jesus teach His Disciples to learn by Heart, *TU* 88 (1964) 105-118.
111. *Jesus als Lehrer. Eine Untersuchung zum Ursprung der Evangelien-Überlieferung*, Dissertation Universität Tübingen (in Vorbereitung).
112. Vgl. CD 6,11; 7,18; 4QFlor 1,11; 4QMessAr 1; *TestJud* 24, 2f; *TestL* 18,1-7; *PsSal* 17,42f; 18, 4-6; *Targ Jes* 53,5.11; *ÄthHen* 46,3; 49,3f; 51,3; 69,29; *Memar Marqah* 4,12; *Midr Ps* 21, 19a; *GenR* 98-99; *Tanch Waje̱hi* 57b.
113. Vgl. Mk 8,38/Lk 9,26; Mt 7,24-27/Lk 6,47-49; Mt 24,35/Mk 13,31/Lk 21,33.

# The "Criteria" for Authenticity

Robert H. Stein
Bethel College
3900 Bethel Drive
St. Paul, MN 55112

It is evident from even a cursory reading of the literature that scholarly attitudes toward the historicity of the gospel materials vary drastically.  On the one side we have those scholars who possess a positive attitude toward the gospel materials and state 'In the synoptic tradition it is the inauthenticity, and not the authenticity, of the sayings of Jesus that must be demonstrated'. /1/  On the other side we have those who possess an equally negative attitude toward the materials

> . . . clearly, we have to ask ourselves the question as to whether this saying should now be attributed to the early Church or to the historical Jesus, *and the nature of the synoptic tradition is such that the burden of proof will be upon the claim to authenticity.* /2/

The latter view clearly presumes that the gospel traditions are "guilty," i.e. historically not true, unless they can be proven "innocent."

## The Burden of Proof

The question of the historicity of the gospel materials has been dealt with in a number of ways in the past.  One popular method was to evaluate the general historicity of the gospel materials by comparing those historical portions of the gospel materials which have parallels in secular or non-Christian historical records and see whether these records support or tend to deny the historicity of the gospel parallels.  By this means perhaps some general attitude might develop toward the accuracy or inaccuracy of the gospel accounts as a whole.  Another attempt has been to establish if a gospel writer was an eyewitness to the accounts he records in his Gospel.  If he was an eyewitness, then this would lend credence to the historicity of his account.  The problems with this approach, however, are two-fold.  For one, only two of our

Gospels are associated traditionally with eyewitnesses and it
is a much debated question as to whether any of them actually
were written, as we now find them, by an eyewitness.
Secondly, even if they were written by eyewitnesses, this does
not in itself demonstrate that what they wrote are accurate
historical accounts of the life of Jesus.  It does not of
necessity follow that eyewitness accounts of historical events
are *a priori* accurate historical accounts!  Such accounts are
of course, all other things being equal, better historical
records than non-eyewitness accounts.  We cannot, however,
assume that we have proven the historicity of the gospel
accounts if we can demonstrate that behind them stands the
testimony of an eyewitness.  On the other hand it seems
logical to assume that, if eyewitness testimony of the gospel
materials could be established, then the burden of proof
should rest upon those who would deny the historicity of the
events reported.

     A final example that shall be mentioned with regard to
the attempt to establish a general attitude toward the
question of historicity and our Gospels is to evaluate the
process by which the tradition was preserved and passed on.
In this method, sometimes called Form Criticism and sometimes
Tradition Criticism, /3/ various arguments are frequently
raised in support of the substantive accuracy of the gospel
accounts.  Some of those mentioned most frequently are:

     1.   The existence of the eyewitnesses during this period
would have had the effect of seeing that those traditions
would be faithfully preserved and that non-historical traditions would not be added. /4/

     2.   The existence of a center of leadership (the
Jerusalem Church) would have caused the traditions to be
passed down carefully and accurately. /5/

     3.   The high view found in the New Testament toward the
traditions (cf. Romans 6:17--the church does not preserve the
traditions but the traditions preserve the church;
1 Corinthians 7:10 and 12--note how Paul carefully
distinguishes between what Jesus has said about divorce and
what he has not said) indicates that during the oral period
the traditions were carefully preserved and safeguarded.

4.  The faithfulness of the early church in transmitting various difficult sayings of Jesus (cf. Mark 9:2; 10:18; 13:32; Matthew 10:5) witnesses to the reliable transmission of the gospel materials.

5.  The view that much of the gospel material was simply created by the early church *de novo* to meet its religious needs and solve various religious problems is difficult to accept in the light of the fact that several of the major problems that the early church encountered never show up in the gospel materials. Since the first and most important issue that the early church faced was the question of whether Gentile Christians had to be circumcised, one would expect to find some saying of Jesus that dealt with this issue, if the church were creating material to solve certain problems.

6.  We must also not forget that the ability to remember traditions and pass them on faithfully is not limited by our present-day inability to do this or to conceive of this.  The introduction of cheap writing materials into the world has had a negative impact in that it has paralyzed our abilities to memorize and to use the mind, rather than notebooks and files, as a data-bank.

Although the above-mentioned attempts to establish the historicity of the Gospels are worthwhile and provide a general attitude toward the Gospel materials, when we seek to discover what the resultant general attitude is, we find no consensus at all.  The present writer believes that the arguments listed above are sufficient to establish that the burden of proof ought to be with those scholars who deny the historicity of the gospel materials.  To assume the inauthenticity of the gospel materials, unless proven otherwise, appears to be an extreme skepticism unwarranted both in the light of the various arguments listed above and a violation of a common courtesy every witness deserves. /6/  A witness should be presumed innocent until proven guilty.  Of course, if through the investigation of an account one arrives at a "general attitude" toward its historical veracity which is negative, then one cannot help but change the burden of proof, so that the historicity rather than the unhistorical nature of the accounts must be demonstrated.  For this writer, however, this has in no way been demonstrated with regard to the gospel materials.

Besides these general arguments which are primarily
helpful in establishing a general attitude toward the gospel
material, there exist certain tools which can be used to
ascertain the historicity, or at least the historical
probability, of a specific saying, teaching, or action of
Jesus found in the Gospels.  These 'tools' or 'rules of thumb'
have been referred to as 'criteria' by which the authenticity
(or unauthenticity) of certain material can be established.
Before we investigate these criteria, however, we must discuss
briefly what is meant by the term 'authentic.'

## The 'Authenticity' of Jesus' Sayings

At first glance it would appear somewhat superfluous to
discuss what is meant by an "'authentic' saying of Jesus," but
because of the particular way in which this term has been
defined by James M. Robinson such a discussion is mandatory.
In contrast to the more traditional way of defining 'authentic'
as 'being actually and exactly what the thing in question is
said to be,' /7/ so that an 'authentic saying of Jesus' would
mean 'an actual saying of the historical Jesus,' Robinson has
defined the term according to his own existential concepts of
historiography.  Robinson states

One may however observe that material regarded as wholly
'unauthentic' in terms of positivistic historiography may
not seem nearly as 'unauthentic' in terms of modern [read-
existential] historiography.  For a saying which Jesus
never spoke may well reflect accurately his historical
significance, and in this sense be more 'historical' [or
authentic] than many irrelevant things Jesus actually
said. /8/

In so redefining the "hopelessly ambiguous term 'authentic'"
Robinson, however, has not contributed anything to clarity.
To claim that a saying which was created by the early church
and was therefore not uttered by the historical Jesus is an
'authentic saying of Jesus' whereas an actual saying which
the historical Jesus uttered is not an 'authentic saying' can
only lead to more confusion rather than clarification.  We
shall therefore define an 'authentic saying of Jesus' as an
actual saying which was uttered by the historical Jesus
before his death.  We shall leave out of the question
entirely the issue of whether such a saying reveals 'Jesus'
existential selfhood.' /9/  All such existential

considerations will be ignored, for the clearest way to avoid all ambiguity is to reserve the term "authentic" for only those words which the Jesus of history actually spoke. /10/ Sometimes the terms *ipsissima verba* (the exact/very words of Jesus) or *ipsissima vox* (the very voice of Jesus) are used to distinguish between the degree of exactness which is assumed. The latter expression would be used in a saying when the words of that saying are not necessarily the exact words Jesus, himself, used but nevertheless accurately express his intention and meaning.

It needs to be pointed out that the term "authentic" is not to be construed as synonymous with the term "authoritative." Evangelicals would, of course, maintain that "authentic" material in the Gospels are "authoritative," for Jesus' words were, are, and will remain authoritative (Mark 13:31). Yet, if a saying attributed to Jesus in the Gospels were inauthentic, its authoritative quality would remain, for the Evangelists not only recalled what the historical Jesus said and did but were taught by the Spirit and empowered by Him to interpret what the historical Jesus said and did (John 14:26; 16:14). Thus in the Gospels the risen Christ also speaks through his Spirit by means of his prophets and apostles. These words are also authoritative even if not authentic. As a result if the inauthenticity of a saying should be demonstrated this should not be taken to mean that this saying lacks authority.

## The Criteria for Authenticity

The criteria discussed below are not new or unique, and some are of more value than others in seeking to establish the authenticity of the gospel materials. The order in which they are presented should furthermore not be interpreted as implying any judgment as to their respective value. They are discussed in this particular order simply because in general they have been suggested in this order.

1. *The Criterion of Multiple Attestation or The Cross-Section Approach.*

One of the earliest criteria suggested for ascertaining the authenticity of a gospel tradition was the criterion of multiple attestation. The basic idea behind the use of this criterion is that a word is 'confirmed by the evidence of two

or three witnesses (Matt. 18:16).' Essentially this criterion
involves the use of literary criticism. Building upon the
generally accepted solution of the synoptic problem, this
view assumes that behind our Synoptic Gospels lie various
sources--Mark, "Q," "M," and "L". /11/ To these can be added
the Gospel of John. Since each source is essentially an
historical witness, if a particular teaching or activity of
Jesus is witnessed to in Mark, "Q," "M," "L," and John then
the authenticity of this teaching or activity is "confirmed
by the evidence of five witnesses."

One of the earliest scholars who advocated the use of this
criterion was F. C. Burkitt. Burkitt stated

It appeared to me that the starting-point we require may
be found in those Sayings which have a real double
attestation. The main documents out of which the
Synoptic Gospels are compiled are (1) the Gospel of Mark,
and (2) the lost common origin of the non-Marcan
portions of Matthew and Luke, i.e. the source called Q.
Where Q and Mark appear to report the same saying, we
have the nearest approach that we can hope to get to the
common tradition of the earliest Christian society about
our Lord's words. /12/

Burkitt then went on to list thirty-one of these 'doubly
attested sayings.' /13/ An example of the application of this
criterion might be the attempt to establish whether Jesus
taught that the kingdom of God was realized in his own
ministry. Witnesses that would support the view that the
realized eschatology of the Gospels was authentic would be:
Mark 2:21-22; "Q" (Luke 11:20); "M" (Matt. 5:17); "L" (Luke
17:20-21); and John 12:31. In general this criterion would
appear to be more helpful in determining the authenticity of
general motifs in Jesus' teaching rather than in establishing
the authenticity of a particular saying. /14/

Of all the criteria to be discussed this criterion has
the advantage of being 'the most objective of the proposed
criteria.' /15/ A number of criticisms, however, have been
raised with regard to its use. It is obvious from the start
that the usual application of this criterion is based upon a
particular solution of the Synoptic Problem. Recently this
solution, that of Lachmann and Streeter, (Matthew used Mark,
"Q," "M;" Luke used Mark, "Q," "L") has been challenged and

in the minds of some scholars "refuted." /16/  If the
"traditional" solution to the Synoptic Problem is not
acceptable any longer, this will, of course, bring about a
major revision of what sources lie behind the Synoptic
Gospels.  If the Griesbach hypothesis (Luke used Matthew; Mark
used Matthew and Luke) is correct, this would mean that we
have essentially only the following sources for the Synoptic
Gospel: Matthew /17/ and "L" (the material in Luke not found
in Matthew), for Mark's contribution would be minimal since
95% of Mark is found in Matthew or Luke.  The criterion of
multiple attestation would still be usable but would be of
lesser value since we shall have lost entirely one witness--
"M" and due to size (the 5% of Mark not obtained from
Matthew) for all real purposes have lost another--Mark!  On
the other hand the question must be raised as to whether the
appearance of the same tradition in Matthew-Mark-Luke should
be considered as only one witness, whether Mark (à la Lachmann
and Streeter) or Matthew (à la Griesbach and Farmer).  Does not
the fact that two Gospel writers chose to incorporate the
account of another Gospel writer into their works witness to
a three-fold testimony to that tradition?  Unless we assume
that the later Evangelists were totally unfamiliar with the
traditions found in Mark (or Matthew), then we must grant
additional credence to the testimony of an account found in
the triple tradition, for in their acceptance of the
traditions in their source they give corroborative testimony
to the primitiveness of those traditions.

   Another criticism of this criterion is that all that one
ultimately can be sure of is that, if a tradition is found in
all or most of the various sources laying behind our Gospels,
that tradition is deeply embedded in the earliest traditions
of the early church.  Multiple attestation does not prove
*absolutely* that the tradition is authentic!  On the other
hand the criterion of multiple attestation can, if we are
able to establish the existence of various sources lying
behind the Gospels, establish the probability that such a
motif is authentic.  McArthur states in this regard

   My own proposal would be that the order of priority
   should be reversed so that the criterion of multiple
   attestation is given first place, at least in order or
   procedure [instead of the criterion of dissimilarity].
   Furthermore I would propose that when three or four of
   the synoptic sources concur in providing evidence for a

given motif in the ministry of Jesus then the burden of
proof should be regarded as having shifted to those who
deny the historicity of that motif. /18/

McArthur's point would appear to be valid.  The multiple
attestation of a motif in the Gospels should place the burden
of proof upon those who would deny the authenticity of that
motif, for the tradition has been "confirmed by the evidence
of two or three witnesses."  On the other hand C. F. D. Moule
has argued that the negative use of this criterion is
illegitimate. /19/  There is no reason or need to deny the
authenticity of a tradition simply because it is found in only
one source.  The most that can be and should be said about
such a tradition is that it is difficult or impossible to
establish the authenticity or inauthenticity of such a
tradition on this basis alone.  To assume the inauthenticity
of such a witness is to assume that anyone who testifies to any
event without corroborating evidence is to be assumed a "false
witness."  Historical research may not be able to assume that
the witness of a single source is true, but it has no right to
assume that it is false.  The wisest course in such an instance
is to withhold judgment unless other evidence is available.
This, interestingly enough, is what the Old Testament
does. /20/

It would appear then that despite various objections, the
criterion of multiple attestation is a helpful tool for
ascertaining the authenticity of a gospel tradition.  It is,
of course, not conclusive in and of itself, but its value
cannot be denied.  Surely the multiple attestation of a
tradition places the burden of proof upon those who would
argue against the authenticity of such a tradition or motif.
Furthermore, if other criteria are found to support the
historicity of such a tradition, then the historian *as
historian* should assume that such a tradition is indeed
authentic.

2.  *The Criterion of Multiple Forms*

Closely related to the criterion of multiple attestation
is the criterion of multiple forms.  This criterion was first
suggested as a tool for authenticity by C. H. Dodd who listed
six gospel motifs as authentic because they appeared in
multiple forms, i.e. in different form-critical categories. /21/
Surprisingly this criterion does not appear to have received

much attention in the literature. /22/ The basic assumption of this criterion is that the various forms of the gospel materials, such as pronouncement stories, miracle stories, stories about Jesus, parables, sayings, etc., centered in different contexts and spheres of interest in the early church and were therefore preserved and passed down through different channels. As a result if a motif is found in multiple literary forms, that motif came from a broad section of the early church and was deeply embedded in the earliest church traditions.

An example of the use of this criterion might be to see if Jesus' teaching that the kingdom of God was realized in his ministry meets the criterion of multiple forms. Thus we shall see how broadly based such a teaching was in the gospel traditions. In this instance it is evident that this motif is found in: pronouncement stories (Mark 2:18-20; Luke 11:14-22); miracle stories (Luke 5:36-39); and sayings (Matt. 5:17; 13:16-17). It is evident from the above that the various forms of the gospel materials portray Jesus as teaching that the kingdom of God came in his ministry. Does this, however, "prove" that this is an authentic motif of Jesus' teachings? Again we must answer in the negative. The appearance of this motif in multiple literary forms of the materials does not "prove" conclusively its authenticity, but at least 'the criterion has some value in distinguishing comparatively early from comparatively late traditions, but it is not as decisive as that of multiple attestation by a number of sources'. /23/ Assuming that the establishment of the early date of a tradition is a positive factor in the establishment of its authenticity, it would appear reasonable to suppose that the appearance of a tradition or motif in multiple forms is supportive, even if not conclusive, evidence for its authenticity. Furthermore if these different oral forms were passed on via different routes of transmission, /24/ then a common motif in these various forms assures us not only of the primitiveness of that motif but possesses a "multiple attestation" not unlike that discussed under our previous criterion.

3.  *The Criterion of Aramaic Linguistic Phenomena*

Another tool for authenticity that has been suggested involves the presence of Aramaisms in the gospel materials. Since it seems certain that the mother tongue of Jesus was Aramaic, and in particular a Galilean dialect of Aramaic, /25/

the presence of Aramaic linguistical characteristics in our
Greek gospel materials argues in favor of the primitiveness of
those particular traditions and the more primitive a tradition
is, the more likely it is that it stems from Jesus.  As a
result the Aramaic background of a saying '. . . is of great
significance for the question of the reliability of the gospel
tradition', /26/ and '. . . the closer the approximation of a
passage in the Gospels to the style and idiom of contemporary
Aramaic, the greater the presumption of authenticity'. /27/
Some of the earliest pioneering work done in this area was done
by Gustav Dalman, /28/ C. F. Burney, /29/ and C. C. Torrey,
/30/ but the two people who have done the most work in this
are Matthew Black /31/ and Joachim Jeremias. /32/

     This criterion has been applied in a number of ways to the
gospel materials.  Through the work of Burney, Black, Jeremias,
and others it is now evident that one form which Jesus
frequently used in his teachings was antithetical parallelism.
Jeremias lists over 138 examples of this form in the Synoptic
Gospels alone, /33/ and whereas some of these may be
inauthentic, it is impossible to deny that many of these
examples of antithetical parallelism come from Jesus, himself.
As a result, although no one would argue *a priori* that every
example of such parallelism in the Gospels is authentic, there
is good reason to believe that the probability of any example
of antithetical parallelism being authentic is greater than
that of other sayings not found in this form.  (This, of
course, must be qualified by an "all other things being
equal.")  By the use of this parallelism it may even be
possible to arrive at the more primitive form of a saying by
retranslating that saying back into a more perfect parallelism.
Thus the original form of Mark 8:35 may possibly be obtained by
the elimination of those words which disturb the parallelism.
Note how much more balanced the antithetical parallelism
becomes by omitting the words in parenthesis.  'For whoever
would save his life will lose it; and whoever loses his life
(FOR MY SAKE AND THE GOSPEL'S) will save it.'

     Another way in which this tool is used is to note the
presence of certain puns which are only puns in Aramaic but
not in Greek.  There are some puns which are puns in both Greek
and Aramaic such as Matt. 16:18 and John 3:8, and puns based
upon different meanings of the same word frequently carry over
into other languages.  (Compare: Luke 9:59-60; Mark 1:17; 4:9.)
An example of a pun which is only a pun in Aramaic is Matt.

23:23-24.

> Woe to you scribes and Pharisees, hypocrites! for you tithe
> mint and dill and cummin, and have neglected the weightier
> matters of the law, justice and mercy and faith; these you
> ought to have done, without neglecting the others.  You
> blind guides, straining out a gnat and swallowing a camel!

In the Greek New Testament this does not appear as a pun, but
when retranslated back into Aramaic the pun is evident because
the term for gnat is *galma* and for camel is *gamla*.  Thus we
have this pun: 'You blind guides, straining out a *galma* and
swallowing a *gamla*.' The possibility that this saying arose in
a Greek environment and by chance is converted into a pun when
translated into Aramaic is minimal.  It seems quite reasonable
to conclude that Matt. 23:23-24 arose in an Aramaic-speaking
environment.  One of the most intensive attempts to use this
linguistic criterion in order to arrive at the *ipsissima verba*
of Jesus is Joachim Jeremias' work on the Lord's Supper.
Jeremias /34/ has sought to argue for the authenticity of the
Markan account of the Lord's Supper on the basis of some twenty
Semiticisms, i.e. Aramaisms, which he finds in the Markan
account.

A number of criticisms have been raised, however, against
this criterion.  It has been objected that the presence of
such Aramaic linguistic phenomena in a tradition establishes
only that the tradition arose in an Aramaic-speaking context,
but that context could be the Aramaic-speaking church rather
than the historical Jesus, and such Aramaisms may not even be
therefore a sign of a saying's antiquity. /35/ Another
criticism is that the presence of Aramaisms in the gospel
materials may be due to Septuagintal influence on the part of
the Greek church or the Gospel writers. /36/ Whether this
influence was conscious or unconscious is beside the point.
Still another criticism of this criterion is that the
assumption that the gospel materials can be accurately
retranslated into Aramaic is itself questionable.  It would be
overly negative to argue that this cannot be done, but on the
other hand it may be that Black and Jeremias are a bit overly
optimistic about this.

As a result of these criticisms some scholars have
minimized the importance of this criterion or see it as
possessing only a negative function, /37/ i.e. if a tradition

contains non-Aramaic features then it (or at least those
features) cannot be authentic. Such criticism is unwarranted,
however, for at least two reasons. For one this criterion can
serve a negative function only if we can assume that Jesus did
not speak Greek and there is good reason to believe that he
did. /38/ As a result we cannot conclude with Fuller that
'. . . any saying of Jesus, if it is authentic, *should* exhibit
Aramaic features . . .', /39/ in that this precludes that at
times Jesus may have taught in Greek. Secondly such minimizing
of the value of this criterion is unnecessary. Certainly it
must be admitted that the mere presence of Aramaisms does not
prove that a tradition is authentic. Even Jeremias
acknowledges this. /40/ Yet if we can establish due to the
presence of Aramaisms (allowing, of course, for the possibility
of Septuagintal influence on the formation of the gospel
tradition in the Greek-speaking church) that a tradition must
go back at least to the Aramaic-speaking church, then we can
use this criterion as supportive testimony for the possibility/
probability that this tradition may have come from Jesus,
himself. Clearly the presence of such Aramaisms increases the
probability of such material being authentic, for to have been
translated from Aramaic into Greek and to have been used in
Mark and/or "Q" argues at the very least for the primitiveness
of such traditional material. Although the criterion of
Aramaic linguistic phenomena cannot alone establish the
authenticity of a saying or tradition, when used in conjunction
with other criteria this criterion becomes a valuable tool and
provides supportive testimony to the possible authenticity of
the saying or tradition.

## 4.   *The Criterion of Palestinian Environmental Phenomena*

Closely related to the previous tool is the criterion of
Palestinian environmental phenomena. According to this
criterion if a tradition betrays Palestinian social, domestic,
agricultural, religious, etc. customs, this argues that the
tradition originated in a Palestinian environment and cannot
be a later creation of the Greek, i.e. non-Palestinian church.
Again the argument here is that the closer we can trace a
tradition to the time and environment of Jesus, the more likely
it is that that tradition is authentic. /41/ Probably no
writer has used this tool more fully than Jeremias in his work
*The Parables of Jesus.* Jeremias argues, for instance, that

the pictorial element of the parables is drawn from the

daily life of Palestine.  It is noteworthy, for instance,
that the sower in Mark 4.3-8 sows so clumsily that much of
the seed is wasted; one might have expected a description
of the regular method of sowing, and that, in fact is what
we have here.  This is easily understood when we remember
that in Palestine sowing precedes ploughing . . . What
appears in the western mind as bad farming is simply
customary usage under Palestinian conditions. /42/

It has been pointed out, however, that Palestinian
environmental phenomena may not be as useful a tool as
originally presumed, for not all of the teachings of Jesus
or incidents in his life are so narrowly "Palestinian" that
they could not have arisen outside of Palestine.  Furthermore
Jesus, himself, may have said things that betray a Greek
environment more than a Palestinian one.  An example of this
is the following saying of Jesus on divorce.  'Whoever
divorces his wife and marries another, commits adultery
against her; and if she divorces her husband and marries
another, she commits adultery (Mark 10:11-12.)'  Frequently
the authenticity of this saying is denied on the grounds that
it betrays a non-Palestinian social and religious environment,
for in the saying there is the assumption that wives can
divorce their husbands and this was not permissable in Judaism.
This assumption has been challenged of late by some of the
material associated with the Bar Cochba revolt, /43/ but it
seems reasonable to assume that a Jewish wife divorcing her
husband would certainly have been an extremely rare incident
whereas among the Greeks this was not uncommon.  Yet there is
a realistic *Sitz im Leben* in the ministry of Jesus for just
such a saying, since the ruler of Galilee had a wife who had
done just that and John the Baptist had been executed at least
in part for having denounced this divorce and the subsequent
marriage.  Downing's statement that 'A Palestinian first-
century background is a necessary but not sufficient condition
for acceptance as authentic; if it were Palestinian Gentile,
the critic should be worried but not dismayed' /44/ should be
carefully noted.  Whether Mark 10:11-12 is authentic or not is
not the issue at hand, however.  What is important is to note
that it is conceivable and quite probable that Jesus could
have said things that reflect a non-Palestinian environment,
if we assume that Palestinian means non-Gentile or non-Greek.
Thus this criterion, like any criterion, is limited in its
application.

The main criticism against this criterion is that at best it can only root the tradition in question in Palestinian Christianity. It cannot demonstrate that the tradition goes back even further to the historical Jesus. This is, of course, true, but the presence of such Palestinian environmental phenomena does nevertheless increase the likelihood that a tradition possessing such phenomena stems from Jesus, himself.

5. *The Criterion of the Tendencies of the Developing Tradition*

Whereas the previous criteria serve a positive function, this proposed criterion serves a primarily negative function. It is a negative tool which has been proposed by the form-critics. According to form-critical theory the passing on of the tradition during the oral period proceeded according to certain "laws" and by understanding these "laws" we can determine what aspects of the tradition are late, i.e. inauthentic. Bultmann states

> . . . the study of the laws which govern literary transmission, can be approached by observing the manner in which the Marcan material was altered by Matthew and Luke; and also how Matthew and Luke worked over what they took from the *Logia*. Here we observe a certain regular procedure which becomes still more evident when we carry the investigation to a later tradition, particularly to the apocryphal gospels, and see how in these the gospel material received further literary development . . . The ability to make the necessary distinctions can be developed by studying the general laws which govern popular transmission of stories and traditions in other instances, for example, in the case of folk-tales, anecdotes, and folk-songs. /45/

This criterion then serves as a negative scalpel to remove the later accretions and modifications of the early tradition, but in so doing it serves also a positive function by helping in the recovery of the earlier form of the tradition, and the earlier the form the greater the possibility that we have an authentic saying or incident in the life of Jesus.

A possible example of how this criterion may be applied to the gospel materials is the parable of the lost sheep which is found in Matt. 18:12-14 and Luke 15:4-7. It is generally

agreed that "Matthew" wrote his Gospel to Jewish Christians.
On the other hand it is clear that certain parables of Jesus
were originally addressed not to believers but to his
opponents.  In Luke 15:1-2 Luke describes the following
parables as having been used apologetically by Jesus to defend
himself against those who murmured that he received sinners
and ate with them.  The parable of the lost sheep, at least
according to Luke, is therefore a defense of Jesus' behavior
in eating with the outcastes of Jewish society.  That this is
the correct setting of the parable is evident from the fact
that this seems to have been a frequent charge leveled against
Jesus (see Mark 2:16-17; Matt. 11:19; Luke 7:39; 19:7).
Furthermore there would appear to be no real reason why Luke
might have changed the audience from the "Church" to Jesus'
opponents (if the parable was originally addressed to the
"Church" as we find in Matthew) whereas there is good reason
why Matthew might have changed the audience from Jesus'
opponents to the "Church" (if it was originally addressed to
Jesus' Jewish opponents as we find in Luke).  It would appear
therefore that whereas Luke seems more authentic in his
setting of this parable, Matthew seeks to apply its teachings
to his own audience which does not consist of opponents of
Jesus but rather of his followers!  As a result, whereas
originally this parable of Jesus was primarily a defense of
his actions in associating with publicans and sinners, for
Matthew and his readers there is no great need for such a
defense of Jesus' behavior, and so the emphasis lies most
heavily upon the content of that defense: God's great love
for the outcastes of society and the inbreaking of the kingdom
of God by God's visiting the rejected of Israel. /46/  Matthew
applies this great truth to his own *Sitz im Leben* by
addressing the parable to the disciples (Matt 18:1), i.e. the
leaders of the church, in order that they may exercise loving
pastoral leadership to those in the church community that have
made themselves outcastes and apostates.  Even as Jesus sought
the outcastes of Judaism, so the leaders of the church should
seek to restore to the kingdom of God its own outcastes. /47/
From the above it is evident that if we recognize certain of
the "laws" which the tradition experienced during the oral
period, such as the changing of the audience in the first and
the second/third *Sitz im Leben*, we shall be better able to
ascertain what is authentic.

   The main criticism of this criterion involves the
establishment of these "laws" by which the tradition was

passed on.  It must be pointed out that Bultmann and the form-
critics arrived at these "laws" based on a particular view of
the relationship of Matthew-Mark-Luke.  If this traditional
view is untenable, much of their argument and their results
will have to be changed, for the "laws" obtained on the
premise that Matthew used Mark will be quite different from
the "laws" obtained on the premise that Mark used Matthew and
Luke!  Recently E. P. Sanders has raised some very serious
questions about the whole matter of the "laws" of the
tradition. /48/  Although it would be overly pessimistic to
conclude that we know nothing about the tendencies present in
the passing on of the gospel materials during the oral period,
it seems clear that no such "laws" ruled with an iron hand over
the traditions.  Tendencies during this period indeed existed,
but "laws" did not!  As a result we need to exercise much more
care and reserve in determining what could or could not have
taken place and not speak of what must have taken place.
Furthermore we must also note that whereas we may ascertain
certain general tendencies or rules which were operative and
worked on the tradition, this does not tell us what happened
in any single specific instance.

The value of this criterion has been criticized of late
and rightfully so, but if it can be shown, by a careful
application of these tendencies, that certain aspects of the
gospel traditions seem to be later additions or modifications,
then the burden of proof would be upon those who argue that
these additions and modifications are authentic.  In stating
this it is of course self-evident that we must have a clear
understanding of what these tendencies in fact were, and
Sanders' criticisms must be given serious consideration.

6.  *The Criterion of Dissimilarity or Discontinuity*

Of all the criteria suggested for ascertaining the
authenticity of the gospel materials, the criterion of
dissimilarity (or distinctiveness) has been heralded as the
most useful.  The exact origin of this criterion is uncertain,
but the most important reference to this tool was clearly
Ernst Käsemann's famous address to the "Old Marburgers."
Käsemann suggested that

In only one case do we have more or less safe ground under
our feet [in seeking authentic material]; when there are
no grounds either for deriving a tradition from Judaism or

for ascribing it to primitive Christianity. . . . /49/

Earlier Schmiedel had made use of something similar to this
criterion for obtaining his seven "Pillar Passages" which could
not have arisen out of the early church, /50/ and Bultmann had
also said,

> We can only count on possessing a genuine similitude of
> Jesus where, on the one hand, expression is given to the
> contrast between Jewish morality and piety and the
> distinctive eschatological temper which characterized the
> preaching of Jesus; and where on the other hand we find
> no specifically Christian features. /51/

Although this criterion is usually treated as a single
tool, it consists essentially of two different parts which
could be and have been separated into two different criteria.
/52/   The first "part" involves whether we can find in the
Jewish thought of Jesus' day elements similar to the
particular teaching or motif in question.  If we cannot, the
assumption is then made that the said material could not have
arisen out of Judaism and later have been attributed to Jesus. An
example of how this works is Jeremias' investigations
involving the term "Abba" in the Gospels.  Where did this
designation for God in prayer arise?  Could it have arisen in
Judaism and then have been read back upon the lips of the
historical Jesus?  To this Jeremias gives a vehement "No."

> There is something quite new, absolutely new - the word
> *abba*.  With the help of my assistants I have examined the
> whole later Jewish literature of prayer, and the result
> was that in no place in this immense literature is this
> invocation of God to be found. . . Abba was a homely
> family word, the tender address of the babe to its father;
> O dear father - a secular word.  No Jew would have dared
> to address God in this manner.  Late Judaism never
> addressed God as *abba* - Jesus did it always. . . . /53/

The use of "Abba" as a designation for God in the Gospels
therefore satisfies, according to Jeremias, the first part of
the criterion of dissimilarity.  Other expressions frequently
suggested as meeting this part of the criterion are: the use
of "Amen" as an introductory expression; Jesus' offer of
salvation to the outcastes of Israel; Jesus' particular use of
parables; and Jesus' use of the title "Son of man." /54/

The second part of this criterion involves the question of whether we can find in the early Christian church elements similar to the particular teaching or motif in question. If we cannot, the assumption is then made that the material in question could not have arisen out of the early church and then read back upon the lips of the historical Jesus. Meyer has suggested that this part of the criterion alone established the authenticity of any gospel saying. For him '. . . the requirement of simultaneous discontinuity with Judaism and the post-paschal church errs by excess' /55/ in that 'Discontinuity with the post-paschal church is sufficient by itself to establish historicity'. /56/ Turner /57/ has also sought to modify this criterion somewhat by claiming that total discontinuity with the teachings of the early church is not necessary for even if they overlap somewhat with the gospel materials the criterion is met as long as there exists a marked difference between the church's teaching and the sayings in question. According to this modification there need not be an absolute qualitative difference to satisfy this criterion. Although Turner's suggestion seems reasonable, for the sake of argument we shall deal with those examples which do not even overlap. An example of this would be the use of "Amen" as an introductory expression. Since this is not found in the New Testament outside of our Gospels, this demonstrates its authenticity, for it meets both parts of the criterion of dissimilarity! /58/ Other teachings or motifs that would appear to meet this requirement are: the "Pillar Passages" of Schmiedel; Jesus' use of the parables; and the apocalyptic title "Son of man" which is found only in Acts 7:56 outside of the Gospels. /59/

Despite the great optimism with which this tool was embraced, there has recently been a heavy barrage of criticism leveled at this tool. The most detailed and vigorous criticism has come from Hooker. /60/ Some of these criticisms, however, are not so much criticisms of the criterion, itself, but of the misuse of the criterion. It has been objected that the criterion assumes the inauthenticity of a tradition if that tradition does not meet its standard. /61/ To be sure, some scholars have argued in this manner and are incorrect in so doing, but the criterion does not demand this conclusion! The criterion used as a *positive tool* does not deserve this criticism. A more serious objection is that this criterion eliminates the great majority of gospel materials, because most of this material does not conflict with both the Judaism of Jesus' day and the theology of the early church.  This criticism, of course, is true, for there is little material that really qualifies as authentic via this criterion.  But again this criticism does not in any way impugn upon the validity of the criterion for the material that meets its standards.  It only points out that the criterion is limited, perhaps extremely limited, in its application.  For the limited amount of material which qualifies under this criterion, however, the criterion of dissimilarity would appear to be an extremely valuable tool with regard to the question of authenticity.

A more substantial criticism of this criterion is that it presumes that we possess a sufficient knowledge of the Judaism of Jesus' day and the primitive Christian community to determine if a particular gospel tradition could not have arisen out of these environments.  Is our understanding of first-century Judaism and the early church, however, complete enough for concluding what could have and what could not have arisen out of Judaism and the primitive church? /62/  It is certainly true that our knowledge of both these areas of history is incomplete, so that to a certain extent this lack of knowledge makes our use of this tool an argument based on silence. /63/  The discovery of additional data no doubt may modify our present picture of both, but it would certainly be overly pessimistic and negative to assume that we are entirely ignorant of Palestinian Judaism in Jesus' day and of the early church or that future knowledge would change completely our present portrait of them.  Certain modifications and refinements can and no doubt will take place, but when and if our understanding changes we shall then simply incorporate this in our use of the criterion.  Again the validity of the tool is not in question in this criticism as long as we are cautious and exercise care in the use of the data available for our understanding of first-century Judaism and the early church.

Another cogent criticism of the criterion of dissimilarity is that what is distinct in Jesus' teaching may not necessarily be characteristic of it.  Hooker points out that

the English word "distinctive" can have two senses--as usual, the Germans use two words: "distinctive" can mean "unique" (what makes it distinct from other things, the German *verschieden*), or it can mean "characteristic" (the German *bezeichnend*).  In which sense is it being used

here?  Clearly the method is able only to give us the
former--but what we really *want* is the latter; and the
two are by no means necessarily the same. /64/

Hooker is clearly correct!  A movement arising in some way or
other from the life and teachings of Jesus which did not have
much in common with Jesus' actual teachings would be
impossible to conceive.  It would be like trying to conceive
of late sixteenth-century Lutheranism which was totally or
even primarily "distinct" from the teachings of Luther.  On
the contrary one would expect that what was "characteristic"
of Jesus' and Luther's teaching would be "characteristic" of
early Christianity and early Lutheranism respectively. /65/
Again we must be careful, however, not to assume that a valid
criticism of the misuse of this tool is in reality a valid
criticism of the tool, itself.  The tool does not claim to be
able to arrive at what is "characteristic" of Jesus' teaching,
even if some scholars have falsely assumed that what was
distinct was in fact the essence of his teaching.  The tool is
primarily concerned with ascertaining "a critically assured
*minimum*." /66/  If we take into consideration the limited aim
of this tool, it is possible to question how useful such a
tool is since so much of the gospel materials simply do not
qualify under this tool, *but* this in no way negates the value
of this tool for ascertaining the authenticity of those gospel
materials which meet the standards of this criterion. /67/

In concluding our discussion of this tool, it would appear
that despite many of the criticisms raised of late, when used
correctly in conjunction with its innate limitations, the
criterion of dissimilarity is nevertheless a most valuable
tool in the quest for the *ipsissima verba* or *vox* of Jesus.  It
may in fact be the single most valuable tool for authenticity,
for if a saying or action of Jesus in the gospel tradition
meets the demands of this criterion, the likelihood of it
being authentic is extremely good. /68/  It is true that this
tool cannot necessarily deliver to us that which is characteristic in Jesus' teachings or even to produce "an adequate
historical *core*," /69/ but it does give us a "critically
assured minimum" to which other material can be added via
other criteria.  Care must be taken, however, to apply this
tool more objectively than in the past, for McArthur has
pointed out that some 'advocates of the criterion relax its

its rigors when, on general grounds, they are convinced
material is authentic, but that they tighten it on the other
occasions.' /70/  It may be that the most objective way in
which we can make use of this tool is to exclude from our
sources for the theology of the early church all the gospel
materials and seek to arrive at our understanding of what the
early church believed only from Acts-Revelation and from any
non-canonical materials which may be relevant.  In so doing we
would avoid the kind of circular reasoning which concludes that
certain sayings or motifs in the Gospels are the creation of
the early church even though these sayings or motifs appear
nowhere outside the Gospels.  Perhaps the greatest example of
this is the total rejection of the authenticity of any of the
Son of man sayings by some scholars on the basis that these Son
of man sayings originated in the early church.  Yet the proof
that the early church possessed a Son of man theology is based
upon the very Son of man sayings under discussion.  Without
denying that the Gospels are a valuable source of information
for the history and theology of the early church, it would
nevertheless appear that caution would suggest that for the
particular saying or motif in question we should exclude the
gospel materials from serving as sources for the theology of
the early church.  Such caution will ultimately bring even
greater objectivity to the use of this tool.

### 7.  The Criterion of Modification by Jewish Christianity

This particular criterion is frequently associated with
the criterion of dissimilarity.  Käsemann has even given the
impression that this criterion functions primarily as a third
part of the criterion of dissimilarity.

> In only one case do we have more or less safe ground under
> our feet; when there are no grounds either for deriving a
> tradition from Judaism or for ascribing it to primitive
> Christianity, *and especially when Jewish Christianity has
> mitigated or modified the received tradition, as having
> found it too bold for its taste.* /71/

One example frequently given of how Jewish Christianity
allegedly modified the original teachings of Jesus in order to
fit better with its own situation is the famous "exception
clause" found in Matthew 5:32 and 19:9.  In contrast to the
Markan parallel in Mark 10:11-12 which reads, 'Whoever
divorces his wife and marries another, commits adultery

against her; and if she divorces her husband and marries
another, she commits adultery' and the "Q" parallel in Luke
16:18 which reads, 'Every one who divorces his wife and marries
another commits adultery, and he who marries a woman divorced
from her husband commits adultery,' Matthew has in both of
these sayings the exception 'except on the ground of
unchastity (Matt. 5:32)' or 'except for unchastity (Matt.
19:9).' In light of this two-fold agreement in Mark and "Q",
as well as the parallel in 1 Cor. 7:10-11 which also lacks an
exception clause, it seems reasonable to conclude that the
*ipsissima verba* of Jesus lacked this exception. /72/

It is clear that as a tool the criterion of modification
will serve both a negative and a positive function. The
presence of a demonstrated modification will of course serve
in a negative way by demonstrating that the modification is
not authentic, so that whereas the absence of modification by
early Jewish Christianity does not prove the authenticity of a
particular saying, the presence of a modification indicates at
least that the modification is not authentic. Yet Walker has
rightly pointed out that it is not easy to distinguish
'whether, when, and by whom the traditions in question were
modified' /73/ and points out that some early Christians no
doubt were more "radical-rigid-bold" in certain respects than
Jesus, himself, so that it is conceivable (although in the case
of the "exception clause" not very likely) that at times the
"harder reading" may not be authentic. Is it not conceivable
that certain groups in the early church, like the Judaizers of
Galatians 2 and Acts 15, may have taken an even harder, more
restricted line on certain issues than Jesus, himself, did?
Such criticisms do raise doubts over the applicability of this
criterion, but in theory, at least, it is of course true that
if we can demonstrate that a particular tradition has been
modified by the early church this not only witnesses negatively
to the authenticity of the modification but also positively
toward the authenticity of the tradition. The fact that the
early church modified such a tradition witnesses to the
probability that the tradition had such an authority and
ancient pedigree that the church or Evangelist could not
ignore the tradition but had to deal with it in the only other
way possible--by modifying it to suit the present context.
The modification of a tradition which the early Jewish church
"found too bold for its taste" therefore serves as a positive
testimony to the antiquity of the tradition and to its
dominical lineage.

8. *The Criterion of Divergent Patterns From the Redaction*

This criterion is essentially the second part of the criterion of dissimilarity applied to the third *Sitz im Leben*. Whereas in the criterion of dissimilarity we assume that dissimilarity between the theology of the early Jewish church and the gospel materials demonstrates that the material in question could not have arisen out of the early church and therefore is likely to be authentic, this criterion argues that such dissimilarity between the gospel materials and the redaction of the Evangelists argues in favor of such material (1) not having originated from the Evangelist and (2) being of such lineage that the Evangelist did not feel free to omit it. As Calvert says

> . . . the inclusion of material which does not especially serve his [the Evangelist's] purpose may very well be taken as a testimony to the authenticity of that material, or at least to the inclusion of it in the tradition of the Church in such a clear and consistent way that the evangelist was loath to omit it. /74/

The inclusion by the Evangelist of material that does not fit his theological scheme serves therefore as a non-intentional witness to the antiquity and authenticity of such material. Calvert lists as an example of this such kinds of material: positive statements about the disciples in Mark and negative statements about them in Matthew. Perhaps a better example of the inclusion of material by an Evangelist which seems to conflict with his main thrust would be the statement in Matt. 11:13 'For all the prophets and the law prophesied until John. . . .' This seems to conflict with Matthew's heavy emphasis on the permanent validity of the law found elsewhere in his Gospel--Matt. 3:15; 5:17-20; 7:12; 12:5--note the Markan parallel here; 23:1-3, 23. This "despite the author" kind of evidence is furthermore the very kind of evidence that historians often find most valuable.

> Nevertheless, there can be no doubt that, in the course of its development, historical research has gradually been led to place more and more confidence in the second category of evidence, in the evidence of witnesses in spite of themselves. /75/

An example of this kind of testimony is found in the Acts of

Paul and Thecla.  Whereas the work is clearly one in which the
Apostle Paul is eulogized, we find the following rather
negative description of the physical make-up of the Apostle.

> And he saw Paul coming, a man small of stature, with a
> bald head and crooked legs, in a good state of body, with
> eyebrows meeting and nose somewhat hooked, full of
> friendliness. . . . /76/

This "despite the author" negative description of the hero of
the work is surely of such a nature that it deserves serious
consideration.

It must be pointed out that this criterion does not and
cannot demonstrate the authenticity of any of the material
which meets the criterion.  All this criterion demonstrates is
that the Evangelist was "loath" to omit such material and
that this material had therefore a firm place in the tradition
of the church. /77/  The assumption seems legitimate, however,
that the more firm the place that a tradition had in the
church, the more likely it is that such a tradition was old
and well-known, and the older and better known a tradition,
the greater the probability that it is authentic.  This
criterion therefore, while not providing "proof" of
authenticity, does provide corroborative testimony to other
criteria that such a tradition possesses the "likelihood" of
being authentic and may serve as a link in a chain of arguments
which seeks to demonstrate the authenticity of the tradition.
On the other hand the criterion cannot be used negatively, for
if a tradition is in support of the theme of theology of an
Evangelist, this does not prove its inauthenticity unless it
can be demonstrated that such a theme or theology contradicts
the situation of Jesus, and if this is true it would be
primarily the concern of The Criterion of Contradiction of
Authentic Sayings. /78/

## 9.  *The Criterion of Environmental Contradiction*

This criterion serves a negative function and argues that
if a saying or motif in the gospel materials presupposes a
situation in the life of Jesus which was impossible, then the
saying or motif must be inauthentic. /79/  There would seem to
be little debate over this criterion, for if a saying was not
possible, by definition it could not have occurred!  In effect
this criterion is simply a tautology which states 'If a saying

or motif could not have been taught by Jesus, Jesus could not
have taught that saying or motif.' The basic problem with
this criterion is that 'It is difficult to assess what would
be unthinkable to Jesus, and the decision must often be that
of individual judgement.' /80/ Calvert gives as an example of
this problem Matt. 22:7 which supposedly reflects a post-A.D.
70 situation. Yet he points out Beasley-Murray's argument
that such a view depends upon the position one takes
concerning the possibility of prophetic prediction. J. A. T.
Robinson has furthermore argued, not without weight, that

> the wording of Matt. 22.7 represents a fixed description
> of ancient expeditions of punishment and is such an
> established *topos* of Near Eastern, Old Testament and
> rabbinic literature that it is precarious to infer that
> it must reflect a particular occurrence. /81/

It must nevertheless be acknowledged that the presence of
non-Palestinian environmental characteristics do argue against
the authenticity of such a saying. /82/ The problem is that
it is not easy to determine what could not have arisen in the
*Sitz im Leben* of Jesus. For some the statement found in Mark
10:12 is impossible in the first *Sitz im Leben* because Jewish
women could not divorce their husbands, but we have already
pointed out /83/ that John the Baptist was beheaded for
condemning just such a divorce, so that it is clearly not
impossible for Jesus to have uttered such a statement. This
criterion is therefore a valid negative tool for determining
inauthenticity, but possesses a very serious handicap in that
it is extremely difficult to determine what Jesus could not
have said in the first *Sitz im Leben*.

10. *The Criterion of Contradiction of Authentic Sayings*

Like the previous criterion this one also serves a
negative function "'A saying is unauthentic if it contradicts
a recognized authentic saying.'" /84/ Calvert admits that
this criterion is very limited in its application, for there
are few instances when one can say with certainty that two
sayings are contradictory. Furthermore the very nature of
Jesus' teaching which frequently used Overstatement, Paradox
and Hyperbole /85/ means that we must be extremely careful
that such a contradiction is not merely formal but actual,
i.e. that the contradiction of the two statements consists in
the meaning of the statements. Are, for instance, the

following two statements contradictory?

> If any one comes to me and does not hate his own father
> and mother and wife and children and brothers and
> sisters, yes, and even his own life, he cannot be my
> disciple (Luke 14:26)

> You have a fine way of rejecting the commandment of
> God, in order to keep your tradition! For Moses said,
> 'Honor your father and your mother'; and, 'He who
> speaks evil of father or mother, let him surely die'
> . . . (Mark 7:9-10; cf. also Luke 6:27).

Or is the command 'Judge not, that you be not judged (Matt.
7:1)' in contradiction with 'Do not give dogs what is holy;
and do not throw your pearls before swine. . . (Matt. 7:6)'
which demands that one "Judge" between "swine" and "non-swine"
and "dogs" and "non-dogs." /86/ We must exercise extreme care
therefore before we conclude that a real contradiction exists
between an authentic saying of Jesus and the saying that is
being compared with it.

Yet we must raise several other questions. Can we
assume *a priori* that Jesus did not make contradictory
statements? On what grounds? And can we assume that what we
consider contradictory could not have been seen by Jesus as
standing in a certain harmonious relationship? Is it possible
that the apparent contradiction between Jesus' teachings on
reward and grace /87/ may be more of a problem for western
minds than for the oriental mind of Jesus? Such considerations
should cause us to move with great caution before we say that
Jesus could not have said "A" because it conflicts (*in our way
of thinking*) with "B" which we know is an authentic saying of
Jesus. On the other hand this criterion does increase the
probability that any saying or motif which seems to contradict
an authentic saying or motif in Jesus' teaching is
inauthentic.

11.  *The Criterion of Coherence (or Consistency)*

This particular criterion has been placed last because it
is the last tool that should be applied in the quest for the
authentic sayings of Jesus. Its validity is dependent on the
presupposition that by wise and judicious use of the
previously listed criteria historical research can arrive at

authentic material, so that this "critically assured minimum" can now function as a template by which other material may be judged to be more or less authentic. According to Perrin 'material from the earliest strata of the tradition may be accepted as authentic if it can be shown to cohere with material established as authentic by means of the criterion of dissimilarity.' /88/ A good example of how this criterion has been used is provided by Carlston. Upon having concluded that Jesus' message was one of repentance in the light of the eschatological coming of the kingdom of God, he states concerning the parables 'An 'authentic' parable will fit reasonably well into the eschatologically based demand for repentance that was characteristic of Jesus' message. . . .' /89/

On purely logical grounds it would appear that the criterion of coherence is a valid tool, for if we can ascertain that that certain sayings of Jesus are authentic, then other sayings claiming to be uttered by Jesus which are in harmony with the ideas and motifs of the authentic material are more likely to be authentic than those which are not in harmony with such ideas and motifs. Certainly coherence does not prove that the materials being considered are authentic, for the early church could have created material which "cohered" with Jesus' authentic teachings. As a result the criterion of coherence cannot serve as an absolute proof of authenticity. It must also be acknowledged that this criterion will tend to magnify any previous mistakes that might have been made in establishing certain sayings as authentic, for if the template is in error, then any product of the template will contain the same error. /90/ Again, however, whereas this latter criticism is a valid one, it is not a criticism of the validity of the criterion but rather a criticism of the incorrect use of the criterion, i.e. using as our standard material that is not authentic. If we can in fact ascertain authentic material in the Gospels, then this criterion is a valid one. On the other hand we must be quick to acknowledge that the criterion cannot prove absolutely that consistent material is authentic or that non-consistent material is inauthentic. What this tool can do is to provide for the historian a greater likelihood that material which coheres with authentic material is also authentic, and this in turn can become one additional argument in the chain of arguments that must be brought to bear on the material in question. /91/

## Conclusion

Having investigated the most commonly suggested criteria
of authenticity, we need now to come to some general
conclusions as to the value of these criteria.  How useful are
they for arriving at our hoped for goal of ascertaining
authentic sayings of Jesus?  It would appear that taken alone
no one criterion can "prove" that a saying in the Gospels is
authentic, although one, the criterion of dissimilarity, is
sufficiently functional so as to place a heavy burden of proof
upon anyone denying the authenticity of any saying which meets
its standards.  Only the strongest kinds of negative evidence
can hope to disprove the authenticity of a saying or motif that
satisfies the criterion of dissimilarity.  It is nevertheless
the cumulative evidence of the various criteria which serves to
demonstrate a saying's authenticity.  If a particular saying or
teaching of Jesus meets most (or ideally all) of the positive
criteria listed above, then we can claim with reasonable
certainty that this teaching is authentic.  Each criterion
serves as an individual chain in the investigative process.
Some are stronger, i.e. of more value, than others in
establishing the probability of authenticity, and whereas no
one criterion, with the possible exception of the criterion of
dissimilarity, is strong enough to tie a gospel saying or motif
absolutely to the historical Jesus, the cumulative effect of
the various "chains" can bring the historian to the place that
he 'has to acknowledge [this material] as authentic if he
wishes to remain an historian at all.' /92/

Even if, however, the weight of evidence is not sufficient
to demonstrate the authenticity of a saying beyond a reasonable
doubt, it may well be that there needs to be an acknowledgement
of where the burden of proof lies.  McArthur suggests that if a
saying or motif meets the criterion of multiple attestation,
then 'the burden of proof shifts to those who deny the
authenticity of that particular motif.' /93/  It may be debated
whether this one criterion alone can bring about such a shift
in the burden of proof for some scholars, but we must
acknowledge that there is also a middle ground between the two
extremes of a gospel tradition being clearly authentic or
clearly inauthentic. /94/  In such instances if a saying
satisfies several criteria the probability of the saying being
authentic will be increased and any burden of proof will
surely be on those who hold a negative view towards its

authenticity.  On the other hand, it must be pointed out once
again that the failure of a saying or motif to satisfy the
criteria of: multiple attestation, multiple forms, Aramaic
linguistic phenomena, Palestinian environmental phenomena,
dissimilarity divergent patterns from the redaction, says
nothing for or against its authenticity.  This simply
indicates that the case for authenticity cannot be established
because of the inadequacy of our tools.  Only four criteria
can be used to argue for the inauthenticity of a saying: the
criterion of the tendencies of the developing tradition, the
criterion of modification by Jewish Christianity, the
criterion of environmental contradiction, and the criterion of
contradiction of authentic sayings.  Yet these criteria must
be used carefully with the important qualifications mentioned
in the discussion above. /95/

Finally it should be pointed out that if by the use of
these various criteria, certain sayings in our Gospels can in
fact be demonstrated as being authentic and this in turn can
establish a continuity between the historical Jesus and
kerygmatic Christ, there is then no *a priori* reason to be
skeptical about the general portrait of Jesus found in our
Gospels.  On the contrary it would then be clear that the
burden of proof lies with those who would reject the
authenticity of the gospel materials rather than with those who
accept their authenticity. /96/  We can say this in another way
using the terminology of the law court.  If by the criteria
discussed above, the authenticity of certain sayings and
motifs in the Gospels can be demonstrated which establish a
continuity between the Jesus of history and the Christ of
faith, then we should assume that the other sayings and motifs
in the Gospels are "innocent until proven guilty," i.e. a
saying in the Gospels proporting to come from Jesus is true
(authentic) until proven false (inauthentic).

Footnotes

[1] Joachim Jeremias, *New Testament Theology*, trans. by John Bowden (Charles Scribner's Sons, 1971), p. 37.

[2] Norman Perrin, *Rediscovering the Teaching of Jesus* (Harper & Row, 1967), p. 39.

[3] Technically these terms are not synonymous but in practice they essentially are.

[4] For the contrary view see: D. E. Nineham, "Eye-witness Tradition and the Gospel Tradition," *JTS*, 9 (1958), pp. 13-25, 143-152, and 11 (1960), pp. 253-260.

[5] For this view see: Harald Riesenfeld, *The Gospel Tradition and its Beginnings* (A. R. Mowbray, 1957) and Birger Gerhardsson, *Memory and Manuscript: Oral Tradition and Written Transmission in Rabbinic Judaism and Early Christianity* (C. W. K. Gleerup, 1961).

[6] R. T. France, "The Authenticity of the Sayings of Jesus" in *History, Criticism & Faith*, edited by Colin Brown (Inter-Varsity Press, 1976), p. 107, states 'Earlier generations of scholars assumed in their simplicity that the tradition is innocent until proven guilty, but now we are assured on every hand that it must be reckoned guilty until proven innocent.'

[7] *Webster's Seventh New Collegiate Dictionary* (G. & C. Merriam, 1965).

[8] *A New Quest of the Historical Jesus* (SCM, 1959), p. 99 n. 3. A good example of this way of thinking is found in Plutarch, *Solon*, 27.1. Here Plutarch accepts "historically" the meeting of Solon and Croesus even though they lived at different times because the meeting is so true to the characters of both men that he will not reject it upon such trivial grounds as the "so-called canons of chronology." I am indebted for this example to C. J. Hemer, "Luke the Historian," *BJRL*, 60 (1977), p. 30.

[9] Robinson, p. 100 n. 3; cf. also pp. 107-111.

[10] So D. G. A. Calvert, "An Examination of the Criteria for

Distinguishing the Authentic Words of Jesus," *NTS*, 18 (1972),
p. 209.

[11]"M" and "L" are symbols used to refer to the special
material in Matthew and Luke not found anywhere else in the
Synoptic Gospels. Whether "M" and "L" were written documents
is of no major consequence, because whether written or oral
they represent a different and separate tradition than Mark
and "Q".

[12]*The Gospel History and Its Transmission* (T. & T. Clark,
1911), p. 147.

[13]Some others who make reference to this criterion are:
C. H. Dodd, *The Parables of the Kingdom* (Charles Scribner's
Sons, 1961), pp. 26-27; T. W. Manson, *The Teaching of Jesus*
(Cambridge University Press, 1935), pp. 10-11; Nils Alstrup
Dahl, "The Problem of the Historical Jesus," *Kerygma and
History*, edited by Carl E. Braaten and Roy Harrisville
(Abingdon, 1962), pp. 153-154; Joachim Jeremias, *The Prayers
of Jesus*, trans. by John Bowden (Alec. R. Allenson, 1967),
p. 115; Harvey K. McArthur, "Basic Issues: A Survey of Recent
Gospel Research," *INTERP*, 18 (1964), pp. 47-48; "The Burden of
Proof in Historical Jesus Research," *ExpT*, 82 (1971), p. 118;
Reginald H. Fuller, *A Critical Introduction to the New
Testament* (Gerald Duckworth & Co., 1966), pp. 97-98; William O.
Walker, "The Quest for the Historical Jesus: A Discussion of
Methodology," *Angl. Theol. Rev.*, 51 (1969), pp. 41-42; Calvert,
p. 217; R. S. Barbour, *Tradition-Historical Criticism of the
Gospels* (SPCK, 1972), pp. 3-4; N. L. McEleney, "Authenticating
Criteria and Mark 7:1-23," *CBQ*, 34 (1972), pp. 433-435; John G.
Gager, "The Gospels and Jesus: Some Doubts about Method,"
*Journal of Religion*, 54 (1974), p. 260; C. Leslie Mitton,
*Jesus: The Fact Behind the Faith* (Eerdmans, 1974), pp. 80-83;
Rene Latourelle, "Criteres d'authenticite historique des
Evangiles," *Gregorianum*, 55 (1974), pp. 619-621; Richard N.
Longnecker, "Literary Criteria in Life of Jesus Research: An
Evaluation and Proposal," *Current Issues in Biblical and
Patristic Interpretation*, edited by Gerald F. Hawthorne
(Eerdmans, 1975), pp. 219-220; Perrin, pp. 45-47; France,
pp. 108-110, David R. Catchpole, "Tradition History," *New
Testament Interpretation*, edited by I. Howard Marshall
(Eerdmans, 1977), p. 176; K. Grayston, "Jesus: The Historical
Question," *Downside Review*, 95 (1977), pp. 264-265; Grant R.
Osborne, "The Evangelical and *Traditionsgeschichte*," *JETS*, 21

(1978), pp. 119, 126; Ben F. Meyer, *The Aims of Jesus* (SCM Press, 1979), p. 87.

[14] So Perrin, p. 46.

[15] McArthur, "Basic Issues," p. 48.

[16] The man most responsible for this challenge and the revival of the Griesbach hypothesis (Matthew was first and was used by Luke; Mark used Matthew and Luke) is William R. Farmer, *The Synoptic Problem: A Critical Analysis* (MacMillan, 1964).

[17] It is, of course, true that behind Matthew there would be sources that could serve as witnesses, but it would be for all practical purpose impossible to ascertain just what these sources were even as it is "impossible," assuming the Lachmann-Streeter thesis, to ascertain the sources used by Mark.

[18] "The Burden of Proof in Historical Jesus Research," p. 118.

[19] *The Phenomenon of the New Testament* (SCM Press, 1967), p. 71. Cf. also Burkitt, pp. 167-168.

[20] See Deut. 19:15.

[21] Henry Ernst William Turner, *History and the Gospel*, (A. R. Mowbray, 1963), pp. 91-102. Some others who discuss the use of this criterion are: McArthur, "Basic Issues," pp. 49-50; Walker, pp. 42-43; James M. Robinson, "The Formal Structure of Jesus' Message," in *Current Issues in New Testament Interpretation*, edited by William Klassen and Graydon F. Snyder (Harper & Brothers, 1962), pp. 96-97; McElenery, pp. 435-436; Calvert, p. 217; Grayston, pp. 264-265; Meyer, p. 87.

[22] See, however, Etienne Trocme, *Jesus as Seen by His Contemporaries*, trans. by R. A. Wilson, (Westminster, 1973) who seeks to arrive at a coherent picture of Jesus from the "Dominical Sayings," "Apophthegms," "Biographical Narratives," "Parables," and "Miracles Stories."

[23] McArthur, "Basic Issues," p. 50.

[24] Cf. Trocme, p. 110, who states 'As we have seen, all the strata of oral tradition have come to us by way of

particular and limited groups."

[25] See Robert H. Stein, *The Method and Message of Jesus Teachings* (Westminster, 1978), pp. 4-6.

[26] Jeremias, *New Testament Theology*, p. 8.

[27] Turner, pp. 77-78.

[28] *Jesus-Jeshua* (MacMillan, 1929).

[29] *The Poetry of Our Lord* (Clarendon Press, 1925).

[30] *Our Translated Gospels* (Harper, 1936).

[31] *An Aramaic Approach to the Gospels and Acts* (Clarendon Press, 1946).

[32] *The Parables of Jesus*, trans. by S. H. Hooke (SCM, 1963); *The Eucharistic Words of Jesus* (MacMillan, 1955); *New Testament Theology*; etc.  Some additional references for the discussion of this criterion are: Walker, pp. 43-44; Fuller, p. 97; Perrin, pp. 37-38; McEleney, pp. 438-440; Calvert, p. 216: Barbour, p. 4; Longenecker, pp. 220, 223; France, p. 109; Osborne, p. 125; Gager, pp. 260-261; T. W. Manson, pp. 45-86; E. P. Sanders, *The Tendencies of the Synoptic Tradition* (Cambridge University Press, 1969), pp. 190-209; Latourelle, pp. 630-632; Meyer, p. 87.

[33] Jeremais, *New Testament Theology*, pp. 15-16.

[34] *The Eucharistic Words of Jesus*, pp. 118-126.

[35] So Reginald H. Fuller, *The New Testament in Current Study* (Charles Scribner's Sons, 1962), pp. 33-34;  Walker, p. 44; Perrin, p. 37; Calvert, p. 218.

[36] Longenecker, p. 223; Walker, p. 44; Sanders, p. 202.

[37] Gager, pp. 260-261.

[38] See Stein, p. 6.

[39] *The New Testament in Current Study*, pp. 33-34; author's italics.

[40]*The Problem of the Historical Jesus*, trans. by Norman Perrin (Fortress, 1964), p. 18.

[41]For a discussion of this criterion see: Jeremias, *The Parables of Jesus*, pp. 11-12 in particular; Dahl, p. 154; Charles Edwin Carlston, "A *Positive* Criterion of Authenticity?" *Biblical Research*, 7 (1962), p. 34; Walker, p. 44; Calvert, p. 216; F. Gerald Downing, *The Church and Jesus* (Alec R. Allenson, 1968), p. 113; Rene Latourelle, "Authenticite Historique des miracles de Jesus," *Gregorianum*, 54 (1973), p. 238.

[42]*The Parables of Jesus*, pp. 11-12.  Cf. b. Sabb. 73 b; Jub. 11:23.

[43]See J. Duncan M. Derrett, *Law in the New Testament* (Darton, Longman, & Todd, 1970), p. 382.

[44]Downing, p. 113.

[45]"The New Approach to the Synoptic Problem," *Journal of Religion*, 6 (1926), p. 345.  For additional discussion of this criterion see: Rudolf Bultmann and Karl Kundsin, *Form Criticism*, trans. by Frederick C. Grant (Harper, 1962), pp. 32-35; McArthur, "Basic Issues," pp. 48-49; Walker, pp. 44-46; Calvert, p. 213; McEleney, pp. 436-437.

[46]Stein, p. 57.

[47]For the present writer this redactional interpretation of Jesus' parable by "Matthew," should be understood in the light of John 14:25-26 which speaks of the Holy Spirit not only bringing the words of Jesus, i.e. the *ipsissima verba*, into remembrance but "teaching" their significance as well. Cf. also John 15:26; 16:14.

[48]Sanders, pp. 272-275.

[49]"The Problem of the Historical Jesus," in *Essays on New Testament Themes*, trans. by W. J. Montague (Alec R. Allenson, 1964), p. 37.

[50]Paul W. Schmiedel, "Gospels," *Encyclopedia Biblica*, edited by T. K. Cheyne and J. Sutherland Black (Adam and Charles Black, 1914), col. 1881-1883.

[51]*The History of the Synoptic Tradition*, p. 205. Some other scholars who discuss this criterion are: Walker, pp. 46-47; Oscar Cullmann, *Salvation in History*, trans. by Sidney G. Sowers (Harper & Row, 1967), p. 189; Perrin, pp. 39-43; Gager, pp. 256-259; Moule, p. 62; M. D. Hooker, "An Examination of the Criteria for Distinguishing the Authentic Words of Jesus," *NTS*, 18 (1972), p. 209 and "On Using the Wrong Tool," *Theology*, 75 (1972), pp. 570-581; Calvert, pp. 215-216; McEleney, pp. 440-442; Barbour, pp. 5-27; Fuller, *A Critical Introduction to the New Testament*, pp. 96-97; Longenecker, pp. 221-225; Osborne, pp. 118-119; Catchpole, pp. 174-176; Hans Conzelmann, *Jesus*, trans. by J. Raymond Lord (Fortress, 1973), p. 16; Turner, pp. 73-74; Mitton, pp. 84-85; McArthur, "Basic Issues," pp. 50-51; Heinz Zahrnt, *The Historical Jesus*, trans. by J. S. Bowden (Harper & Row, 1963), p. 107; F. F. Bruce, *Tradition: Old and New* (Zondervan, 1970), pp. 47-49; Helmut Koester, "The Historical Jesus: Some Comments and Thoughts on Norman Perrin's *Rediscovering the Teaching of Jesus*," in *Christology and a Modern Pilgrimage*, edited by Hans Dieter Betz (Claremont: New Testament Colloquium, 1971), pp. 124-136; France, pp. 108, 110; Latourelle, "Criteres d'authenticite," pp. 622-625; Grayston, p. 264; and David L. Mealand, "The Dissimilarity Test," *Scot J Theol*, 31 (1978), pp. 41-50; Meyer, pp. 81-87.

[52]See Calvert, pp. 214-215.

[53]"The Lord's Prayer in Modern Research," in *New Testament Issues*, edited by Richard Batey (Harper & Row, 1970), p. 95. See however, Geza Vermes, *Jesus the Jew* (Fortana, 1976), p. 211.

[54]It is quite possible that outside of Dan. 7:13 we do not possess a single pre-Christian apocalyptic Son of man reference, for 2 Esdras 13 is clearly late first-century and although the book of Enoch is pre-Christian, the Similitudes (chapters 37-71) probably are post-Christian. See J. T. Milik, *The Books of Enoch* (Clarendon Press, 1976), pp. 89-107.

[55]Meyer, p. 86.

[56]Meyer, p. 86.

[57]*History and the Gospels*, pp. 73-74.

[58]The question of whether "Amen" as an introductory

formula is found in pre-Christian Judaism has been greatly
debated of late.  For a succinct discussion of the more
recent debate see Bruce Chilton "'Amen': an Approach through
Syriac Gospels," *ZNW*, 69 (1978), pp. 203-211.

[59]There are, of course, critics who deny the authenticity
of certain "Pillar Passages," certain parables, and all the
Son of man sayings.  There have been and still are critics who
deny that Jesus ever lived!  To this writer, however, an
objective use of the criterion of dissimilarity as suggested
on p. 21 below, argues for the authenticity of this material.

[60]"On Using the Wrong Tool,"pp. 570-581, but see Mealand,
pp. 41-50, for a corrective.

[61]See Fuller, p. 96, France, p. 107, and Gagner, p. 258
who states 'The proper use of the criterion cannot allow the
claim that such a story [which does not meet the standards of
this criterion] is inauthentic, merely that we can never be
confident of its authenticity under the circumstances.'

[62]See Hooker, p. 575.

[63]Hooker, p. 575.

[64]Hooker, p. 574.  Cf. also Catchpole, p. 174, and
Walker, p. 48.

[65]Longenecker, pp. 224-225.

[66]Dahl, p. 156; cf. also Barbour, p. 26.

[67]Thus the criticism that the Jesus of this criterion
must by definition be "anti-Jewish" and "anti-Christian" is
true only with regard to those scholars who deny the
authenticity of any material which does not meet the criterion
of dissimilarity.  On such a basis the portrait of Jesus must
by definition be "anti-Jewish" and "anti-Christian" and
ultimately docetic.  On the other hand if we accept the fact
that this criterion can only produce a solid core of authentic
material, the problem this criticism is directed at is
greatly diminished.

[68]Jan Vansina, *Oral Tradition: A Study in Historical
Methodology*, trans. by H. M. Wright (Aldine, 1965), p. 107,

states concerning African historical traditions,

> When features which do not correspond [i.e. are dissimilar]
> to those commonly attributed to an ideal type nevertheless
> persist in a tradition, they may usually be regarded as
> trustworthy.

Cf. also Schmiedel, col. 1872. It should be noted that Vansina
combines the criterion of dissimilarity with a form of multiple
attestation ("features which . . . persist in the tradition").

[69] Barbour, p. 26.

[70] McArthur, "The Burden of Proof," p. 117; cf. Catchpole,
p. 175; Hooker, pp. 576-577.

[71] Käsemann, p. 37; author's italics. Cf. also McEleney,
pp. 442-443, and Perrin, p. 39, who adds to the criterion of
dissimilarity the following: 'and this will particularly be
the case where Christian tradition oriented towards Judaism
can be shown to have modified the saying away from its
original emphasis.'

[72] Although Robert Banks, *Jesus and the Law in the Synoptic
Tradition* ("Society for New Testament Studies Monograph Series -
28"; Cambridge University Press, 1975), pp. 152-153,
acknowledges the exception clause as being Matthean, he does
not see this addition as a weakening or lessening of the
intensity of Jesus' words. He suggests the following
translation on p. 156. 'I say to you, whoever dismisses his
wife - the permission in Deut. 24.1 notwithstanding - and
marries another, commits adultery.'

[73] Walker, p. 49.

[74] Calvert, p. 219; cf. also Moule, pp. 62, 67; Harald
Riesenfeld, *The Gospel Tradition*, trans. by E. Margaret Rowley
and Robert A. Kraft (Fortress, 1970), p. 72; Osborne, p. 123;
Andre Bareau, *Recherches sur la Biographie du Bouddha* (Paris:
Ecole Francaise, 1963), p. 380, who applies this principle to
the "quest for the historical Buddha"; Schmiedel, cols. 1872-
1873; and Longenecker, pp. 225-229.

[75] Marc Bloch, *The Historian's Craft*, trans. by Joseph R.
Strayer (Alfred A. Knopf, 1953), p. 61.

[76]Acts of Paul and Thecla, 3, in *New Testament Apocrypha*, edited by Wilhelm Schneemelcher, trans. by R. McL. Wilson (Westminster, 1965), II, p. 354.

[77]Hooker, p. 579.

[78]See below pp. 25-26.

[79]Calvert, p. 212.

[80]Calvert, p. 212.

[81]*Redating the New Testament* (Westminster, 1976), p. 20.

[82]See above pp. 12-14.

[83]See above p. 13.

[84]Calvert, p. 213.

[85]See Stein, pp. 8-12, 19-20.

[86]Cf. also Luke 12:57 in this regard.

[87]See Stein, pp. 105-106.

[88]Perrin, p. 43.   Cf. also: Fuller, p. 98; Bultmann, *History of the Synoptic Tradition*, p. 105; Joachim Jeremias, *Unknown Sayings of Jesus*, trans. by Reginald H. Fuller (SPCK, 1964), p. 71; Catchpole, pp. 176-177; Calvert, pp. 217-218; McEleney, pp. 443-444; Longenecker, p. 221-222; Barbour, pp. 9, 26; Gager, pp. 259-260; Grayston, p. 264; Walker, pp. 49-50; Osborne, pp. 119, 121; Schmiedel, col. 1873; Latourelle, "Criteres d'authenticite," pp. 625-627; France, p. 108.

[89]Carlston, p. 34.   Cf. also Rudolf Bultmann's similar use of this approach in *Theology of the New Testament*, trans. by Kendrick Grobel (Charles Scribner's Sons, 1951), pp. 4-11, and the approach of James M. Robinson, "The Formal Structure," p. 99.

[90]So Hooker, p. 577; Barbour, p. 26; Osborne, p. 121.

[91]See James D. G. Dunn, "Prophetic 'I'-Sayings and the Jesus Tradition: The Importance of Testing Prophetic

Utterances Within Early Christianity," *NTS*, 24 (1978),
pp. 193-196, for an interesting discussion of the importance
of the criterion of coherence for testing prophetic 'I' sayings
in the early church.

[92]Käsemann, p. 46.

[93]McArthur, "The Burden of Proof," p. 119.  It is, of
course, a matter of debate as to whether one should *a priori*
assume the inauthenticity of any saying in the Gospels before
the investigative process begins.

[94]See Meyer, p. 84, who states, 'In the first place, there
will be three columns for historicity judgments on the
material: yes, no, and question mark.'

[95]See pp. 16, 22, 25-26.

[96]See Jeremias, *New Testament Theology*, p. 37.